HIGH ROLLER

HIGH ROLLER

The Woman Who Embezzled 6.2 Million Dollars

Jan Welles

NEW HORIZON PRESS
Far Hills, New Jersey

Library of Congress Catalog Card Number: 92-85166

Welles, Jan
High Roller: The Woman Who Embezzled 6.2 Million Dollars

ISBN: 0-88282-119-9
New Horizon Press

1997   1996   1995   1994   1993   /   5   4   3   2   1
Manufactured in the U.S.A.

They will never find it all . . . never! Put me in any banking institution or credit union and I will show you a hundred ways.

—Gerrie Powell

This is to state that the facts and events depicted here within the Gerrie Powell Story are true accountings of my deeds with the Henry Vogt Employees Credit Union, and of the episodes in my life with Cindy Kelly. Though I regret many of the happenings, they are true to the best of my knowledge and recollection.

Additionally I would like to extend my sincere apologies to the Henry Vogt Machine Company and its employees.

—Geraldine W. Powell

Contents

Acknowledgments

To Jo, to whom I am most indebted, for without her encouragement and tireless efforts none of this would be possible.

I am also deeply grateful to Gerrie Powell for her honesty with me as her sole and exclusive confidant. She has been and still is my friend. Throughout this book, you may sense my empathy for her; nevertheless, the facts are true.

And to Ingrid Anderson, Alicia, June Vals, and Lynn Diebolt, my special thanks for contributions to the creation of my book.

In addition I am grateful to the following institutions for their cooperation: Churchill Downs, Turfway Park, and Louisville Downs.

And to Mr. Henry V. Heuser, Jr., of Henry Vogt Machine Co., my very deepest thanks for your help.

Author's Note

This is the actual experience of a real person, Geraldine Powell. The personalities, events, actions, and conversations portrayed within the story have been reconstructed from extensive interviews and research, utilizing court documents, letters, personal papers, press accounts, and the memories of the participants. In an effort to safeguard the privacy of certain individuals, the author has changed their names and the names of certain places and, in some cases, altered identifying characteristics. Events involving the characters happened as described; only minor details have been altered.

Prologue

The phone lines stayed busy all evening, as Cindy made calls to everyone she could think of, telling them the news. In her story she was blameless. "Gerrie stole the money," she said, "but she lost everything gambling!" Distant acquaintances believed her story, but not close friends who had known Gerrie before she started gambling. They knew the truth.

As Cindy was busy phoning, Gerrie drove from place to place through the outskirts of the city, trying to avoid police cruisers. Her expensive clothes were in garbage bags in the trunk of her car. She could hardly be recognized as the same person in her old Buick. The car was dirty and in need of repair; it was quite a step down from the shiny Cadillacs of the past. On the seat beside her lay a tape recorder and her most prized possession, her little dog. Besides finding a place to sleep for the night, the important thing was to destroy the paper trail, and in doing so protect Cindy and the money.

She had no idea how many millions she had stolen from the company over a period of twenty-five years. But for that many years she had fooled the auditors.

Because of her long, loyal service, credit union members looked to her as they would a mother, a consoler, a confidant.

On that June night, her one consolation was that the wealth she had accumulated was protected. "Everything is safe," she whispered, "the money, the horses, the farm . . . they will never find them!"

Her hand left the steering wheel for a moment to give a comforting pat to her little dog, Tootie, a black pocket-size poodle that lay beside her.

She looked around for a place to stop. Parking her car on the banks of the Ohio River, she watched the pleasure boats making their way to the marina. Fog rising from the water obscured their navigating lights and hovered around her car like a blanket of gray, leaving her to think . . . without distraction. . . .

This spot had often been flooded because of spring rains that, in time, exposed large flatbeds of limestone rock in the river. Adding to its vulnerability for flooding were low-lying banks on the eastern side and a turn in the river where it reached this area. At one time this part of Kentucky was referred to as the "Falls of the Ohio." Captain Thomas Bullett and his small company of land surveyors had landed at the mouth of Beargrass Creek on July 8, 1773. About thirty yards from where Gerrie was sitting, the men had set up camp on the banks of the Ohio River. They were among the first explorers of a place that was later named Louisville.

The flat terrain and fields of grass made conditions ideal for raising thoroughbred race horses. Bred for excellence, the high-spirited animals crossed the finish line in a race named the Kentucky Derby, at Churchill Downs, for the first time on May 17, 1875. It would become an event that would affect all the people of Louisville, and especially Gerrie Powell's life.

HIGH ROLLER

With her tape recorder on the car seat beside her, Gerrie began speaking of events that had transpired, perhaps for no other reason except to help her understand . . . not *what* she did, but *why*.

CHAPTER 1

A Taste of Power

The first time Gerrie Powell walked through the steel doors of the Henry Vogt Machine Company in 1951, she felt the excitement. Entering the plant, she heard the vibrant hum of massive motors. The sound came from the manufacturing of the world's largest and most complete line of high-pressure, forged steel valves and fittings.

The company built module steam generators, boilers, heat exchangers, and other metal products. Perhaps they were best known for their Tube-Ice machine, a machine that freezes ice automatically in vertical tubes, momentarily thaws the ice loose from the tubes, and then cuts it into short cylinders. The familiar cylinder-shaped ice with the hole in the center is renowned for its sparkling clarity.

Looking behind and beyond the small reception room door into the factory that morning, Gerrie was awed and ran her trembling fingers through her brown hair, which she had cut in a Dutch-boy bob just for the occasion. Huge steel machines glistened, aisles were filled with the murmurs of men at work. It gave Gerrie her first taste of the immense power of a factory. More than anything, she wanted to be a part of that power.

Stopping at the glassed-in reception center, Gerrie nervously tapped on the window. A tall, red-haired, fortyish woman looked up. "You here for a summer job interview, hon?" she asked, cracking the gum she was chewing. Suddenly shy, Gerrie just nodded in reply. The woman smiled. "First job?"

Again, Gerrie nodded. "I've worked after school."

"Now don't be nervous," the receptionist said kindly. "I'm Ginny Hayes. Look, I'll walk you down to Leonard Brinkman's office. He'll be interviewing you."

On the way, as Gerrie listened avidly, the talkative receptionist told her that the company had been named for the founder. He had one child, a daughter, who inherited the business after his death. Through the years the business remained family owned and operated.

"Good luck," the receptionist smiled and stuck her head in the door. "Leonard, your appointment's here."

Gerrie gulped, gathered her courage, and walked in. Then there was a long interview by Leonard Brinkman, the olive-complected, balding manager of personnel. Finally, twirling his moustache, he asked, "Geraldine, when can you start work?"

She had a previous commitment to coach the girls basketball game the following Wednesday afternoon. Not wanting to disappoint the team, she replied, "If it would be alright, can I start Thursday?"

"Good!" Leonard said, standing up. "Report for work at 8:00 A.M. You'll be starting at sixty cents an hour."

In time, that hiring proved to be the most costly decision ever made by the company's personnel manager. But Gerrie was elated! For forty hours of work, her gross pay would be twenty-four dollars! She knew it was going to be difficult to convince Stella, her mother, to accept the fact that her "baby" might not continue with her studies after this summer. The pride of a college degree was far more important to Stella than to Gerrie. Gerrie was tired of scrimping and saving so she could go to school. She felt she had been deprived of buying nice things for long enough.

That first morning of work, Gerrie wore a new baby-blue rayon dress which she was sure everyone would think was real silk. Stella drove her to the factory and dropped her off at the front door. "Here we are, hon." Gerrie began work as a messenger girl, making the rounds of the plant delivering memos and mail. In addition to this she would be doing clerical work in the Cost Department.

The plant extended over twelve acres. Exhilarated, she wanted to walk the entire campus during that first hour, but Leonard insisted she make the rounds on a given schedule. "I'll be watching you, and if I'm not, Mike McCrossen your supervisor will be."

Gerrie nodded. Her schedule began with the blacksmith shop. In front of open furnaces that were fed twenty-four hours a day, men in goggles labored with long silver tongs, hammering hot metal for the forging shop. There they created the molds from steel. Then came the sheet metal department. Here blueprint patterns were drawn with chalk on large 5'×10' sheets of metal to be used in making various parts.

After the sheet metal department Gerrie continued walking under giant yellow cranes used to transport massive products. Her eyes opened wide. From there she went to the laboratory and then to Department 20, where metallurgists worked to economically extract metal from ore. On and on she trod. Her route took her to the stockroom and Shipping

Department 12, where trains and trucks at platforms were readied for loading. After that Gerrie ambled through the small maze of offices and the first-aid room, leaving the mail. Then she journeyed on to Department 8, where the electricians worked.

At each place Gerrie, a born investigator, asked a million questions.

Leonard caught up with her at one point and stood to one side. "Are you planning on owning this place?" he chuckled.

"I want to know about every phase of the operation," Gerrie soberly replied.

"You'll get over that enthusiasm the first week, I bet," Leonard grinned.

But she didn't. Gerrie loved the job. She was not satisfied to know that something happened; she wanted to know *why* it happened.

In those early months on her rounds she met and talked with every worker in the company. Some were middle-aged, thrifty people who worked hard and saved their money; others, old and young, hardly managed to make it until the next payday. In six months she knew each man's name and habits. This relaxed familiarity affected the completion of her work. She liked to chat with the guys and grew fascinated with the immensity of the production itself.

A simple "Hi, Gerrie, how's it going today?" brought on a long conversation with anyone who offered the greeting. Daily she would make her rounds, talk to a hundred people and remember to ask about the wife or child who was ill, or if they had found their lost pet; little details were important to Gerrie. When her immediate supervisor Mike McCrossen rebuked her, "Look, you're spending too much extra time making rounds," with polite disagreement she informed him that she was "learning."

Gerrie worked all summer and only grew more enthusiastic about staying on through the fall. She had several heated discussions with her mother, who was adamant about the benefits of a college degree in physical education.

Though Stella offered several times to help with her daughter's tuition, Gerrie felt it was now her turn to care for her mother. She felt strongly about her obligations and told her mother, "You've worked nineteen years for me, now it's my turn. I'm going to work for you." She vowed, "Mother, you'll never want for anything!"

Because of her decision, Gerrie decided to talk to Mike McCrossen about staying with Henry Vogt. "You know you have a raise coming," McCrossen said, wanting to keep the diligent young girl who, despite her propensity to chatter, seemed to have made so many friends. "We're all hoping you'll stay," he added. Without hesitation Gerrie decided to continue on with the friendly people, even though it meant a six-mile walk each morning and night.

During that first year, Henry Vogt promoted Gerrie to clerk in the company credit union. Her new salary was eighty cents an hour, and in a few months the position would pay a dollar an hour. She was progressing. She was thrilled.

In Gerrie's starting position at Vogt, she had gotten to know all the workers' names. Now, as a clerk, she began to connect the names to their clock numbers. After a while, to her dismay and later to theirs, the people themselves became numbers, no longer names and faces.

Her position called for her to take deposits from members, cash payroll checks, and do the posting. She was efficient, and her memory was outstanding.

In 1952, $1,000 was the maximum amount a person

could have deposited in their account. The amount available to borrow on a signature was limited to $50. To borrow more, one needed collateral or a co-signer. There were equal amounts of loans and co-signers. If a car cost $1,000, the credit union would loan only 80 percent of the total cost—with an "okay" from the manager.

Gerrie purchased her first car for $1,200; she was twenty-two. The car was a beige 1951 Chevy Belair. When Gerrie was not using the car, she gave it to Stella and the family to drive wherever they wished. What belonged to Gerrie she felt was also theirs.

On weekends, she liked to take a group of friends for a drive. Since very few girls on the team she coached owned cars, they would call Gerrie during the week to arrange to be part of the fun trip.

One Saturday they had planned to drive to Cincinnati to a football game. In planning the trip, Gerrie was too proud to admit that she was broke. The payments on her car were taking all her extra money. It was eight days until payday.

That morning an employee came in with a cash deposit of one hundred dollars. She gave him a receipt and put the money in the cash drawer. Instantly she murmured, "That's what I need for the trip." Looking quickly about the room, another thought flashed: "But what if they catch me?"

For the rest of the day she debated whether to take the money. Each time she waited on a customer she could feel her hands begin sweating. Two hours before quitting, she opened the drawer to give change to a fellow worker. When he left, the drawer remained opened. A few minutes later she reached for the money. Momentarily, hesitantly like an illusion in her mind, she saw a smaller hand . . . the hand of a child . . . her hand.

*   *   *

When she was little her dad kept his change in a Mason jar in the bedroom and his "folding money" in a cigar box on a dresser. Often she saw her mother cry, because there was no money for food. Gerrie would remind her of the money in the bedroom. "No!" Stella would say, "That is from gambling. It's not the Lord's money! I want no part of it!" Gerrie felt differently.

However, Stella was stubborn. A direct descendant of the Cherokee Indians, she was a little woman, five-feet, two-inches tall and weighing 108 pounds. She had brown hair and piercing brown eyes. Her voice, although soft, demanded the respect of her children. The staunch Christian woman devoted every minute of her life to the teachings of the Bible.

The Powells had four children: Kathleen, Thomas, Bridget, and Geraldine Wray. Gerrie was named after the actress Fay Wray, of *King Kong* fame.

Gerrie cherished vivid memories of her mother working to "make do" with the two or three dollars a week her father gave her. Stella spent most of her days at the sewing machine, mending her children's clothes; always cutting something down, or making it different, and the children loved her for her efforts. However, there was never enough food in the house. Gerrie was always hungry.

It was a situation Gerrie couldn't take. Starting at the age of five, she would go to the box on the dresser and grab a handful of her dad's money to give to her mother. In order to get it to Stella without letting her mother know what she had done, Gerrie slipped change into her mother's coat, dress, or apron pocket, and Stella, who was often preoccupied, would think it had been overlooked on a previous search. Other times, Gerrie would gather an arm full of junk, go into the alley, and return later, telling her mother she had sold the items to the rag man. At the rear of the house on Prentice Street stood an old shed with a low roof. The daily fun for the kids was to slide down the roof into the alley. There they waited for the clippety-clop of the rag man's horse. Every Wednesday the old-white haired gentleman came by, calling out, "Raaaag man! . . . Got somethin' for the raaag man?" At the sound of his voice, kids in the neighborhood would run up one side of the alley and down the other like scurrying ants, gathering anything available they could sell to the rag man for a penny or two in return. For those who were lucky, a piece of iron or lead or an old bicycle part sometimes brought three cents. And then Gerrie would run quickly to retrieve a quarter or two of her dad's money to add to the pennies, to give to her mother. Stella was so proud of her little money maker. She praised her often, never dreaming that the little girl was stealing from her father.

As time went on and Gerrie got older, she often questioned herself as to why she took the money. Was it that she wanted to help her mother, or did she resent her father for having it? Regardless of the fine line between the two reasons, she continued picking his pockets while he was sleeping off a "drunk." It was never missed; he never knew.

Her dad was a handsome man of French-English descent. He loved betting the horses and was a snappy dresser. His friends never saw him without a jaunty hat. Jokingly, his card-playing buddies asked if he wore a hat because he was bald, or if he was bald because he wore a hat. Bill would just laugh it off. He was a friendly guy when he wasn't drinking. He loved to eat, and Stella loved to cook. Because they were poor, though, meals were most often pasta and starches. The combination added many pounds to his five-foot, ten-inch frame. In time it also added a strain on his heart.

During the next years, Gerrie continued to slip money to

her mother, sometimes only a few quarters. Many times this was the only way her family had food, and Gerrie felt proud to be helping.

Her mind spun back to the present. She was grown now, a trusted employee with a fine company. Things were different and yet they were the same. She needed money once again. She shook her head. No, she couldn't take it now. She slapped the drawer shut and went on with her work, at the same time convincing herself that she could bet on the football game in Cincinnati, win, and put the money back. It sounded so easy, to just sort of borrow it until payday. While the time ticked by, her mind went back and forth.

It was a few minutes before five, almost quitting time. Checking around the office, she realized that she was alone. She made a snap decision, stealthily reached in the drawer, clasped the hundred dollars, and quickly put it in her purse.

She won her bet on the game but had a miserable weekend. Her theft haunted her mind: *What if a supervisor came into the office on Friday night and had an audit?* she agonized. Often they did that. Sinking deeply in guilt, she could hardly wait to get into the office to put the money back. It hadn't been fun; she was miserable!

She swore, "Never again!" Nothing was worth going through the hell she had been through that weekend. However, the ice had been broken.

The cash in the drawer was too tempting. With Gerrie's penchant for spending, she lived from payday to payday.

"The money was always there, and I'd borrow little amounts now and again to take a friend to dinner. Nothing big, maybe $40 or $50. Then I'd put it back," Gerrie recalled while talking into her recorder.

There were so many things she wanted: clothes, cars, a luxurious home, things she had dreamed of as a poor child.

Her family had never stayed very long in one house. They were moving continuously, though not too far away and always in the west end of town, in the California area of Louisville. Gerrie was aware of the many times they were evicted because the rent hadn't been paid. Being young, it wasn't until several years later that she understood why she so often had to play on the living room couch that was sitting out on the sidewalk. Later, remembering the incidents, she was humiliated.

Gerrie attended California Grade School. Seeing the obvious poverty of the family, the principal offered help with food and clothing. It hurt to go to school and have some child recognize an old dress she had discarded. Stella did her utmost to give her children what they needed. However, although a gallon of milk was only sixty-two cents and a loaf of bread cost ten, there were many times when there wasn't even a slice of bread in the house. Those were the times that help seemed to "come from God." Stella called it "God sent." She'd find a quarter in an old sweater, or someone from church would call for help with ironing or cleaning. She insisted on working for everything and never accepted donations of money.

The children knew they were poor. They saw others who dressed nicer and felt proud to be their friends. Gerrie remembers the respect she had as a child for her cousin Charles. His clothes, his manners at the dinner table, and the way he spoke were so "proper." Everyone looked up to him. More than anything, she wanted to be respected in that way. As a small child she thought that money generated respect.

Charles was thirteen, six years older than Gerrie, when he visited the family one Sunday. He wore an expensive pair of gray flannel slacks and a pair of "nifty" looking boots, the kind with a pocket knife sheath at the top. They were the most wonderful boots she had ever seen. It was all she could talk about, even though she felt she'd never have them.

Christmas had little or no monetary meaning for the children in the Powell family. It was primarily a religious time; however, Stella tried to make the holiday something special. All the children received a stocking full of fruit and a small toy. They knew better than to ask for anything. One year when Gerrie was ten, she talked constantly about a pair of high-top, lace-up boy's boots, the kind with a knife in the leg like Charles had. That year her aunt and uncle came in with gifts for everyone, and Gerrie's gift was the pair of boots. Stella was upset with them for buying her daughter boy's boots, but Gerrie loved them.

Charles was dressed in the best clothes money could buy, and in time they were handed down to young Tom. An expensive pair of gray flannel slacks caught Gerrie's eye, the same pair he had worn a few years earlier. Stella altered the pants for Gerrie, and she was proud to wear them. She wore them until they were thin from wear.

Gerrie began to model her life after Charles and his family. "They were proper, quiet; they had nice white linen tablecloths with napkins that matched. They were respected." Gerrie vowed to somehow achieve that respectability.

The principal at California Grade School became close friends with Stella and was instrumental in encouraging the children to channel their interests in a craft or sport. Gerrie was encouraged to play on the girls' softball and basketball teams. It was here she found her niche.

One of her teachers, Anna Hoover, a very tweedy and

masculine-looking woman, felt sympathetic to the family. Ms. Hoover, aware of Gerrie's family situation, sometimes bought clothes for Gerrie and saw to it that she went to all the school functions.

In her teens, Gerrie was tagged "bean pole," but most of her high school friends described Gerrie as kind, sociable, friendly, and giving. She always wore a gentle smile, copying her manners after her cousin Charles and his family. With a soft voice and a nod, she'd say, "Hi-do!" to a group of people. She had a quiet charm that made people reach out to her. In addition, her skill at sports made her acceptable if not accepted.

It was because of her skills at athletics that Gerrie was asked to coach the girls' basketball team after she graduated high school. She became so involved with the games and the girls she had no time for boys. At least, that's the way it appeared. The team members were closeknit and had a good relationship, but were never "out of hand." With the money Gerrie received from coaching, she tried to repay the money she took from the drawer, but she couldn't because she always needed more. She would take her friends to Fountaine Ferry Amusement Park and treat them to horseback rides and sodas. When she shopped, she over-bought, always buying something for a friend. The gratitude she received from giving made her feel wonderful. Nothing pleased her more than giving her friends something they had never had. She soon felt that the more she gave, the more they admired her. For this reason, she gave more. In fact, she simply could not resist giving, wanting so much to receive adoration in return.

Gerrie was capable of giving more when she was promoted to credit manager. The credit union's assets at that time were $100,000 with five hundred members. At that time, the government had no control over credit unions. Very few laws affected them. Audits were done by the Department of Banking. Two examiners would appear for one half day, talk to the manager, ask to see the year-end statement, voice a few simple questions, and leave. That was the extent of the outside audit. The credit union had a charter, but there were only a few written policies. It was a very small operation.

From a total of fifteen volunteers within the company, members elected persons to govern and audit the credit union. The men on the board of directors were responsible for the election of a president, a secretary, a treasurer, and a credit committee. This committee of three people would meet and make decisions on all loan applications. Three more people were elected to serve as a supervisory committee. Besides their regular job, they were responsible for holding quarterly audits of the credit union's books and policies. The board of directors set up guidelines and policies for the committee to follow. In the beginning Gerrie was not part of the audit committee, but she watched and learned.

The treasurer, Mike McCrossen, was her immediate supervisor. He had been the functioning manager of the credit union and cost accountant for Henry Vogt. He was expected to run the credit union and still do his full-time job at accounting. No one up to that moment had expressed too much interest in the department because it was small. Because of a lack of interest it remained small. It was merely there for the convenience of members.

Henry Vogt's owners were civic-minded people. They supported institutions in Louisville, but the salaries they paid their employees were low. Gerrie's primary function was to serve members and run the positing machine. Everyone liked her. She soon gained their confidence. The deposits began to grow.

As credit union manager, Gerrie started doing the book work. She kept a close account of the money she had taken, sometimes working extra jobs to repay her debt before the examiners arrived. However, she continued to borrow more in ever-increasing amounts and she had very few areas of flexibility. A person who had worked twenty years for the company could only borrow a small amount without collateral, and the amount of money in each member's account was small. Gerrie didn't like these rules. Slowly, she began to make suggestions. She felt that if a person had worked there for ten or twenty years, he wasn't about to leave. Faithful employees loved the company. Even during the depression, hours and days had been cut, but no one had been laid off. "This type of company creates loyalty and long-time employees," she argued. "Henry Vogt was security to every man and woman there, the backbone of the community. You had to do a lot to warrant being fired. A whole lot."

She had a multitude of ideas for the company, and many of her suggestions were passed by the board. However, the one most important to her wasn't: they didn't want to raise the limit of deposit. Given Gerrie's needs, increasing membership was her only alternative. She began a membership drive. Membership was raised to eight hundred. Ultimately the credit union's assets grew to $300,000.

Once again Gerrie talked to the credit committee and to the board of directors about policy changes on signature loans. The amount was raised from $50 to $75.

As the union instituted more policies, more rules and regulations were initiated, making Gerrie's borrowing more hazardous, but she enjoyed the challenge. Now it was her job to attend the board of directors' meetings.

With the increased revenue and membership the union moved into a large new office that previously had been the office of the president. Within three years, the credit union grew to a $750,000 operation. Gerrie saw an even greater potential.

Still initiating changes and increasing the limit on signature loans to $200, she suggested financing new furniture, bicycles, and luxury appliances. The board agreed. In the beginning the limit of deposit had been $1,000. In the next years it was raised to $2,000 with Life Savings and Loan Protection insurance coverage. This encouraged many loans. For a low-income family, the loss of the breadwinner could be devastating. The plan afforded member confidence and security. Money on deposit was doubled by the insurance company up to $2,000.

In a statement to a friend, Gerrie said, "The credit union has continued to grow, and so have I." She learned about loans, financing, and collections, and in the minds of her associates she knew her job. Extremely proud of her accomplishments, she reveled in being at banking seminars, mingling with other credit union managers and boards of directors. All this time she was keeping the secret of her thievery to herself. She also was keeping another thing to herself: the fact that Gerrie was discovering she was a homosexual.

There had been signs. . . . As a youngster Gerrie felt more comfortable in her brother's old clothes. She ignored the teasing she took from kids for always playing with boys. She enjoyed trading comic books with her friends, playing around cars, and sucking fumes from the gas tanks to get high. The neighborhood tomboy, that was Gerrie. She grew up getting into one scrape after another, always in more trouble than her siblings. As punishment, her mother ordered her to stay in the front yard. She made the most of a handicap by inviting all the neighborhood boys to her domain. She and her buddies were heavy marble players and played daily until one side of her yard was completely bare of grass.

During her teens she had crushes on women teachers. At fifteen, she had begun to question why she felt more comfortable around boys. She finally concluded that the boys were her buddies, people to chum around with, but she seemed to always want to impress the girls. One in particular, Heidi Graham, was the first woman she had feelings for that she didn't understand. Gerrie felt warm and tingly around Heidi and wanted to get closer to her, to touch her. With this insight, Gerrie realized she was different. Heidi, a tall, blond beauty, was about fifteen years older than Gerrie and was respected by everyone. All the teams loved her. Heidi taught Gerrie everything she knew about refereeing and was influential in getting Gerrie on the Board of Recreation in Louisville.

When Gerrie found she was heading in a direction that was sexually and emotionally out of the norm, she tried to change. Until that time she had no idea what the word *lesbian* meant. When she found out, she knew that her mother would disapprove. She vowed not to give into these feelings. Yet the sensations she had when she was around Heidi and other women were turning into something more than superficial crushes. She told no one how she felt. She was terrified at the thought of being different and perhaps being rejected. In an attempt to suppress her inner feelings, at seventeen she began seeing Todd Van Horne, a fellow who lived near her family and had been studying to be a priest. Blond, good-looking, and gentle, Todd came home one summer on his last leave before making his final commitment to the priesthood.

The leave of absence was to allow him time away from the seminary, to reach complete assurance that he had chosen the vocation best suited for him. Following that time, he was to have one final year of theology before being ordained. That summer he and Gerrie spent many quiet hours enjoying life. They went everywhere together: bicycle riding, walking, and fun things. For Gerrie it was a purely platonic relationship. For Todd, Gerrie was his first love. As the summer passed, Todd decided he didn't want to be a priest. He never returned to the seminary.

Todd joined the Army Reserve for eighteen months, and he asked Gerrie to marry him the following year. The day before Gerrie's graduation, when she was eighteen, Todd gave her an engagement ring. She accepted it but had mixed feelings. She felt she was doing the proper thing in marrying Todd. She knew it would please her mother, but when she forced herself to think of the sexual duties of a wife she became physically sick. Then she'd remember that her mother was happy, and that was important to her. Yet Gerrie continued to feel deeply concerned about the closeness she wanted with women, a closeness she didn't want with Todd. Finally when Todd returned she realized she could not go through with a marriage to him or any other man and broke off their engagement.

About this time her assignments as a referee led her to a high school where she met a petite Italian girl named Gina Lucci. Gina was a soft-spoken girl, kind and reserved. Fascinated but trying not to get involved, Gerrie took her to dinner. They began a long and lasting friendship. The two went everywhere together. Neither had ever been with a woman before; however, it seemed so natural. Gina said many times, "Gerrie is the most generous person you could ever meet! She will go out of her way to help a friend, family member, or stranger, financially or otherwise, in any way she can." They enjoyed each other's company, but never actually lived together and rarely stayed overnight. Gerrie knew her mother worried constantly when she came home late and when she didn't come home at all. Moreover, Gerrie's guiding force in wanting to remain at home—besides wanting to please her mother—was in not wanting anyone to suspect that she was a homosexual.

At the office, therefore, Gerrie hid the truth when speaking of her social life. Several weekends a year, the credit union held weekend work sessions. At office social functions, the only person appearing with Gerrie was her mother. The other credit union managers and their wives or husbands began to know Stella as well as they knew Gerrie.

At the seminars, credit union managers were alerted by the Kentucky Credit Union League to any law changes coming out of Frankfort or Washington. The league also informed them of new requirements by the National Credit Union Association, which insured deposits of up to $100,000 with government money. It was also a source of information to keep credit union managers on top of new laws and policies regarding collection, bribery, and the Internal Revenue Service. In addition to the seminars the league held education sessions twice a year. At these sessions they would always have activities for the spouses of the credit union people. Since most heads of credit unions were men, the activities provided were bingo or other things of interest to a woman. Gerrie took Stella, who loved the activities.

Gerrie was a devoted daughter. Every year, she and her mother went on a one-week vacation wherever Stella wanted to go. Of course, to do so Gerrie had to "borrow" from the company, but seeing Stella in Florida, suntanned and walking in the ocean, Gerrie felt that giving her mother everything that she missed throughout her life was worth the risk Gerrie was taking. Gina often went along on their trips. These were fun times—St. Augustine, seagulls, shrimp boats, Gerrie, Gina, and Stella strolling the beach, hand in hand. Gina would be on one side of Stella with Gerrie on the other.

During these vacations, Gerrie took her mother and Gina to nice restaurants. Gerrie loved the feeling of being waited on. She remembered a time when she was "hired help," working in a soup kitchen at fourteen, a time when she washed dishes for twenty-five cents an hour and would gaze out through the little window in the kitchen door and wonder what it would be like to be a customer. As money became more plentiful, Gerrie upgraded and enjoyed the fruits and fancies of even finer restaurants with Stella or Gina. For the first time in her life she was served by a tuxedo clad waiter and tasted caviar. It was at this point that Gerrie began to overeat, perhaps because of her constant hunger as a child. Her appearance changed from the "bean pole" of her youth, and the well-muscled athlete of her teenage years, to a fuller, more voluptuous shape.

She tried to reduce but could not stand depriving herself. Indeed, she was quickly becoming accustomed to more and more luxury. Through the credit union Gerrie soon financed her first boat, a weekend cruiser she called *Sweet Sixteen*. When she found herself low on funds, she made payments on her loan with money from the drawer. She called the funds her "resource."

The free, fresh feeling of boating with Gina—turning the key in the ignition and just taking off—became addictive. It was her entrance to a world of forgetting problems, work, and family; it was her escape. Gerrie would be seen going up and down the Ohio River, often alone. She would open the throttle to its maximum speed, letting her hair blow in the wind. To her it was a feeling of power and control, and yet she felt dizzy with freedom.

Gerrie was in her prime; Gina was maturing. In time, however, the love they had for each other began dwindling. Gerrie began seeing other women.

After a short while, Gerrie's one-night escapades turned into more serious affairs. She began spending her salary on clothes and women, but why not? There was always more cash from the drawer to replace it. The women she went out with seemed to love the attention she gave and the money she spent on them. In turn, the adoration and respect she received was like a tonic. Unknowingly, she was blocking out all guilt and criminal consequences of her embezzlement.

In Gerrie's circle at the time were approximately fifty girls. "They loved me," she said, "I could do no wrong." At least that was what she thought. She had a mania to be accepted by everyone. With time the scope of this need accelerated. Gerrie began to aspire to being accepted by more and more exclusive elements of society, to open doors that had always been closed to her.

Although the South is well known for its hospitality, it is difficult for an individual—especially one from a different class—to be accepted. And like its hetero counterpart, there is an established hierarchy for gays. Louisville had no gay bars for women at that time, but small groups of friends formed their gay cliques. There were beer drinkers, ball players, card players, boaters, and then there was the "500 Club." This clique was composed of college graduates with degrees. All were well off financially, had maids, played golf, and belonged to a prestigious country club. They were successful lesbian women in skilled professions who gathered over cocktails to share each others opinions of the latest newsworthy events. They were unknown as "gay" to the "straight" world. Being discreet and hiding behind the comforts money afforded, they lived comfortably with their companions. The 500 Club accepted very few new friends. As Gerrie watched them, she began having visions of herself as a member.

At every opportunity she tried to become friendly with them. However, the group looked down their noses at Gerrie. She was hurt, but the rejection made her more determined. Being welcome in every other group, she went from one woman to another, bed-hopping with all types, even some rather unsavory characters, but she was always in circulation and always searching for that next rung on the ladder that would allow her to climb up socially. She decided she needed a better occupation than bookkeeper to advance herself.

A business property was for lease on Fairground Road. It was attractive inside with booths, tables, and a twenty-five-foot bar. In the back there was a small club with a bandstand and dance floor. The owners wanted $2,500 for the business, while assuming a lease for $200 a month. Gerrie examined the books and found the bar was clearing $200 a week. All she needed was the cash to get going. Then she remembered: she had her "resources!"

Gerrie "borrowed" $1,500 from the office. This was the largest amount she had taken at one time, but she felt confident that she could bring in enough business to repay the money before the next audit. The small shortages were easy to explain: $2,000 or $3,000 in cash remained on hand to cash payroll checks, and this money wasn't counted during an examination of the books.

Gerrie partnered with an old friend of hers. Denise Simms was a stereotypical butch. She wore sport clothes, short hair, no makeup, and was liked by the regulars of the bar, working men in the area. She conversed continuously, which made her an asset as a "front" for the business and enabled it to keep previous customers.

The club began growing. Once a month Gerrie hired a band on Saturday night, and for the first time in Louisville, gay couples had a place to socialize. The bar became popular immediately. However, Gerrie soon realized that with payroll and expenses, it would take a while for her to be able to pay off the amount she had borrowed. And the auditors were due to check the credit union's books.

The night before they were to arrive, Gerrie stayed in the office working diligently on the books to cover her tracks. She confused transactions, removed files, and worked until 1:00 A.M. Gerrie lay awake most of the night, exhausted. At 6:00 A.M., she dressed in a powder-blue silk dress, and at 8:00 she went to the office. The next two hours inched by.

The auditors arrived promptly at 10:00, a tall balding man with watery blue eyes behind rimless glasses, followed at three paces by a non-descript, ageless woman and a younger, dark-haired man with piercing brown eyes.

"Fred Haines," the older man said.

"Gertrude Baker," the woman chimed in.

"R-r-r-obert Shoenberg," the younger man stuttered.

Almost on cue the three stared at Gerrie. She flushed.

"I'm Geraldine Powell, the credit union manager," Gerrie said, trying to make her voice sound normal. She wondered if the look on her face would reveal her secret and alert them to dig deeper into the books.

"Well," said Haines, nodding, "let's get down to the books, Miss Powell."

Trembling, she led them over to the bridge tables and chairs she had set up.

"If there's anything you need . . . ," she began.

Haines again spoke for the three auditors, "We'll let you know."

Sitting rigidly at her desk, Gerrie waited. Bent over the books, the three worked for hours. During the entire time they exchanged only a few words. Haines would say, "See this, Robert," or "Look here, Gertrude." That was all.

The other two confined their answers to "Yes sir" or "No sir."

Gerrie listened. She tried to ascertain what aspect of the books were they studying. Trying to be discreet, and agonizing over each word, she could not figure it out.

It was 4:00 P.M. when Haines stood up. "Okay," he said, taking off his glasses and cleaning them with a crumpled tissue he pulled from his pocket.

He turned to Gerrie. "Everything is in balance, Miss Powell. We'll see you in three months."

The deliverance of final relief was unnerving. As soon as Gerrie was sure they were out of the building, she left the office and drove to the bar. Hurrying inside she called out, "A round of drinks for everyone!" She kept her reason for celebrating to herself.

In the months to follow, as Gerrie's extravagances grew, the income from a neighborhood bar was far too limited to establish the type of cover she needed, and being involved in the business with another person kept her from using the bar as a means to launder money. Within the first year she sold out her part of the business and began looking at other projects to explore.

Despite these drawbacks, the customers she had met had become her friends.

One person in particular that she became acquainted with was a professional dancer, Lucy Kohler.

CHAPTER 2

And Other Appetites

Lucy Kohler managed a dance studio. She lived with her mother on sixteen acres of rolling hills in east Louisville. They lived quite comfortably due to the sharp eye of Mrs. Kohler, who turned real estate deals to her advantage. The estate was landscaped with natural beauty in a way that only time and the elements can create. The years had wound a creek around the guest cottage, under a walking bridge and up to the front of the main house where Mrs. Kohler lived. Lucy occupied the "rambling ranch" guest cottage. The layout impressed the ambitious Gerrie. To impress Lucy in turn, Gerrie wanted to entertain her at the finest supper clubs, and this meant taking larger amounts from the drawer.

On their first dinner date, Lucy wore a short sweater-dress and tights. She was talkative, very youthful (almost to the point of being immature), but charming. The first evening Gerrie was well aware of Lucy's beautiful legs and innocent child-like smile. Lucy was "on stage" at all times. Her dark hair was meticulously coiffured. She was striking, playful, and lovable. With funds from the credit union, Gerrie took her out several times a week. She reveled in Lucy's bubbly conversation at their candlelight dinners as they imbibed French wine.

They began spending more time together, and Gerrie moved some of her clothes into Lucy's guest home. Nevertheless, Gerrie didn't want to get too close to any one person. When she could get away from her mother at night, she was living the life of a free-spending playgirl. She wanted it to stay that way—no strings attached, no commitments—otherwise someone might suspect.

Meanwhile she did the book work alone, went to the board of directors meetings, and had total responsibility of the credit union. By this time, the board of directors trusted her completely and agreed with almost every suggestion she initiated. And she had many . . . new plans, new ways to keep up an ever-increasing flow of cash.

Gerrie had full control of posting and managing; she *was* the credit union. Gerrie and the credit union were continually growing. She hired a part-time employee, Harriet Neely, to work for her. Neely worked afternoons from 2:00 to 4:30 P.M. It was a great relief to Gerrie, and the company was impressed with the way the credit union prospered. In conjunction with this, Haines and the other auditors invariably gave a good report. "No problems," Haines said, speaking for all three. "Everything ran smoothly, everything balanced." Haines respected Gerrie. "She's always smiling, always friendly." She had a contagious warmth that generated trust. The employees were happy. On many occasions they came into the office to sit and talk to her about their problems and their families. She made herself available to them at all times.

Smiling, confident, she seemed to use an inner defense mechanism with the men on the board of directors and became indignant if asked questions about the operation. Therefore, their questions were few.

Gerrie, always astute in her job, and always needing more money, continued making suggestions which by now were invariably followed. Maximum deposit was raised, because of her suggestion, to $5,000. She constantly generated more cash flow. The credit union kept growing, and the officers trusted her completely. Twenty or more loans were approved weekly, and Gerrie's input was invaluable to them. She knew the people and therefore controlled everything going through the credit union.

In her private life Gerrie's affair with Lucy grew more heated. It was Lucy and Gerrie at the Hilton, at the Top of the Tower; it was champagne dinners at the most expensive spots in town. Gerrie was having a ball. When she invited a group of friends out for dinner, without exception, she paid for everything . . . with, of course, the ready cash from the company. After a while, however, friends, aware that money always seemed plentiful, started asking questions. In the beginning, Gerrie laughed off their remarks, but she soon realized she had to get a more believable cover. She needed a "front," something believable, so people would say, "So *that's* how she makes her money!" She had grown up listening to her dad talk about horse racing. She hadn't paid much attention and had never been drawn to the sport enough to want to learn the skill of handicapping. Nevertheless, she realized now this could be her cover. If she at least looked like a gambler to her friends, it would account for the money she was spending.

At that time, the little bit of wagering Gerrie did was on ball games and cards. However, a new racetrack that had just opened in town, Louisville Downs, featured harness racing, with trotters and pacers.

On July 14, 1966, opening night, 3,480 fans had bet over $100,000. A few days later, Gerrie drove into the parking lot for the first time. She passed the marquee, the white fence, and the large iron gates, seeing the sprawling one-level structure with the entrance reading "Club House." She was impressed by the view in the center of the track—a clear, cool lake with white swans and ducks.

She took a seat in the stands and looked down at the track. There were the trotters. In awe, Gerrie watched the beautiful horses pulling a perfectly balanced sulky with a driver. "I love the atmosphere," she murmured. She adapted quickly, as though she were born to it.

Next to her sat an old lady, with silky white hair, studying her racing form. "Hi," she said, "I'm Dorothy. This your first time?"

Gerrie smiled. The woman reminded her of some of the workers at her company. "Sure is."

"Would you like some help?"

"That would be very kind of you," Gerrie said politely.

Dorothy taught her to read the tote board, how to figure current odds for each horse, and how to handicap. Gerrie had arrived with $50 in her pocket and bet $2 on a horse in the first race.

"You can play him to win, place, or show," Dorothy told her.

"I'm scared. I'll bet the horse to show," Gerrie laughed.

"Novice," she chuckled.

Gerrie's horse finished third, and she won $3.20. She liked a longshot in the second race; using the same system she won $15.30.

"Not bad, dear," Dorothy said.

"Not bad? It's wonderful!" Gerrie exclaimed.

Excited with her new-found luck, she kept betting the horses to show, staying on the safe side. She picked her horses by the name, then she listened to her hunches. When she was $25 ahead after the fifth race, Dorothy told her, "Time to get a racing form. You should learn to decipher the speed ratings of each horse and how far around the track the horse was at the first call, second call, and stretch call and how he finished." Fortified with that information, Gerrie learned to find the track records of each horse and check their past.

Gerrie left the track that day $406.60 ahead. After that she could be seen nightly at Louisville Downs. As each day passed, she became more excited about her plan to use the sport as a front for the money. When the season closed she had over $2,000 in clean money.

Louisville Downs closed for the season. Miles Park had the next racing dates. Thoroughbred racing, which was a faster pace, was different to Gerrie, far more exciting than harness racing.

Miles Park Race Course was one of the smaller tracks offering thoroughbred racing in the city. It was owned by the Jacob family, the "Sportservice" concessionaires. The track was built on land in the west end of town that at one time was the Old Kentucky State Fairgrounds.

With an extra $500 that she had taken from the drawer, Gerrie was eager to get to the track on opening day. She called ahead for a reservation for one in the dining room and was seated at the first "deuce" table on the second tier overlooking the finish line. When that evening was over, she was hooked. In the days that followed she lunged into studying the art of handicapping as a means of getting more money and creating a cover. She was hungry to learn, to find a system . . . if there was one.

The races started at 7:30 P.M., but Gerrie was there each night at 6:00, studying. As each race began, she joined the crowd in the excitement and watched from the rail, cheering for her horse to win. Going to the track night after night, she met other regulars. Many were people with no other job— professional gamblers. They followed the track openings and lived from race to race. As one meet ended, they headed for the gates of the next track.

Paul McFarland, a muscular, ruddy-faced redhead, was one of the fellows that Gerrie saw every night. He was a "touter" who spent his mornings on the backside of the track with trainers and groomers. He always wore the same brown pants and tan shirt, clean, but always the same. He sported the typical look sometimes seen at a race track, hands in his pockets rubbing two quarters together. He clenched a lit cigarette in his mouth at all times, prompting a cock to his head and a squint in his eye. He listened to anyone who would give him a tip on a horse that was racing that day. With that information and the knowledge of past performances printed in the racing form, he would pinpoint his winners.

Paul could be seen stalking several different people before every race. He was drawn to the ones who spent money freely. Of course, he spotted Gerrie. "Get on #6 in the first, to win." If the horse won, Paul would come back for a little gratuity. He survived on the tips he gave to racing fans. When he gave a tip on a loser, he'd disappear. If a touter likes two horses in one particular race, he will divide the tip with two people. The person who gives the greatest gratuity in return receives the best information. Touters make it their business to be likeable people, and they constantly compliment the gamblers. Some people refer to them as leeches because, they say, "You can't get rid of them."

With cash from the company and nightly trips to Miles Park, Gerrie improved her skills. With her mind firmly set, she'd approach the window to place a bet then, remembering a tip, would often go against her own hunches. She started betting the favorites to show; she was winning. This progressed to betting "across the board": $2 to win, place, and show ran her $6 a race. She was picking winners, but the winnings were slim on $2 bets on the favorites. Watching her, Paul told her, "Wait till the opening of the larger track, Churchill Downs."

"Churchill Downs?" Gerrie said quizzically.

"Yeah. Thoroughbred owners, like Claiborne or Calumet, never enter horses at the small tracks." Gerrie nodded. She couldn't wait for the opening at Churchill.

A week later the Miles Park meet ended. The next day Gerrie left work and drove to 4th Street and Central Avenue, south of downtown Louisville, for the beginning of the meet at Churchill Downs. She was an hour early for the first race. At the gift shop she bought a Derby Pin, picked up tidbits of information from friendly strangers, and waited for Paul to join her.

"How do you like it?" he asked.

"I like it," she smiled.

Gerrie learned that the 180 acres of ground were first purchased from the Churchill family. When established, the track was known as the Louisville Jockey Club. Several years later a writer gave the race course the present name of Churchill Downs. Gerrie asked question after question. She wanted to learn all she could.

The same was true with her betting. Always asking questions, she learned and progressed to betting $10 Exactas. With an Exacta she had to pick the first and second horse in the race. Paul suggested, "Why don't you 'wheel' the #3 horse?"

"Wheel it . . . ," she said slowly.

"Sure. If you like the #3 horse to win, put it with each of

the other horses, okay? Let's say you bet the #3 with #1, #3 with #2, #3 with #4, and so on. That's wheelin', see?"

She nodded. She was a quick learner.

Every day she made sure she was seen studying, breaking down each race into fractions and class, in preparation for the next day of racing. Methodically, she seemed to be getting the art of picking horses down to a science, but since she was spending more than the payoff on a favorite would be, she had to bet larger amounts of money to make it feasible.

A few weeks after the meet opened, she had won $2,400. Gerrie was not one to have extra money for any length of time. There were so many things she wanted; it was so hard to choose. She decided to shop for a larger boat. She came across a twenty-three-foot Chris Craft cabin cruiser. It was something she had always dreamed of having. It slept four and had everything one would want on a boat. She christened the cruiser *Wave Dancer*. It became her escape. "When I was alone on my boat, there were no problems, no tomorrow. I liked myself and enjoyed the time in my space." During the week she docked *Wave Dancer* at Harrod's Creek, off the Ohio River. Gerrie looked forward to a summer of fun and parties.

On weekends, she docked at Six-Mile Island. Several gay friends with boats pulled up side-by-side and tied off together. Gay couples played cards and enjoyed drinks. In the evening someone always started a fire on the shore, and the group congregated around it and pretended they could sing. It was fun, and Gerrie was relaxing between audits.

At the office Henry Vogt began a "fleet policy" for company cars. This also came under Gerrie's control. She learned the insurance business and the handling of claims. It grew into a full-time responsibility. She was accountable for premiums and collections. She loved her work and tried to keep her two lives separate, but gambling at the races had gotten into her blood and without meaning to she began talking of going to the track at the end of the day.

At about this time, Louisville Downs began what was called the "Big L." It involved the seventh and eight races of each day. To hit it, one had to pick the win and place horses in the seventh race and exchange the winning ticket for one's pick of the win and place horses in the eighth race. This is difficult to do, but the pay off is enormous. Gerrie's main goal became winning the Big L.

One day, because of betting several horses in the same race, Gerrie had cashed four winning tickets when the seventh race came up, and she was going to try for the Big L again. Gerrie was hoping to win with a longshot, #4, Native Sun. She "wheeled" it with every horse in the seventh race. There were seven other horses: it cost $14.00. She could hardly stand the wait. The horses were on the track; it was nearly post time.

Over the loudspeaker a voice shouted, "They're off!" The horses broke from the starting gate somewhat abreast. At the first call, one-quarter mile, the #1 horse, Dream Date, pulled out two lengths ahead of the others. All the horses began making a move, including Native Sun. They moved up on Dream Date, with Native Sun on the rail, right behind the leader. They heard the stretch call. They had one-eighth of a mile to go; Native Sun came up on the inside and took the lead. Then it was neck and neck. Scanning the track, Gerrie jumped up and down as Native Sun came over the finish line, with #1, #2, and #8 in a photo finish for second. She had them all; she knew she had an exchange ticket for the eighth race. She had one leg up for the big one, with twelve minutes to post time for the next race. This time she couldn't wheel her bet. She had one chance to pick the win and place horses in the final race.

In the eighth race, Paul McFarland, her touter friend, liked the #1 horse, Brave Secret. "Gerrie, I know he's a shoe in! Brave Secret's gonna win that eighth race! Put him on top of what you like. You can't lose!" Gerrie had been studying her racing form the night before, and she felt strongly about two horses, #6, Bright Promise, and #2, Willow. She still had seven minutes to make up her mind. She drank a screwdriver, but kept hearing Paul's voice interrupting her thoughts: "Go with Brave Secret, he can't lose. I'm positive." Still she kept telling herself, "The #6 and #2 have a good chance." She confused herself with her indecision, and beads of perspiration dripped down the side of her face.

From the rail, she studied the beautiful four-legged athletes on the field. As the horses were nearing the starting gate she made up her mind. With two minutes to post time, she went to the window to exchange her winning ticket from the seventh race for what she hoped would be a win and place ticket in the eighth. Sticking with her hunch, she picked #6 Bright Promise to win and #2 Willow to place. There was less than a minute to go. This was her supreme test. With only one exchange ticket, she had to pick it right. All the money in her pocket couldn't help her now.

The horses broke from the starting gate, the track was fast. All eyes in the crowd turned toward the action as the #1 horse, Brave Secret, bolted out in front. Gerrie heard Paul yelling, "Brave Secret, Brave Secret!" She had a sick feeling in the pit of her stomach. Paul hadn't seen Gerrie's ticket. He only assumed she had taken his tip.

Three-quarters of the way around the track, Brave Secret broke his stride, slowed, and tried to regain his position. Suddenly Willow came up to take the lead; #4 Taggert was second, #3 Gentle Wind was third, and Bright Promise was on the rail in fifth place. Gerrie's heart seemed to stop. She murmured, "I've lost it."

Into the turn, Gentle Wind dropped back, Willow was still ahead, Taggert moved up to take over the lead. With Bright Promise in fourth place, #5 Silly Putty charged up on the outside. Silly Putty and Bright Promise came challenging on the rail.

There they were, horses 4, 2, 5, and 6, all in a line, fighting for first position as the spectators screamed. Then into the stretch, #7 Tailspin moved up, and now there were five horses abreast. Numbers 4, 2, 5, 6, and 7, side by side, looking like the Rockettes. The crowd's roar was deafening. In seconds the horses were at the wire. It was a photo finish.

On the tote board the numbers were put up: #6 for win, #5 for place, and #2 for show; Gerrie had 6 and 2. Without warning the #5 began to flash off and on, which meant an inquiry for second place.

Her gut was grinding, but she sat with a stoic façade and sipped her drink while waiting for the results. She looked around, suddenly noticing that her friend Paul, thinking he had touted her onto the wrong horse, had disappeared.

Finally #5 came off the board and #6 and #2 stayed. Grabbing her ticket, she stared at the numbers, as if she thought by some twist of fate she had been issued the wrong ones. She had #6 to win and #2 to place. She jumped up and twirled around and around. She had done it. She had the only winning ticket on the Big L, and she had done it by herself.

Paul came rushing toward her, obviously watching from a distance. He blurted out, "Did ya' get it, Gerrie? Did ya' have the 6 and 2?" Once again, figures were put on the tote board. The Big L paid $6,725. Gerrie clutched the ticket to herself, grinning broadly. Only one ticket was sold, and Gerrie had it. "You look just like a gambler," Paul said. The instant respect and admiration he had for her was obvious, and she wanted more.

"Can I cash the ticket for you, Gerrie?" he asked. "I'll use my Social Security number. I've got three kids for deductions. I'll cash it for ten percent. How 'bout it?" This was another way Paul made money.

"Thanks, but I can cash it myself," she laughed.

She hurried to the cashier and turned in the ticket, signed the forms and left the window with $5,100 in cash. She peeled off $300 and gave it to Paul for past efforts he had made to give her a win. She knew he needed money. He was happy, but not nearly as happy as Gerrie. For the first time she had handicapped the races herself.

Later Gerrie remarked to a friend, "Paul never left my side at the track. We were both handicapping, and I had the money. He was well paid."

During the weeks that followed, Gerrie's handicapping improved. She was winning, but sometimes only a few dollars on a bet. "It's not enough," she decided. "I could borrow larger amounts from the office and bet $50 instead of $2, then return the money and keep the winnings."

The next day she waited on customers, taking deposits and payments and handling thousands of dollars. Convinced of her skills at handicapping, Gerrie took $1,000 from the drawer, and that night she began betting fifties and hundreds. The day after that she replaced the money when she won; and when she didn't, she had to take more to recoup.

After work every day she went to the track and gambled with company money. She continued winning, spending, and replacing what she could; she felt that she was on top of the world. This was the kind of high she had been searching for; and forever after she would find herself trying to reach that ultimate high.

She began throwing extravagant parties at Lucy's home. They had open house with hors d'oeuvres and champagne for fifty to seventy people. Any occasion called for a party. The Derby, the Breeders Cup, the Rose Bowl, Halloween—all were occasions to celebrate. Her reputation as a free spender grew, and everyone wanted an invitation. They all wanted to be her friend. The attention seemed to feed a hunger within Gerrie that could never be satisfied. She made the parties more and more lavish. The bigger the party, the better Gerrie felt; the better she felt, the more friends she wanted.

Besides the food that was catered by ever-classier firms, she began to have music—at first smaller combos, but later orchestras. Her reputation as both a hostess and a successful gambler grew. The list of guests expanded until the event had to be held at the dance studio. The cost was well in the thousands. She became obsessed with the things money afforded her: newer cars, better clothes, big cluster diamond rings, and heavy gold chains. Big money brought respect and friends. Then the inevitable happened—she began losing. At first, it was $500 a day, then $700 and more.

After a losing streak that lasted two months, she totaled her debt to the company. It was $43,000. Gerrie concentrated on covering the shortage as she took larger amounts in a desperate attempt to win.

Meanwhile, the company's assets were escalating. More applications were received monthly to finance boats, cars, and mortgages on houses; Gerrie saw this as still another means of getting money. "If an account became delinquent, I followed the correct procedures of repossession. However, many times when the credit union received the property, I'd go to my resources, 'borrow' the money to pay off the account, change the title, and resell the car. The loan department appeared to have very few delinquent accounts," Gerrie said. "We had a near-perfect record. I made certain that our rates were competitive, always offering lower rates than banks." So, despite her losses at the track, she still had more money because of extra money she received from the sale of repossessed cars.

Eventually even Lucy began to question Gerrie's strange behavior. Flighty as the dancer was, she knew Gerrie was hard to live with when the auditors were due to arrive.

"Not that I want to complain, but where are you getting all this money, Gerrie?" Lucy asked.

Gerrie flushed. "Just lucky, I guess," she said, turning away.

Her debt to the company soon reached $58,000. In her mind, the only way to repay it was to borrow more and go for the big win.

But as the pressure mounted, she had a constant fear of the auditors appearing. Several times a month, Gerrie went to the office on Sunday to work, to get things in order. The examiners never came in December or January, but the time between February 1 and November 30 was her cancer. And she lived with the cancer that was consuming her.

Aside from the stress at work Gerrie's worry over her mother finding out was another issue that plagued her.

The 1:00 A.M. curfew Stella set for her daughter could not always be met. To avoid a confrontation over being late, Gerrie would stay out all night. If she had been drinking, she would not call for fear that her mother would suspect. Her guilt over her behavior with drinking, women, and the money she had been taking grew. It began depressing her to the point of making her physically ill. She had bouts of nausea and a loss of appetite. Both Gerrie and her mother worried about Gerrie's deteriorating health. When her condition became critical, she had to be hospitalized.

Going into the hospital added further stress. It meant Gerrie would be out of the office. After many tests, Garren Hayes, her doctor, called a conference. He told Stella, who refused to leave her daughter's side, that Gerrie had a spasmodic stomach from nerves. His orders to Gerrie were "Find a hobby of some sort that would serve as therapy, and begin living in an apartment of your own." He looked badgeringly at Stella, who had telephoned him at every opportunity. "I know you mean well, but Gerrie's nervousness is partially due to your rigid control over her personal life, as well as pressure at work." Outwardly Gerrie appeared calm, almost stoic. But inside there was turmoil. Only Gerrie really knew what was causing her problem.

Confident that he had found the reason for Gerrie's illness, Dr. Hayes took Stella aside after the meeting and advised her to turn Gerrie loose.

"But my daughter needs me," Stella objected.

Hayes pushed back his thick, graying hair. "Ah, Stella, we parents like to think that. But you have to let her live her own life."

Gerrie later admitted, "I suppose, aside from the pressure of taking the money, I resented my mother for refusing to give me freedom. She wanted me to account to her for everything. I was her crutch, and she wouldn't let go and I couldn't tell her what I was doing." In fact, even Stella had begun to question Gerrie about her dates and her excessive amounts of money.

After his discussion with Stella, Dr. Hayes talked to Gerrie. "Tell your mother you need a life of your own," he advised.

She stared at him for a while, then nodded.

On leaving the hospital, Gerrie had a long talk with her mother. "Mom, you've grown so accustomed to mothering me that you can't release me."

Stella began to cry. "I know, but I love you so much and I worry about you all the time. There's no one to take care of you but me."

"Mom, I appreciate your caring," Gerrie said gently. "You'll always be first and last and always, but I need to grow up and you need to let go."

"I'll try," Stella promised. "I really will."

Gerrie weaned her mother as one would a small child. Slowly at first, with two nights away from home, working up to four, then seven. She felt this would open the door for her to spend more time with Lucy. But the couple soon realized that added time together increased their differences. Lucy wanted her career. She loved teaching dance day and night, while Gerrie was desperate for the nightly seclusion she found on the river. Moreover, Lucy complained of what appeared to be Gerrie's compulsive gambling and the fact that when the auditors were due to arrive, "Gerrie was like a live wire dangling over water." Lucy explained, "Any wrong move could set her off."

After a while Gerrie's serious demeanor conflicted with Lucy's carefree way of living. Their problems grew. Meanwhile Gerrie's internal pressures were building. Finally they split up. Alone again, Gerrie spent most of her free time on her boat, the *Wave Dancer*. But it came to be a constant reminder of Lucy. Gerrie needed something new . . . something to make her forget.

To get it Gerrie went back to her "resources"—the cash drawer. This time she escalated the amount of her take. With $5,000 in her pocket she left the office and celebrated, telling friends about her successful "win" at the track. The next day she went shopping for another boat.

This time she lost her heart to a 42-foot houseboat offering all the amenities of a small luxury apartment. It consisted of a full kitchen, bath, and sliding glass doors opening to a carpeted living room.

Once again the feeling that she had to have this luxury filled her. She put $3,000 down and financed a $4,000 balance through the credit union. In the ensuing weeks her frantic desires to assume more luxuries grew. She acquired three houses with down payments acquired from the company till.

Not satisfied, Gerrie had the boat refurbished, and Stella made new powder-blue drapes and silk navy slipcovers. After Gerrie moved in, a telephone and stereo were added. She named the new boat *Gemini II*. The floating apartment became her home.

In early spring, still cool with a brisk March wind, she found solace on her boat. Here she was alone with her thoughts. Some were pleasant, but others were tormenting.

In 1971, Gerrie's debt to the credit union rose to $90,000. She worked overtime to adjust the books and cover her theft. By the this time money she won at the track was replacing only a small percentage of the debt.

One restless Sunday night she tossed and turned, trying to get some sleep, but couldn't. For some reason a dark thought kept running through her mind. Somehow she sensed "they" were coming. Gerrie left her bed at 1:00 A.M. to go to the credit union to adjust the books. At her office, she worked until the dawn light streamed in the window. Near exhaustion, she tried everything she could think of to cover the shortage. Finally she left at 6:00 A.M., still worried but feeling better.

Monday morning she found her premonition was justified when Ed Haines and Robert Schoenberg arrived unannounced. Pale and shaken, Gerrie led them to the books. Gerrie explained figures and answered questions. The tension escalated until the sound of her own swallowing seemed to interrupt the heavy silence of the room. The men stayed for eight hours. They left saying, as always, "Everything's in balance, Gerrie. See you in three months." Gerrie had pulled it off again. She drove directly home to her boat. She could hardly believe she had gotten away with it. Now she knew how to keep it going. She would not be caught.

CHAPTER 3

Memories Pull

Gerrie had a certain fascination with the water, but thinking back to when this same muddy river on which she now lived imposed itself upon her family, she also had great respect for it.

She was five when the Powells lived four blocks from the river, on Bank Street, in the Portland area. It had taken Stella five years to make her small house comfortable. Because they had little extra money she had made all the curtains and bedspreads. Indeed she scraped, painted, and patched every inch of used furniture, floors, and walls.

It had been a rugged winter that year. Heavy snow fell in Pittsburgh and other cities north of Louisville. In January, an incessant rain began and the banks of the Ohio swelled until the magnitude of damage surpassed anything to that date. As the snow melted in the north, the rain continued in the Ohio Valley. It rained without interruption for six days in January, elevating the Ohio River to a depth of thirty feet, two feet above flood stage.

That day Stella was anxiously listening to the WHAS radio announcer, Pete Monroe, asking rescuers to send a boat to areas around 41st and Market Streets. Her family lived seventeen blocks east of that area. Neighbors were nervously discussing incidences of friends being "flooded out." Everyone seemed preoccupied with the river rising, but Gerrie, being so young, did not comprehend the impending danger.

Jim, Stella's brother, a foreman at the train station, called Bill at the Brown Foreman Distillery, where he worked the night shift. "You'd better move the family to the train depot at Tenth and Broadway. If you stay where you are," Jim said ominously, "you'll be flooded out."

Bill rushed home before daylight that morning. The children, sleepy-eyed and half-awake, asked each other, "Why's Dad home so early?" He wasn't due home until 7:00 A.M.

As he entered the bedroom, Bill shouted, "Stella, get the kids up. Get dressed. We've got to get out. The water's coming up." Everyone rushed from their beds, scrambling for clothes—all except Gerrie. She watched the others struggle in confusion.

Bill grabbed Gerrie, still in her nightgown, wrapped her in a blanket, and carried her to their 1931 Chevy.

The rain was coming in torrents. Half-drenched, Stella ran to the car with the rest of the family. She herded the children into the back seat, tucked a blanket around them, and got in the front. Bill immediately started the motor and began speeding away. He wanted to reach high ground where all would be safe.

Stella had very few possessions, but as they drove through the flooded streets, she glanced back toward the house and recalled the years of work she had put into gaining those few objects. Her eyes filled with tears and she began to cry softly. Gerrie understood the seriousness of it all when she saw her mother cry.

As Bill reached over to comfort his wife, water came in

over the floor boards of the car, splashed onto Stella's shoes and the back seat floor.

"Daddy, Daddy," the children cried, "we'll be drowned!"

Bill and Stella put aside their own rising fears and tried to comfort them. "No, no, everything will be all right," Stella said.

But Gerrie, her eyes wide with terror, could not stop shaking.

When they arrived at the train depot, people were hurrying inside. Jim and his wife Hazel rushed to the car and assisted the family. Motivated by panic, Jim quickly moved into position to yank the kids from the car. His gray-green eyes flashed back and forth as he waved his hands in the directions they were to go to reach safety. Everyone on the loading dock frantically passed kids between them like bundles of merchandise. Hand over hand they reached and grabbed. Gerrie cried out, "Don't take me away from Mommy! Don't take me away from Mommy!" But a strong, sinewy arm clasped her and the two were separated. Finally her mother caught up to her and Gerrie gripped her skirt as though it were her only salvation. Bill ran up beside them as crowds of people welcomed the family to safety in the three-story structure of the depot. They anticipated a move to an upper level if the water rose any more. In less than an hour, it had.

In 1,500 square feet of space there were over a hundred people—people who had never associated with each other. Rich folks met poor folks, white folks met black folks.

Gerrie's grandfather, who saw the children's terror, pulled up a chair. He was a frail man with wrinkled, rugged, ruddy skin, white hair, mustache and goatee. An American Indian, he began to quietly entertain the children with his famous story telling. They listened for hours. Gerrie was engrossed in his stories about bartering in the Old West when he was a boy. If a child cried or the children sensed fear in the grown-ups, he'd tell another story. Meanwhile, the downpour seemed endless. It lasted into the night and through the next day.

By the third day, Bill's car as well as many others was submerged. The rising water had long since swallowed up the loading dock platform and was halfway up to the second floor.

They were marooned, with no way out except by boat.

The end of the week brought freezing temperatures, producing sleet and hail and refreezing the ground. This swelled the Ohio to fifty-seven feet before the water began to recede on January 27.

Broadway became a river navigated by rowboats, canoes, and makeshift rafts. At Third and Broadway the water was five-feet, six-inches deep. The Courier Journal and Louisville Times Building was flooded. It housed the city's only newspapers. Presses had to be temporally shut down. Typesetters and printers worked around the clock keeping the latest news available to everyone. The small handset newspaper was cranked out on old manual presses, then delivered by boat and passed from person to person.

The flood destroyed businesses and wrecked homes; it also brought people together. Before the flood there had been a color barrier, a barrier of hate that had broken when the water came, and returned when the water receded. Louisville, with her 325,000 residents, was the largest city to feel the full impact. The massive floods took 500 lives and forced 164,500 people out of their homes. Bank Street, where the Powells lived, was under twelve feet of water.

The Powell family lost their meager belongings—all they

had scraped together was totally destroyed. Bill saw no hope. He began drinking at work and within weeks was fired from his job at the distillery. After that he couldn't keep a steady job. As the last resort he began working for President Roosevelt's Work Projects Administration, or W.P.A., organized during the Depression. The workers built roads and bridges and were paid as little as ten cents an hour. However, Stella never saw his paycheck. He'd lose it between Friday afternoon and Saturday night playing cards in the back room of some seedy corner saloon. If he came home, he would be drunk and she would know she was in for a weekend of hell. Devastated by the flood, Bill never fully recovered.

Stella had to resort to menial jobs outside her home, such as scrubbing floors, or other domestic work. From then on she accepted numerous servile jobs from women of the church to supply the family with food.

Gerrie watched the swift-moving, muddy water from the *Gemini II* and sadly thought of the muddy waters of long ago and the final submersion into poverty the water had brought her family and especially her mother.

Trying to shake off her dismal thoughts, Gerrie decided to leave the *Gemini II* and go to the track. Her intentions were to stop first at her old flame Gina's and ask her to come to the races with her. Although Gerrie and Gina's affair had long since ended, they had remained friends.

Gina had begun raising miniature Schnauzers as a pastime. Eventually, it developed into a profitable business. Gina had worked hard and saved her money. When she had accumulated enough, she built a stone house with a pool on three acres of land on a country road east of the city. There she opened a kennel and boarded dogs.

As Gerrie pulled into the driveway, she immediately rec-
ognised the five-year-old tan Cadillac as belonging to another
fried of theirs, Josephine.

Josephine was an attorney, a classy lady who now lived
with a woman but at one time had been married to a very
wealthy man, a millionaire with a summer home in Malibu.

The other car, a metallic blue Chevrolet convertible,
Gerrie did not recognize.

As Gerrie walked in, Josephine, with her paisley
muumuu and amaythst beads, her platinum hair and air of
Zsa Zsa Gabor, leaned toward the striking woman seated on
the couch next to her and loudly whispered, "My dear, here
comes a very wealthy woman. And let me tell you, if you
want a . . . . I *know* what I'm talking about." In an instant
the classically featured, thirtyish woman pulled the plastic
curlers from her lustrous, salt-and-pepper hair. Combing it
quickly with her fingers as Gerrie walked closer, she smiled
and exhaled a melodic, "Hi!"

Gerrie nodded, accepted Gina's offer of a scotch and
soda, and was introduced to Cindy Kelly, the woman who
was to play the most devastating role in her future life.

Cindy's childhood had been spent in Eastwood, Kentucky,
a small country town twenty-five miles from Louisville. Her
father, Charles Whitehall, was a successful farmer with an
eye for business. Years before he had accepted an offer to sell
off part of the family land for quite a large sum of money.
After that Charles Whitehall and his family lived comfortably
in a large stately home surrounded by hundreds of acres of
farm land on Johnson Road.

Cindy was raised as a rich little girl. At a young age she
had an eye for expensive things: Shirley Temple dresses, vel-

vet and fur-trimmed coats, a piano and private lessons—she had it all. But the thing she loved the most was her palomino pony and cart.

Her father was the ruler of the household, and Cindy was ever aware of that fact.

Charles was the type of man who found it difficult to show affection openly. When he said no, he rarely gave in. He believed in stern, strict discipline. Unlike her mother, however, the child discovered other means of getting her way. If being sweet didn't work, pouting would. If that failed, she could always accuse her father of not loving her . . . and that worked every time.

Although the child learned how to get what she needed materially from her spartan father, the lack of affection from Charles was more than her mother Katherine could handle; so she began to drink. Being a self-made man, Charles admired only those who were "doers." The more Katherine drank, the more Charles rejected her. Tormented by loneliness, Katherine's bottle became her only comfort.

Cindy's father and mother divorced. He was awarded custody of Cindy. Following the divorce, Cindy attempted to spend time with her mother, but found the visits depressing because of her mother's constant drinking.

When she was eleven her father remarried to a woman with two daughters, ages four and six. Charles had not only a new wife, but a whole new family.

It would be an understatement to speak of the turmoil invading Cindy's mind as mere jealousy. For a young child it was simply too much to handle, yet she had to put up a pretence of accepting it. Seeing her step-sisters wearing beautiful dresses like the ones she had outgrown while she was now buying bargain basement clothes hurt her deeply. It was difficult for the child who had been so spoiled in her early years to suddenly feel she was second-class.

Having lost her father's attention, Cindy's material possessions became the only "real" things she had to depend on for security. Hiding her resentment taught her to be a little actress when the family was together. However, she was finding it more difficult to keep up her act of being in control when her sisters took everything of hers for their own, including her pony and cart. Or later, when Cindy was in a part of the house that was now shared with the sisters, she heard the sound of a piano . . . her piano. She wanted to run to them and say, "No! No, that's mine!" But she kept it inside, concealing her pain. It was no wonder she was jealous. Sometime later, Cindy's piano lessons were stopped and her pony and cart were sold; this further devastated the child.

As a teenager, Cindy drove an old Army jeep like a general. The jeep, her status symbol, came to be the envy of her peers. Cindy seemed to enjoy their envy. A piquant-faced brunette with a beautiful figure, she was a bouncy, nubile cheerleader. With the boys, she flirted and acted fragile and vulnerable. She was never at a loss for a date. Her father and step-mother passed judgment as they were introduced to her boyfriends.

However, the mere fact that her parents liked a boy would cause Cindy to rebel and drop him. Against her parents wishes, she chose James Kelly. He spent money on her. They had fun together. But most of all, he was the one boy her parents disliked.

The new Mrs. Whitehall had chosen another boy for Cindy to marry. He was in the upper realm of Kentucky society; however, all attempts to stop the relationship between James and their daughter merely made Cindy more determined. In spite of threats that she would be disinherited, they

were married when she was eighteen, one year after graduation. She never believed her father would carry out his
threat.

The marriage was only three weeks old when the new
bride accused her husband, probably unjustly, of seeing another girl. Cindy's attempt to return home was met with
harsh words from her father: "You've made your bed," he
said, and he repeated his threat to eliminate her from his will.

She was devastated, but a born survivor, she returned to
her husband and vowed to make it in spite of her father. She
said, "One way or another, I will show that son of a bitch."
And she set out with a determination that was to guide her
for the rest of her life.

Disenchanted with her marriage, Cindy had dreams of
starting her own business. She began working toward that
goal. After three years of marriage, however, James Jr. was
born and her plans for the business had to be put on hold.

Six years later Cindy and James had their second child, a
little girl born on September 4, 1954, named Kim. She was
the most wonderful event in Cindy's life. According to her,
"James started to gamble, and the debts grew." In reality, she
wanted her baby girl to have the best that money could buy,
so perhaps Cindy was the cause for the debts to grow. Whatever the reason, the charges multiplied with every shopping
trip. One month later, on October 25, the couple filed for
bankruptcy.

During this time Cindy held various menial jobs to try to
stay ahead of the bills. Then in 1963, she began raising Stan-
dard Poodles and became a professional dog handler. Her
beautiful, thick, dark hair turned salt-and-peppery when she
was in her late twenties, enhancing her exotic looks.

It wasn't enough that James had a steady job at the
Courier Journal and Louisville Times; he also groomed the dogs

and helped with the housework while his wife traveled to dog shows. But Cindy wanted to climb socially. She had a fixation for being around people with money. She was ambitious, but to her, "James was dragging his feet."

Much of Cindy's adult life had been unhappy. The lack of a close relationship with her mother when she needed her most had left a permanent void. Then a terrible shock after Cindy was grown nearly destroyed her.

She decided to visit her mother just before Christmas one year and found the house locked. The lights were on, her mother's car was there, so she thought her mother was drunk and unable to come to the door. Finally, when she found a way to enter, she discovered her mother's body. She had been dead for several days. Cindy carried this horrible memory with her. Every year after that, Christmas became nothing more than a sad reminder of a terrible loss. Feeling that she had been cheated out of the bonding that she deserved to have with her mother, Cindy wanted to make up for her loss through her children. She would stop at nothing to give them everything that she had missed.

While Gerrie had been expanding her "resources," Cindy and her husband were struggling to stay ahead of their bills. Cindy was spending money for things James couldn't afford. They constantly argued over finances. As James fought to stay out of bankruptcy court, the marriage became more rocky. Because of Cindy's expensive taste, they were always in debt. For Cindy, though, being in debt was not a deterrent; it only triggered her desire for spending. She had a fixation for, and seemed to gravitate to, people of independent means.

One person who gave the appearance of having independent means was Gerrie's old friend Gina. Cindy had been showing dogs with her and they became fast friends.

During the week Cindy was a regular visitor at Gina's home. They had much in common with the exception that Gina seldom had a drink and Cindy was seldom without one. Cindy met most of Gina's gay friends, men and women. She mixed well, appearing to be curious and quite comfortable with the crowd. They readily accepted her because, as they said jokingly, some of their best friends were straight. One day in the middle of June, Cindy visited Gina at her home to go swimming. After the swim, Cindy oiled her skin, rolled her hair in pink curlers, and relaxed. "I love the feeling of luxury," she explained.

Josephine had come to Gina's that day to pick up her dog, which she had been boarding. Several months earlier Cindy had met Josephine. They were chatting easily about this and that when Gerrie walked in.

C indy Kelly and Gerrie Powell had grown up in two different worlds, yet their worlds were only twenty-five miles apart geographically. One little girl's most valuable possession was a palomino pony and glistening yellow cart, while the other highly valued her special "shooter" marble and the circle of dirt in her front yard. One was a chronic spender willing to gamble on life, willing to do anything to impress people with her importance. The other, in contrast, was destined to take what she wanted, by whatever means, to show Daddy she could do it on her own.

The setup was explosive, ready to ignite when the two met.

Innocently Gerrie walked into this affair with a warm "hello." Turning to Gina she said, "What about dinner and the races?"

Cindy interjected, "Oh, maybe I'll go to the track with

James tonight." She hesitated, looked curiously at Gerrie for a moment, and said, "By the way, haven't I seen you there . . . at the $50 window?"

Gerrie smiled proudly as Gina asked, "Would you and James like to go with us?"

Unequivocally Cindy answered, "Yes. Let me call him."

As Cindy spoke on the phone, the others could hear her voice rising. "The one time I really want to go, you're not going?" She was becoming irate. Finally, Cindy informed him, "You can go or stay, I don't give a damn. I'm going." After arguing for a few moments more Cindy slammed the phone down and returned to the pool.

And as if an inner switch had been flipped, she flashed a radiant smile. Her reply was a cool, confident, "We're going."

Gerrie called for reservations for four. "The evening's set," she announced.

"We'll meet you there," Cindy said sweetly.

When James and Cindy arrived at the track, Cindy looked lovely. The black designer suit she wore accentuated her slender waist and high breasts.

During the evening Gerrie bet as she usually did, hundreds every race. Cindy never bet; she wasn't a gambler, and she became upset at James's $2 bets and constant losses. He was a gallant escort and treated his wife as though he adored her. Yet Cindy did not take her eyes off Gerrie, who as always blossomed in the light of the attention she received, carrying herself with an air of confidence, even superiority. With perfect timing, she flashed a roll of cash from her pocket on the pretense of hiding it, impressing the people around her. With the same timing, she informed a waiter, "Put all of this on my check," giving those witnessing the bankroll a taste of her wealth. The evening ended around 1:00 A.M., and as always Gerrie picked up the tab.

After that the foursome had a few parties on the boat. James appeared interested in helping Gerrie with various projects. However, when fall came, Gerrie was working, gambling, or busy with other friends. She saw very little of Cindy and James that season.

One day in the middle of December, Gina and Gerrie were planning a Christmas party at Gina's house. Through acquaintances, Cindy heard about Gina's party. She felt certain she would be invited.

Invitations were delivered to approximately twenty gay couples who were Gina and Gerrie's friends. Although Gina had been in touch with Cindy, Cindy was eliminated from the guest list. "After all," Gina said, "she's straight, and this is a gay party."

A week prior to the party, Gina was out and Gerrie was making last-minute preparations and completing the list for hors d'oeuvres when Cindy came by. She seemed terribly upset. She said her daughter Kim had planned a Christmas party which happened to be on the night of Gerrie and Gina's party. Cindy began to cry. "Christmas has always depressed me," she said. She trembled when she spoke of her mother, "And I don't know where I'll go while Kim is having her party. James will be gone and I don't want to be alone."

Without hesitation Gerrie said, "Look, come to our party. You already know some of the people, so you just come over here."

"I don't know . . . ," Cindy sniffled.

Trying to clear Cindy's mind from unhappy thoughts, Gerrie said, "I really need help with the menu and everything, and you're so good with that kind of thing."

Cindy smiled and began making suggestions. "See," Gerrie said, "I really do need your help. Will you come along while I choose the napkins and glasses and a centerpiece for the table?"

In a nearby mall, Gerrie and Cindy selected party supplies and favors with no regard for quantity or price. "Cindy, now you get whatever you want for your daughter's party as well." At the checkout counter Gerrie paid for everything flashing a large roll of bills.

On the way home, Cindy led the conversation by saying, "If only I had a mother to talk to and hold me, how fulfilling it would be."

Without hesitating, Gerrie answered, "You know I'm gay, Cindy?"

Shocked at the abruptness of Gerrie's remark, Cindy flushed and said, "Oh . . . Yes, I thought so. . . . Would you talk to me about it? I've been associating with these people in one way or another, for years. I think I've *missed* something." Gerrie, feeling a bit uncomfortable, changed the subject.

All that week Gerrie meant to tell Gina she had invited Cindy to the party, but somehow she never got around to it.

Early on the day of Gina's party, Cindy dropped by again. "Just to help with last minute things," she said. She pitched in instantly.

They worked for hours and the scene was set. Everything was finished. Cindy picked up her purse, started toward the door and asked, "What time should I arrive?"

Startled, Gina turned quickly to look at Gerrie, who said softly, "I've invited her, Gina."

"Well . . . ," Gina said hesitantly, "okay." Cindy walked to the door, smiling, appearing happy with Gina's approval. As she was leaving, she said, "See y'all later." Cindy was out the door and down the porch steps in a hurry to go home and dress.

Several guests had arrived when Cindy returned. All heads turned. She was wearing a breathtaking white silk dress with a rhinestone collar and cuffs. She looked like a goddess.

As more guests arrived at Gina's house, Cindy greeted them as any hostess would. It was her first experience at a gay party, and it was amazing the way she fit in. As a matter of fact, she took over, dancing with everyone, circulating, and attending to everyone's drinks and comfort. She was especially solicitous of Gerrie, who cast a lingering glance in her direction every time she brushed by.

After the last guest had gone at 2:30 A.M., Cindy picked up her rhinestone handbag, then turned to Gerrie and Gina, who were relaxing for the first time, and said, "I'll tell you what. I'll sleep on the couch and help clean up in the morning."

"Oh no, you don't have to do that," Gina said. Cindy was persistent and politely refused to have it any other way. Later Gerrie lay in bed thinking over the evening, recalling the way Cindy had flirted . . . but Gerrie wanted no part in a relationship with a married woman.

In the next few weeks Gerrie was busy working overtime. It was the first of the year, dividends had to be figured, 1099s were mailed, and she had to prepare for the examiners' visit sometime in February. Although she felt confident with her "system," there was always the possibility of having a new group of auditors arrive and introduce a change in auditing. Gerrie couldn't allow herself to relax until after the first quarter of the year.

The next spring, after the auditors had once again given their "okay," tension eased. Gerrie went out fishing on her boat. Once again, Cindy dropped by for a visit one day. She had just returned from a shop where she had had a complete makeover—hair, cosmetics, and clothes. Her hair had been cut short, slightly waved on top, close at the neck, and combed back on the sides. It definitely gave her a Demi Moore air. Dressed in a crisp white summer suit, she would have turned any man's head.

"Just out shopping. I thought I'd drop by," she said. Gerrie prepared bone-dry martinis in frosted glasses and they talked for several hours. Cindy was charming company.

"I love your floating apartment," Cindy said. "The get-away-from-it-all feeling."

"I'm glad you like it. I do, too," Gerrie replied.

The two relaxed. It was a peaceful change for Cindy. Her marriage had become one exploding argument after another. The closeness Cindy had with her daughter was diminishing. The teenager, being popular, spent her free time with friends. Cindy and Gerrie were both ready for something new, and it all started innocently when the two spoke of the coming holiday.

The Fourth of July was always a big time at Gina's. It was a pool-side "bring a dish" party for a group of close gay friends. The celebration was an occasion not to be missed. The younger fellows and girls played ball. The older ones played cards or just conversed. "No," Gina said, when Gerrie asked her, "I don't intend to invite Cindy." So as much as Gerrie loved parties, she decided to extend an invitation to Cindy to spend their Fourth of July, on the boat.

After the Fourth, their next rendezvous was for dinner at the Ramada Inn in Indiana. The friendship grew. Gerrie's easy way with money was a breath of spring to Cindy, who had grown tired of listening to her husband saying he couldn't afford things for years. The two women were impressed with each other. Cindy had never been treated so gallantly and Gerrie had never had a date with such an attentive lady.

Aside from being with Gerrie, Cindy also wanted to spend time with her daughter, but Kim didn't have time for her. She had been seeing a man that her mother didn't care for, Martin Walker. They argued over Martin constantly, with Kim maintaining she had the right to see whom she wanted. Then one night Cindy and Kim had a huge blowup. "Mother, there's something I need to tell you," Kim said.

"Not Martin again," her mother grimaced.

Kim, who had her mother's strong will, argued back. "We're engaged. I'm going to marry him and move to Wisconsin."

"You're just a child," Cindy said shocked. "I know you think you're in love, but *marriage?*"

Kim broke in, "I'm eighteen, and in this state that's old enough."

After that conversation, Cindy nearly had a breakdown. The thought of losing her daughter was too much for her to accept. She began drinking heavily, and since her husband accepted the news stoically she needed a friend more than ever. She began visiting Gerrie at the river every spare moment she had. She would drink too much and cry constantly.

Gerrie spent so much time comforting Cindy that little time was left to concentrate on winning at the track and repaying her debt. Whatever she won, she spent on entertaining and impressing Cindy. Friends started joking about her extravagance. "Well, I go to the track every day," she would reply, seeming to take it all in stride. "That's how I make my money." "Sure, sure," they would say, turning away and shaking their heads. It got to a point where Gerrie felt she had to do something to make her story more convincing. She felt that she was being pulled into a whirlpool.

This forced Gerrie to work harder to look like a winner in order to account for the company money she was spending. At the office she borrowed more and more to entertain Cindy and to bet at the $50 window. Regardless of the amount she lost, she needed to be seen winning big to account for the extra income and keep up the façade.

Gerrie, who had begun to care deeply for Cindy, bought gifts to cheer her. Every time Cindy seemed depressed, Gerrie would take her shopping and spend hundreds of dollars on her. It became apparent to Cindy that her new friend could be manipulated. Gerrie was also learning things—that Cindy seemed to have no one, and this made Gerrie feel needed. It drew them closer.

Sitting quietly on the deck of the *Gemini II* one night, Cindy started the conversation by saying, "No one has ever talked to me about . . . gay people. Help me learn, help me understand." She asked, "What is it like to be turned on by a woman?"

Gerrie was taken in by the appearance of innocence. Like a sculptor molding a piece of clay, Gerrie tried to answer the question. "It's the same feeling that anyone has for another person, regardless of the gender. You see someone . . . and you are drawn to take a closer look. You find yourself walking toward them. Some inner contentment makes you smile and want to know them better. The chemistry between the two mixes, and a friendship starts an emotional roll of feelings that need to be satisfied." She fingered her tailored broadcloth shirt and smoothed her flannel trousers. "Whether they are satisfied by simple conversation, or companionship, the need is there. And it has nothing to do with the gender of the body one is standing in. It so happens that a man has never turned me on, but that's not because of my body . . . it's because of my mind."

Gerrie watched as Cindy slid the purple paisely kimono covering her purple and gold swimsuit to the side . . . exposing her figure. She lowered her head, then looked at Gerrie and smiled. Gerrie knew Cindy wasn't gay, so she avoided making a comment, as difficult as it was. However, Cindy kept giving her provocative glances. Trying to act casual, Gerrie picked up a bottle of champagne, walked toward the cabin, and asked, "Would you like a drink?" Cindy looked back over a bare shoulder, and stated with a smile, "I'd kill for it."

That night on the boat Gerrie slept on a couch at one side of the cabin while Cindy slept on the opposite side. Waking in the middle of the night, she found Cindy sitting on her bed, watching her sleep. With a gentle touch, Gerrie pulled her close . . . and continued sleeping. The dawn found them entwined in each other's arms.

At eight, Gerrie slipped from the bed. She bathed and put on the "girl" clothes she always wore to the office. As she was leaving she turned to Cindy, still sipping coffee in the cabin, and asked, "See you tonight?"

"I'll be here," Cindy answered softly. Her deep throaty voice sent a warm sensation through Gerrie. She could think of nothing else while driving to work. At the office, her thoughts were still on Cindy. She was becoming totally consumed.

CHAPTER 4

A Touch of Heaven

That evening after work, returning home to the *Gemini II*, Gerrie found the two sleeping areas in the cabin had been moved together. Opening the closet, she was surprised to see Cindy's clothes, but Cindy was not there. Mixing her usual martini, Gerrie surveyed the situation. "She likes me!" Gerrie murmured out loud. "No! It's more than that. . . . She's latent—that's it! She's really gay, and she likes me . . . *me!*" Gerrie could hardly believe what was happening. Above all she didn't want to mess anything up.

Later that evening, Cindy sauntered onto the boat, looking beguiling in white jeans and white linen shirt with gold insignia and a navy yacht cap trimmed with gold braiding. Seeing her, Gerrie sighed.

"Do I look alright?" Cindy smiled radiantly.

"You look wonderful. I'm so glad you're here," Gerrie replied.

"From now on, I'm staying here with you." Cindy gently touched Gerrie's shoulder. The warmth of her sensual sweetness overwhelmed Gerrie. Gerrie was positive her suspicions were correct. "She's latent and she likes *me!*"

That night, as Cindy lay in bed next to her, hugging the wall, Gerrie said with reassurance, "You can relax. I'm not going to touch you."

"It's not that, Gerrie. I wouldn't mind, in fact, I'd like for you to touch me. I just don't know how to respond. I don't know what to do!"

"That's something that comes naturally in time, but it's something that you're not ready for yet. We're friends, and I value that. Let's just keep it that way; we have a very good understanding of each other." Cindy didn't answer, but it was becoming obvious to her that if a move was to be made, she was going to have to make it.

The next few days were full of warm affection. The mornings found the two women going about their tasks for the day—Gerrie to work, Cindy to her home to take care of the house and kennels. Gerrie gave her an extra hundred or two to keep in her handbag. Cindy's husband James was still taking care of the modest four-room house.

After another week of rapturous meetings, Gerrie came to her senses. "This is not going to work, Cindy. James will not put up with this forever, and I'm going to get my throat cut! Besides, I don't want to break up your marriage."

"No, Gerrie, I'm not staying with James. I've told him that when Kim gets married I want a divorce."

"Cindy, do you know what position that puts me in?"

"You're not in any position!"

"James is not as naïve as you are. He'll figure this out."

"I don't care," Cindy insisted.

The luxury of the boat, dining in fine restaurants, and the money she received pleased Cindy. Gerrie was fun to be with, and, unlike her staid life with James, there were new and exciting happenings every day. The strains of the calliope from the *Belle of Louisville* as it paddled along the Ohio was a far cry from the barking in her ears as she cleaned the floors of the kennel. Parties, shopping, the wharf, the river—this was the type of life Cindy wanted. She loved looking down at the smaller boats as they passed. She did not want to lose the person who was making this new life possible. She had to think of a way to hold on to Gerrie.

They drifted away on the boat, alone, to Eighteen-Mile Island. Cindy was her usual charming self. Once they docked, she went into the bedroom. After a few minutes she called to Gerrie to come into the sleeping area.

The shades were drawn, white candles scented with gardenias were lit, and a radio softly played love songs. Poised on the bed, Cindy was an illusion in blue chiffon. To Gerrie she was beautiful, and she was ready to end the platonic friendship.

Time passed. The candles burned low. They lay still, side by side. Then Cindy rose, leaned over, and began raining gentle kisses on Gerrie's face and neck, and running her hands along Gerrie's shoulders, kneading them. With a low moan Gerrie reached out for her, and the last flame of the candles sputtered into darkness.

Later, on the deck, the two sipped martinis and watched the parade of boats up and down the Ohio. At dusk Cindy went into the kitchen and prepared a meal of chicken breasts with orange slices, grapes and brandy, Caesar salad, marrow stuffed zucchini, and dry white wine. They ate by candlelight.

Gerrie's head was spinning. "Am I living a dream? What more could I ask?" Gerrie murmured. "I just don't want to ever lose you."

"You won't," Cindy replied.

Gerrie began spending excessive amounts of money on Cindy to buy her new clothes and jewelry. Each day she gave

Cindy cash from her "resources," telling her, "This is for you. . . . I had a good day at the track."

Cindy accompanied Gerrie to the track on several occasions. Anytime Gerrie had a "Win" ticket that paid 300 to 1, or more (which would be $600 and up on a $2 bet), the payoff money was claimed with Cindy's Social Security number. It was a situation they both had dreamed of; Gerrie had a girl so beautiful, in her eyes, that she would be envied by men and women, and Cindy had money anytime she asked for it.

Cindy was happier than she had been in years, and so was Gerrie. She didn't even mind that Cindy phoned her several times a day at the office just to talk. One day Cindy playfully recorded her conversation. Toying with her new recorder, she taped a conversation about the night before. "Look's like somebody's had a party!" she said. Gerrie was trying to carry on her duties at work, so she answered.

"Mmm-uh, it does?"

After a long silence, Cindy started rambling on with unimportant chit-chat about the night before in an effort to have Gerrie respond. Finally, after running out of light subjects to talk about, she said, "Oh yeah, I know what I wanted to ask."

Gerrie remained quiet.

"What should I do with this extra?"

"What do you mean, Cindy?"

"These . . . tickets, you know."

"Oh, put it on James's . . . let him claim 'em. It'll mean about $600 for him."

"Mm-hm, well . . . he'll like that," Cindy laughed.

After another long period of silence, Cindy ended the talk with, "Oh well. I can't wait to see ya tonight." Each one had thrown out their line and was slowly but surely reeling the other one in.

Cindy kept her threat to James that she would leave him when their daughter Kim married Martin and moved to Wisconsin. On Kim's wedding day Cindy left her husband. During the weekend she made calls to her home from the boat, asking James to leave.

"I want you out of the house when I get back Monday," she said.

Each time James answered she asked him once again to get out until James no longer answered. He knew her well; he had seen enough of her wrath and wanted no more. Packing as much as he could cram into his car, he grabbed a six-pack of beer and left Sunday evening.

Docked on the island in the Ohio that summer night, Cindy and Gerrie made a commitment to one another and considered themselves united.

On Monday, Cindy returned to the little house. She was happy to be free from James. However, every place she looked, she was reminded of him—an overlooked shirt hanging in the closet, his family pictures, his magazines, his tools, his coffee cup.

All of this reminded her of the past. Quickly she began packing each and every thing away. One way or another she was going to make her future better. She called Gerrie at the office.

"I want to give you the news, that James is gone."

Gerrie mumbled her approval.

"I'll be waiting here for you to finish working," she said in the throaty voice that sent shivers up Gerrie's spine.

At 5:15 Gerrie drove out Shelbyville Road to Eastwood, Kentucky, Cindy's home. Happy the ordeal appeared to be over, she breathed a sigh of relief as she turned onto the road where Cindy lived. It was a barely marked, winding dirt road, paralleling an abandoned train track. The road crossed the railroad track and narrowed to one lane. This remote area featured only a few unmarked bungalows on hundreds of acres of land with hills filled with cedar, sycamore, and hickory trees dotted with wild red poppies.

Approaching Cindy's modest, boxy, four-room house with the small cement-block kennel, Gerrie's feeling of self-worth grew to a climactic peak. This woman needed her. This woman made Gerrie feel precisely as she wanted to feel—important, admired, respected, accomplished.

Dressed in an emerald-green hostess gown, Cindy stood at the open door, waiting for her.

"This is the beginning of our new life together," Cindy said. "Come in."

Gerrie, her heart reflected in her tear-filled eyes, took Cindy in her arms.

In the weeks that followed Cindy and her son, Jimmy, who had always found it difficult to get along, now found it impossible. To Cindy, Jimmy was a constant reminder of his father. Like his father, young Jimmy was trim, muscular, five-foot-seven with blue eyes and straight black hair. On his lean face he wore a mustache and beard, and having been influenced by his father's patriotic beliefs Jimmy was a proud American and sported a tattoo of a bald eagle on his upper arm. After only one month of living with his mother and Gerrie, Jimmy left home. Both of her children resented Cindy leaving their father to live with Gerrie.

When the divorce was final, Cindy changed her name back to Whitehall. Although she made an effort to keep the kennel business going, without James to groom the animals she found all the details impossible to handle herself. She complained that lifting heavy dog crates and working with strong chemical solutions was too much for her. Moreover, with a constant cash flow on request, Cindy soon felt that all the extra work she was doing was superfluous. She closed the kennel.

During the next weeks, she claimed to be understanding more about herself and her abilities to build a relationship with Gerrie. Nevertheless, there were still many sad moments when Cindy cried for hours as she spoke of her childhood. Gerrie was touched by sympathy, and Cindy manipulated the strings.

"The story was so sad," Gerrie recalled. "It was a Cinderella story, and she was good at telling it." There were many beautiful evenings when Cindy would put her arms around Gerrie and kiss her tenderly. Perhaps Cindy felt that it was the only way to remove the heterosexual wall that was stopping Gerrie. As though trying to coax a move from her, Cindy began saying things like, "I've been so confused, because I don't know anything about it or how you feel. I want you to be patient with me, it's all so new."

Gerrie recalled, "Cindy often spoke of hating men, of being unable to cope with them any longer. The more masculine they were, the more repulsive they were to her. Her father was one of those men. Cindy said, 'He is so dominating, so arrogant, with such a superior attitude, I know he was the cause of my mother's drinking.' He had such an upsetting effect on Cindy that even talking about him was anguishing to her. 'Daddy was like a dictator,' she told me, and she trembled as she spoke of her childhood."

It was soon evident to Gerrie that Cindy was constantly competing with her father and step-mother. She wanted the same things they had. Cindy merely stated, "I would like to have . . . ," and Gerrie, who wanted more than anything to please her, financed it, whatever it was. She simply went to her "resources."

When Mr. Whitehall bought a big luxury car, Cindy was

sick with envy—she wanted one. Gerrie took the money from the credit union to buy her a Cadillac. Cindy couldn't wait to drive to her father's home to show him "her Caddy." Never having forgotten how he had supplanted her and her mother with his second family, she was getting even by flaunting her possessions in front of him, saying, "See, Daddy."

Gerrie's plan of putting the stolen funds back into the credit union had evaporated. Gerrie's main concern now was to get larger amounts of money, so she could continue playing the parts of being provider, protector, and big-time gambler.

With Cindy's persuasion, Gerrie financed the remodeling of Cindy's four-room house by taking out a $14,000 mortgage on the property with Union Financial Corporation. At first Cindy spent much of her time at home, claiming she liked to cook. But after being introduced to Louisville's finest eating spots, she soon complained that the preparation of food was tiring to her and she begged Gerrie, who could not refuse her anything, to take her out. During the racing meets, they ate at the track. At Louisville Downs, everyone in the lavish dining room knew them.

A reserved table was held nightly by the maitre d' and waitresses. Anyone observing the large amounts of money they spent assumed that Gerrie was very wealthy, a winner, and a big-time gambler. Gerrie tipped everyone handsomely. Cindy loved the feeling of importance it gave her.

"Hi, Gerrie, who are we betting on?" Jacques, the dark, handsome maitre d', would ask with a wink.

"Got any exchanges for the eighth?" piped in Teresa, the pert, blond waitress.

"Yes, a couple," Gerrie would respond, smiling. Actually she was winning small amounts, but she was stealing more—

so much more that the theft had begun to reduce the assets of the company.

Besides the shortage caused by the theft, the company now suffered a shortage of interest the money would have accrued. To keep the assets from depleting to a noticeable low, Gerrie had to think of ways to recruit new depositors by offering incentives to new members.

Gerrie placed an article in the Vogt company newsletter stating that she was starting a jackpot of $20, adding $20 to the pot every month. Once a month she drew five members' names. If any one of the five members had made a deposit of $20 or more during that month, over and above their payroll deductible, they would receive one-fifth of the running balance of the jackpot. Once again the credit union began to grow, with deposits getting larger as it grew. The larger the deposits, the greater the amounts of funds that were available to Gerrie.

By this time Gerrie had stolen two-fifths of the credit union's assets, so although her jackpot idea helped, she spent all her spare time searching for new ways to keep money coming in. Meanwhile, as her own need for more money increased daily, she had to hit her "resources" in ever-increasing amounts.

As she sweated out her problem, she attracted still more new members by placing notices in pay envelopes:

ANYONE OPENING AN ACCOUNT OR ADDING TO AN EXISTING ONE BY DEPOSITING $500 OR MORE EACH MONTH OVER A PERIOD OF SIX MONTHS WILL RECEIVE A THREE-DAY VACATION FOR TWO AT DISNEY WORLD!

In six months the membership grew and deposits increased by $80,000.

The credit union had now reached over $1 million in assets. The extra work load was beyond one person's capabilities. Gerrie needed help in the office, someone she could trust.

She began watching a friend of hers, Pat Salzman, whom Gerrie had helped to get work at Henry Vogt. Pat was a short, heavy-set woman, brunette, very friendly with an easy sense of humor and a curious mind. Pat attended most of Gerrie's parties. She loved to spend time fishing on Gerrie's boat. Although at times she seemed to be a bit envious, they were good friends nevertheless. Pat also enjoyed playing the horses and attending Gerrie's Derby, Preakness, and Belmont parties.

Gerrie knew Pat was scheduled to be laid off as time-keeper because of the reduction in Vogt's sales and inventory; so Gerrie, having an opening in the credit union in a few months, requested the board of directors hire Pat as her posting clerk. The next month Pat was moved to the credit union office to work under Gerrie. Gerrie relaxed a little, figuring she could control Pat.

Meanwhile, Cindy and Gerrie were moving into a higher social class. They were finally accepted into the 500 Club.

After that, there was no stopping either one of them. Cindy wanted everything the other wealthy women had—diamonds, furs, horses—and Gerrie wanted to keep up the pretense of being rich. She vowed to herself, "Nothing will change my direction."

Gerrie's debt to the credit union had now reached $100,000. The money was easy to take; Gerrie's main concern was in trying to cover her crime. Although she was winning $2,000 or $3,000 every few weeks, her winnings were minuscule compared to her losses. Moreover, she and Cindy had found another enjoyable luxury.

The couple began traveling to the Islands, to Mexico, and all over the United States. They made new friends, and appearing quite affluent they mixed well with the elite. After a short while, Cindy commented, "My little house isn't in keeping with the homes of our new friends." The two women moved into a large comfortable home that Gerrie rented on Brown's Lane, in the St. Matthews area in the east end of Louisville.

"In our bedroom, Cindy and I were lovers, but in public, we were often seen in the company of gay men." Dating this way was the custom of the 500 Club. The couple met Fredric Taylor and Allen Cummings. When the foursome were together, to all outward appearances, they passed as two straight couples. The men owned an antique shop. Gerrie, who was still looking for a means of laundering money, saw the antique business as her answer . . . if Cindy would go along with it. Gerrie could pass money to Cindy and justify the purchase of her cars, furs, trips, and the excessive amounts of cash she was spending.

The men gave Cindy books on antique furniture, glass, and silver, and she studied them. With only this knowledge and a little guidance from Fredric and Allen, Cindy opened an antique business in the Brown's Lane home. Of course, the antiques were purchased with credit union money. Every accessory and piece of furniture in their home had a price tag attached. The fact that Cindy knew little about the subject was unimportant. Money taken from the credit union was turned over to Cindy and was credited as a cash sale. Regardless of the price Cindy received for an item, the money was all profit and income to Cindy, because she received the merchandise at no cost. On a shopping spree, Gerrie often spent up to $20,000 for period furniture. Cindy could then sell an item, or receive cash from Gerrie, and claim the money as income.

They had quite a system. Laundered money continued to flow. As the articles were sold, Cindy rearranged the pieces that were left in the house. With the continual change of furnishings, Gerrie never knew what to expect when she arrived home.

Besides the money Cindy received from the sale of antiques, Gerrie gave her several hundred dollars every week for personal expenses. In addition to that expense, Gerrie continued to pay $235 a month toward the mortgage loan with Union Financial Corporation. Still Cindy wasn't satisfied, so more money passed through Gerrie's hands, triggered by a desire in Cindy to own more . . . much more.

"I want to buy a home with lots of acreage and a swimming pool, like Gina's," she said to Gerrie late one night, her eyes shining. "Consolidating would save money. I'll sell my house, and you can sell your boat and use the profit as a down payment on a larger home."

Once again Gerrie, who couldn't seem to say no to Cindy, agreed.

They looked at property half a mile away from Gina's on Chenoweth Run Road. The house was a pretty, brick split-level nestled on a hill amid pines and cedars, and secluded in the back by a hillside of deciduous trees. The asking price was $52,000.

"It's a great buy," Cindy insisted.

Before selling the four-room house in Eastwood, Gerrie paid off the loan. Cindy cleared $20,000. With that amount she made the down payment, and on October 14, 1977, the deed to the new home was put in her name. Gerrie was in complete agreement with this arrangement, although she knew she was going to have to make all the mortgage payments.

Gerrie felt that if she were caught and had to go to prison, her money would be safe in Cindy's name. Upon her release from jail, the two could either live on the property or sell it and divide the money.

Gerrie said, "If anyone comes after me, they can't touch you. You will be protected. Everything will be safe in your name."

Cindy quickly agreed.

The two moved into the new house, and Gerrie began making mortgage payments.

After a month, bills totaling more than $20,000 for remodeling came in. With the house in Cindy's name, she had to show income in order to pay these bills. They decided to open an antique shop in Nashville, in Brown County, Indiana. It was a quaint little town where narrow brick sidewalks lead visitors from specialty store to specialty store. Candles, leaded glass, antique toys, vintage clothes, and hand-made copper jewelry invited the curious. On weekends the town was alive with customers who browsed for hours, then took their time relaxing at a sidewalk soda shop and enjoying the nostalgia of it all. Gerrie and Cindy found the perfect store here.

Cindy worked hard every weekend, but she soon found that big ticket items did not move well. The visitors wanted articles under $20, traffic items, something different that caught their eye, a whim.

She decided to try her hand at selling calico. Gerrie paid thousands of dollars for bolts of the variegated cotton cloth; however, with low-priced items the income was small.

The drive every week to and from Louisville soon turned

into a tiring, fruitless effort. For Gerrie the slow turnover was not laundering money fast enough; six months later they closed the business.

Looking at places closer to home, they rented one stall in the Antique Mall on Goss Avenue in Louisville. The owners of the mall handled the merchandise for five percent of the sales. Cindy kept it stocked.

After several months the sales barely covered the rent, but the stall was serving its purpose. Any cash received from Gerrie was credited as income from the antiques business. Gerrie was taking enough money to keep the bills paid, plus purchase a few luxury items. But Cindy was never quite satisfied.

"One of my friends has a home with a bigger kitchen and a swimming pool," she told Gerrie enviously. Cindy wanted all those things.

Gerrie had been making $60 monthly payments on a home she and her brother had built on New Cut Road. Appealing to Gerrie again, Cindy convinced her to sell her house and put the additions on Chenoweth Run, consolidating Gerrie's equity into one home. The new remodeling cost was another $22,000.

As long as Gerrie went along with Cindy's requests, Cindy was happy, carefree, and full of charisma. When Gerrie said no, Cindy projected gloom with every word and action. Then Gerrie had to give Cindy money to make her happy again.

To keep her that way, Gerrie bought her everything she wanted and took her on cruises to the Bahamas, gambling in Las Vegas, Atlantic City, Florida. She threw extravagant showy buffet parties with ice sculptures and orchid centerpieces. Besides the champagne that flowed from a fountain, the open bar had professional bartenders to mix special concoctions. There were parties for holidays, Derby Day, birthdays—any and every occasion conceivable. There were lavishly catered parties where a Who's Who of the gay life in Louisville, including wealthy business people, were invited.

Of course, their friends and acquaintances were all wondering where all the money came from.

Gerrie said, "I had Cindy programmed. She was told exactly what to say in defense of having so much money. She never asked why she needed a defense; in fact, she tried to avoid the subject. However, it had to have occurred to her that if I was giving her money I had won at the track, she would not have needed a defense. She could have said it was a gift. Besides the cash from the company," Gerrie continued, "I gave her my winning tickets to put on her Social Security number. I had to bet heavier to win." In order to be sure of having a winning ticket to cash, Gerrie bet hundreds on several horses in the same race.

Gerrie always gave Cindy her winning tickets. This became Cindy's income. In contrast, Gerrie kept bags full of losing tickets to prove that she had gambled with the embezzled money, if she were ever caught.

"Cindy cashed tickets on horses she didn't even know were running," Gerrie later told Jan Taylor, one of her friends. "And many times she wasn't even in the same town. But who, other than Cindy and I, knew this? It was perfect! This was my master plan. At the track I bet, I won, . . . but I never cashed my own tickets over $650.

"Cindy never asked where I was getting all the money or why my winnings were put on her Social Security number. She never complained about my asking to use it; in fact, she seemed to enjoy the idea of fooling the I.R.S. It was accepted as our way of living."

Everything was going well. Cindy needed Gerrie to give

her the life she loved. Gerrie wanted an attractive woman that would make her the envy of her peers, a woman who asked few questions, whatever her suspicions. She had all of this in Cindy. They were the ideal couple, and they went forward at a brisk pace . . . with tunnel vision.

Gerrie recalled, "She avoided the discussion of money problems. She saw my paycheck when she cashed them; she had to know my salary!" Gerrie's salary from the company varied between $20,000 and $30,000 a year, including bonuses—hardly enough to account for the way they lived.

In 1978, the credit union had assets of $1.8 million. Gerrie was in debt to the company for $500,000. Knowing she could never repay this money, she lived in constant fear that the auditors finally would catch her. Every asset she and Cindy had together could have been liquidated and she still could not have reimbursed the company.

Gerrie was becoming worried. The healthy win at the track that she needed to at least ease the burden was not forthcoming. Her winnings of $2,000 or $3,000 were always needed to pay new bills, for Cindy, for something. The demand for money drew her back to her "resources" in order to keep producing.

Then interest rates began to climb. The local banks offered 11%. For Gerrie it was a lucky break. As an incentive to new customers, Gerrie suggested the credit union offer 12¼%. Every month she printed flyers and added them to pay envelopes. Bulletins promoting certificates of deposit were posted in all parts of the factory. The credit union was growing ever more and its potential, Gerrie was sure, was endless.

Moreover, at this point, members of the board relied one hundred percent on Gerrie. She kept them purposely uninformed as to the complete operation and totally dependent upon her to run the department.

As Gerrie's lifestyle became more and more lavish, Gerrie knew she had to upgrade her reputation as a gambler. When Churchill Downs opened in the spring, she left the office in mid-afternoon and made it known that she was gambling. She would give the other women in the office enough work to keep them busy before she left for the track. To appease them for handling the office in her absence, she offered to put up $10 for them on a "show parlay." She'd bet $10 on a horse to show in the first race, then bet those winnings on a horse to show in the second race, and continue this through all the races that day; the women would split the money.

Each morning, they waited anxiously for Gerrie to come to work. She always had money for them, regardless of how the parlay turned out, because that was Gerrie's way of convincing them that she was a *successful* gambler.

Pat was especially impressed. "I want to be like you," she told Gerrie. She began her mornings by going to the drug store to purchase a racing form and scratch sheet. Instead of posting and doing her other office duties, she studied the horses and gave Gerrie her picks of the day to bet for her. In addition, Pat took a flea market stand.

When anyone complained that Gerrie left the office too often, Gerrie told the office workers that she felt entitled to because she made up her time by working on weekends. Of course she didn't tell them why she'd return to the office after the races and work until midnight. Gerrie knew working alone had another major benefit: it afforded her the privacy she needed to take more money and alter the books.

As soon as Gerrie left the office, Pat would stop posting to listen to the stretch run of each race on the radio. In time she resented having to be at work while Gerrie was enjoying herself at the track. Resentment festered. Being close friends socially, Pat began looking upon Gerrie as another co-worker, rather than her superior. She began to act accordingly. On errands for the office, such as going to the bank or courthouse, Pat would spend hours visiting thrift stores, looking for bargains for her flea market business. Seeing the lack of regard Pat had for her job, Gerrie realized her friend was taking advantage of their relationship.

The other office workers also complained about the amount of time Pat squandered reading the morning paper, checking the scratch sheet, running personal errands, or listening to the radio. Gerrie was forced to put friendship aside and take the situation under control.

"Pat," Gerrie said late one afternoon after the others arrived, "you have to change your habits and start work at 8:00 A.M. And no more extra stops along the way while on credit union time." Pat resented the reprimand, especially in front of the others. She smoldered. It had become obvious to Pat that Gerrie wanted to run certain functions of the business in private. On several occasions, just before the auditors arrived, she had observed Gerrie's stealthy, secretive mannerisms. Certain things were off-limits: Gerrie's desk, the bank statements. Pat only had suspicions, no proof as to what was going on, but she watched Gerrie more closely and waited. Months passed . . . September . . . October . . . and on until the end of the year. Pat saw that from the middle of December to the last of January, Gerrie often worked twelve to eighteen hours daily, and at times even through to the next day. Seeing Pat's attitude and having her own pressures mounting, Gerrie grew more nervous. The end of every year was a hectic time, having to deal with the reports to the I.R.S., the Department of Banking, 1099s, and year-end dividends on deposits. She also had to prepare for the auditors showing up anytime after January 31. The supervisory committee conducted audits quarterly in addition to the yearly audit that was done by outside auditors.

"No one will ever know the torment and pressure that I was under, but I brought it on myself. I was living a double life." Gerrie's life was regulated by when the bank examiners were coming. During this period another problem surfaced: it became clear that Cindy was a compulsive shopper. Gerrie insisted that she destroy all of her credit cards. Cindy agreed with that arrangement, but she soon opened new accounts and kept them secret from Gerrie.

Despite the pressure, Gerrie was happy. Never had she felt such passion and had it reciprocated. "No one could ever make me believe Cindy is heterosexual, the way she responds and the way she enjoys sex." In addition to the passion, Cindy was a beautiful ornament whom many of her gay friends envied Gerrie for having. "Cindy was a perfect counterpart at the parties," Gerrie said. "I merely supplied the money to pay caterers, bartenders, and the liquor store for cases of the best wine and liquor. Cindy handled everything. Sure, I could see that she was beginning to have no regard for the amount of money she was spending, and I sometimes would speak to her about it. Then she would smile that radiant smile at me and I'd say, 'Oh well, what the heck . . . if it makes her happy. . . .' "

Gerrie added, "When I looked at her, I was on a cloud, She was my idea of what a woman should be. And when she wanted to turn me on, I was helpless. I didn't care what happened. She was my world . . . and she knew it."

CHAPTER 5

Seeds of Discontent

During the next years life for Gerrie and Cindy went along reasonably smoothly. Gerrie continued stealing large amounts, and Cindy continued spending larger amounts.

In Wisconsin, Cindy's daughter Kim and her husband Martin were happily married. They had two little boys, Brad and Michael. Living so far away from her grandsons prompted Cindy to make frequent trips to visit them. Wanting to keep Cindy happy, Gerrie accepted these trips and paid for them. In fact, the few arguments the couple had were mild. Perhaps the biggest problem between Gerrie and Cindy was caused by friction between Cindy and her son Jimmy. According to Gerrie, "Jimmy stayed away from her house except when he needed money, or help, but usually money would solve whatever problem he had."

Later Jimmy also married and had a child. One day he called saying he had lost his job. "I'm destitute. I want to move back in with you and Gerrie." They took him in; Gerrie tried to help him.

While he had been gone, Jimmy had joined the Army. There he had worked as a mechanic, so Gerrie suggested he apply for a government loan and continue his schooling. His loan went through and he received $125 weekly.

He attended school three days and one night a week. However, he complained to Gerrie, "I have a heck of a time, I look scruffy and I'm trying to get around without transportation." Gerrie bought new clothes for him and gave him a car. From then on he saw her as an easy mark. And the more she gave, the more important she felt. Daily, he would observe Gerrie with a racing form. *Obviously,* he thought, *she always has money. She's one hell of a gambler!* After watching her study the paper hour after hour, he began to read it himself.

His entreaties massaged her ego. He begged her to teach him to be a big-time gambler. She did. She explained the abbreviations to him, and at the end of the day she would show him her "picks" for the next day of races.

He enjoyed going to the track and on trips to Las Vegas or Atlantic City with Gerrie. On each trip she gave him $500 to play seven-card stud. When they went to the track, she gave him $100 each night. Win or lose, it was his!

Once again Gerrie fell prey to someone's feigned admiration. The more attention she received from a person, the more money she spent on them. Jimmy could not help but be enticed, and perhaps Gerrie was, too. The more she thought he liked her, the more she gave . . . from a seemingly bottomless well of money.

However, Gerrie sensed resentment in Cindy whenever she spent money on Jimmy. Conflict resurged again between Jimmy and his mother. It grew to an unbearable level, and in time Jimmy moved out.

Later, when he returned to the scene, he had remarried and had one child, Jennifer. He had been working at odd jobs to keep food on the table. He was barely getting by. Gerrie watched Cindy worrying about them.

"I don't know what to do with him, Gerrie," she murmured sadly. "He's my son. I can't stand to see him suffer."

"I know," Gerrie said sympathetically.

Cindy turned to Gerrie. "Gerrie, you're so smart, perhaps you can think of some way to help him."

Gerrie was sick with the desire to be a hero in Cindy's eyes. All Cindy had to do was ask for something in Gerrie's presence and Gerrie felt she had to get it or lose Cindy's love. For instance, one of Kim's sons spoke of never having seen Disney World. Company money financed the trip for Kim and her family. Not only Jimmy and Kim but all of Cindy's family were recipients of Gerrie's generosity. On birthdays and holidays she deposited money into Cindy's grandchildren's bank accounts toward each of their college funds, plus hundreds of dollars in gifts for them to unwrap. Credit union money paid for all of their clothing, dance lessons, costumes, and other frills.

Jimmy's daughter, Jennifer, spent one weekend a month with her grandmother and Gerrie. On these weekends, they went shopping for new clothes at the best children's boutiques and had dinner at expensive restaurants. The credit union's money flowed like water.

Cindy was happy, and Gerrie was thrilled that her family was happy. For her own birthday, Gerrie bought airline tickets to Disney World for Cindy and Jennifer. Then she bought a customized van with company money, put it in Cindy's name, and surprised her with the gift when she returned home. At the same time Gerrie was making Cindy happy, she was fulfilling her own desires to be recognized as a great provider and a big spender.

In 1982 the credit union had assets of $2.2 million. Two employees were helping Gerrie handle the assets, but, as always, she did all the bookwork. To allow anyone else to do it would have made her vulnerable to discovery; therefore, Gerrie made sure no one else knew how. She prepared everything for the board of directors, including the typing of the minutes.

They studied the abbreviated reports she gave them—no more, no less. She prepared and discussed the treasurer's report at the meetings, explaining and answering their questions and at the same time moving things along quickly and keeping important things obscure. The entire meeting was conducted by Gerrie. When she wanted to keep something from them, it was eliminated. When a minor problem emerged that she felt didn't need to be hidden, she presented it to the men on the board in order to keep them feeling involved in decision making. When she suggested raising interest rates and told them why they should, the men nodded in agreement. Every suggestion she made was approved. They were totally dependent on her. Not only that, but Gerrie was complimented repeatedly on her job performance. Trusting her implicitly, they were at her mercy. At the office she appeared to be a diligent employee—kind, sympathetic, and a good listener. Upon leaving for the day, she would walk out with thousands of dollars in her pocket and change from the mother image to the female version of Diamond Jim Brady.

In 1984 her salary was $22,169.67, but that same year she took $176,637.67 from the credit union. She knew if she had asked for a larger salary, she would have received it, but she didn't ask. Perhaps she wanted to keep what little pride she had left. At that point she had stolen $1.5 million—one-half the assets in the union. Knowing her thievery was growing to immense proportions, Gerrie was intent on trying to build the business.

Gerrie suggested issuing CDs at a higher rate than Share

Savings. The credit union became stronger still. Depositors kept investing more. Many people closed accounts at other institutions and purchased CDs at the Henry Vogt credit union. Money continued to flow. Gerrie suggested making more real estate loans. Again the suggestion brought instant success. The credit union escalated—more cash, more funds available, and more for Gerrie to take home.

Her illusions of self-importance escalated as well. She was on top of the world, living the life of a queen. She felt she had it all, and in a peculiar way, she did.

However, when the local Prudential Savings and Loans went under, it changed the whole credit union system; things grew more pressured for Gerrie. Charles Haines and Robert Schoenberg, the two auditors who had been coming to Henry Vogt for so many years, had also been auditing the savings and loans. They were held responsible for the institutions going under. There was a general shake-up in the Department of Banking. Following this, there were myriad changes. One primary change was that three new examiners were assigned—Dan Roberts, Doreen Butke, and Carl Holiday. It was announced they would remain at Henry Vogt for one full week per audit. Gerrie worried that time was closing in. "For years I had been pitting my mind against all of the men in the department of management, including the auditors, but now with these new examiners? . . . I questioned my method. Was it good enough to cover me?"

The government controlled ninety percent of all credit unions, banks, and savings and loans. The "good times" when the board of directors ran the credit union were gone. From then on, it was done by the government. The union was forced to take out federal insurance—NCUA, National Credit Union Association—similar to the FDIC protection banks had.

There were new restrictions on the type of loans made, with books of new laws for managers to study. Gerrie spent days reading policies and laws to avoid making mistakes. She became a very thorough, astute interpreter of credit union law. But in order to keep up, she had to study constantly.

Not only did Gerrie have more stress on the job, but there was also more at home. Cindy's son Jimmy, unable to make it on his own, moved back in with Gerrie and Cindy for the umpteenth time.

By 1985, Gerrie and Cindy had been living on Chenoweth Run for eight years. Jimmy had been struggling along from job to job and finally took a job as a groom on a horse farm owned by Russell Newlander, a handsome and prominent horse trainer who had sixty thoroughbred horses. "You can't imagine how rich he is—this is real Kentucky horse society," Jimmy said, thoroughly snowed. Although his job called for shoveling manure and performing odd jobs, mingling with famous horse trainers seemed to give him a craving for eminence. He wanted more—he wanted to become a part of the racing game. One day he came home excited about a horse he wanted to buy. "The animal's named Son of Ange, and the selling price is $5,000. I know it sounds like a lot," Jimmy said excitedly, "but we could make millions, Mom. One day we could have a stable full of our own thoroughbred racehorses."

"That does sound incredible," Cindy said, impressed. "I'd really like the idea of you starting a business, but," she signed, "you have no money and only two years experience as a groom. The only way I can get money from Gerrie for you would be to get involved myself, or to get Gerrie involved financially."

"I know," Jimmy said miserably. "I guess it's impossible. Nothing I want ever happens."

"Jimmy, I hate to see you so unhappy. Look, I'll ask Gerrie; all she can do is say no."

"Oh Mom, she won't say no to you. She never does."

Cindy smiled and patted her son's shoulder. "We'll see."

That night she approached Gerrie. "We will do all the work," Cindy said, "if you will finance it." Cindy assured Gerrie that Jimmy's source of information regarding the worth of Son of Ange was valid. For the first time Gerrie, who had spent a tiring day with the auditors, refused Cindy's request.

Shaking her head, she replied, "The extra expenses involved in owning a thoroughbred are out of my reach, Cindy. We would have to pay boarding fees. Besides, strict regulations forbid owners to saddle their own horses. Only a trainer is allowed to saddle a horse for a race. Jimmy's not a licensed trainer; we would have to pay a licensed trainer to saddle the animal, and I can't afford that."

It was true Jimmy was not a licensed trainer; however, he wanted to be an owner, and was not about to allow a minor obstacle like that to stand in his way. He pressed Cindy, "Mom, all we need is $5,000 and sufficient time for me to study and get a trainer's license. In the meantime we can use another trainer to saddle the horse."

The more Cindy thought of it, the better it sounded. But in order to persuade Gerrie and catch her at the exact moment of weakness, Cindy had to be at her best.

The next evening after work, Gerrie arrived at the house to find Cindy dressed in a lavender silk hostess gown. She looked lovelier than Gerrie had seen her in years. She was smiling happily, and a lavish dinner was on the table. After they had eaten they sipped wine and talked by candlelight, and Cindy began working on Gerrie again. Gerrie, trying to convey sympathy and still reject the idea, replied, "I see this as the biggest and most extravagant adventure I have ever been asked to support. I'm truly sorry, but I can only say no, Cindy." Cindy put her head in her hands. Gerrie went on. "Honey, the $5,000 is only the beginning. We can't afford all the expenses involved in boarding, feeding, transporting, training, and entering a horse in a race. It's out of the question."

Tears running down her cheeks, Cindy stood up and left the table. She pouted for days, then alternated sweetness and anger, with tears added for good measure. One miserable week passed with Gerrie enduring Cindy's mood swings of bitterness. They carried into the next, until Gerrie felt compelled to produce or be mentally tortured. In the end Cindy won.

That Tuesday at the office, Ted Torrey, a union member, added $10,000 by certified check from First National Bank in Louisville. Gerrie slipped the check into her purse along with a deposit slip for $5,000 to the First National Bank, asked for the remaining $5,000 in cash for petty-cash, and went home with the money.

Several days after purchasing Son of Ange, Jimmy started his training to obtain his trainer's license. Gerrie wanted to visit the Indiana training track where the colt was boarded. When she arrived she found Jimmy and Seymour Rohn, the veterinarian, in the stall with the horse. Son of Ange had his rear ankles heavily bandaged.

"What's wrong with him?" Gerrie asked.

Jimmy explained, "The horse raced three days ago and ran down."

The vet told Gerrie, "Some horses have this problem. The fetlock hits the ground as they run, causing the skin to rub raw." Gerrie sighed heavily. She knew Jimmy should have known this before the purchase. She also knew she should not have trusted the judgment of a person so new to the business. But what was she to do? She needed Cindy so much. Gerrie swallowed the bitter taste the whole thing left in her mouth and said nothing. The horse required three weeks of patient care. When he was able to go back into training, he wobbled and stood weakly. In the end, Son of Ange was never able to race again. He was sold for $500.

Unlike Gerrie, Jimmy was not discouraged. He continued to study, and he received his trainer's license three months later. "I'm so proud of him," Cindy gushed. "I want to do all I can to help him." Buying more horses was all she talked about. "Jimmy will train them," Cindy said to Gerrie, "and after all, you've already invested five thousand, plus the vet bills. It will be a good chance to get back your investment. Besides, Son of Ange was only a little bad luck."

Days passed, and Cindy pressed on. Gerrie was torn between the guilt of stealing and the guilt of depriving Cindy of something that could make her truly happy for the first time in her life. Gerrie rationalized, *Maybe this will be Cindy's niche. If it is . . . it could make money for us.*

Once again Gerrie gave in to Cindy. She handed over $2,500, with which Cindy purchased Virtual Lady. Cindy wanted a broodmare in order to begin breeding horses and raising their own colts. "I want to produce a winner of the Kentucky Derby more than anything," she told Gerrie. Now it is not unheard of for an owner new to the sport to produce a Derby winner. The goal of every owner, trainer, and jockey in the racing industry is to be in the Derby winner's circle. Cindy was no different. She pestered Gerrie until they bought Margarie L for $8,500.

For Cindy, however, this was only a beginning. Right

afterward she convinced Gerrie to pay $2,500 for Shoot the Dice. The bills of sale on the horses were in both women's names, but the van used to transport the horses was registered to Cindy. These purchases were the beginning of the C & J Stables, named for Cindy and Jimmy.

Once the initial horses were purchased, Cindy said, "Now we can get the other things."

"Other things," Gerrie echoed, her face coloring. Cindy didn't notice.

Then Cindy began another campaign. "We have to hire on a horse trainer and, you know, jockeys."

So Gerrie hired jockeys. Of course, the jockeys needed "silks" and caps. Then Cindy wanted satin jackets for the hired hands and for herself and Gerrie. Gerrie needed to keep producing money—a lot of it.

Gerrie put Jimmy on salary, and he finally moved out on his own. He mingled with other groomers and trainers on "the backside," the barn area. He was learning and trying to develop his skill.

Rumors circulated on the backside about Gerrie—rumors that told of her wealth.

"She must be rollin' in it," one of the grooms was overheard saying. "They say she's the manager of a credit union. The way I see it, she must be hittin' the till, 'cause she sure ain't makin' it on her horses. Makes ya wonder, with that kind of money to throw around, why would anyone keep a nine-to-five job . . . unless there was more in it for 'em than the salary?"

The rumors quickly filtered from the trainers and jockeys to the other owners, like Courtney and Leland Morrison. One evening they met with Cindy and Gerrie to discuss racing fees. Leland said, "Money can't be a problem for you

Gerrie . . . everybody knows you're takin' yours from the credit union."

Trembling slightly, Gerrie laughed it off. She was well covered in the books, and if she had managed to deceive the examiners, no one observing from the outside could possibly have reason to suspect.

The cash continued to flow. Gerrie funneled the flow to Cindy, and Cindy distributed it like a centrifuge—to her business, her house, herself, and her family. As time went on Cindy pressed for more and the centrifuge gained momentum. By now Gerrie was tapping her "resources" every day to furnish money for Cindy to pay the trainer, the vet bills, the farrier, stall rent, entry fees, and jockey salaries. In less than a year Gerrie had funneled $225,000 to Cindy. None of the money was claimed as income to either one of them.

In preparing her income tax for that year, Gerrie reported only $21,925 as taxable income; the tax due on that amount was $3,625. However, her true income was $447,394, upon which the income tax due the government should have been $211,141. Gerrie said, "I gave almost all of the money to Cindy with the exception of the money I used for gambling. Even then, I would win and give the winnings to her. So she actually has as much or more than I took from the company . . . plus my salary." At that point Gerrie's biggest fear was not in being caught, but in figuring out how to account for Cindy's assets since Cindy had claimed no income. Gerrie worried about it constantly.

Then a serendipitous thought struck her. One sure way to protect Cindy would be to hit a big win at the track and have Cindy claim it on her Social Security number. Starting that year, Churchill Downs offered a new type of wagering for Louisville, the "Pick 6" with a carry-over pool. To win, the bettor had to pick the six winning horses in the third through eighth races. Gerrie felt she could do this if she bet every likely combination.

She waited for payday at Henry Vogt. As usual, thousands of dollars were on hand to cash company checks. "Let me relieve you, Pat," Gerrie said in her usual sympathetic way. "You've been looking tired. Take a long lunch." Gerrie was the only one in the office. Once she was alone, the rest was easy. After slipping several thousand dollars in cash from the drawer, she went into her office. Gerrie worked overtime that night to adjust the books, just in case.

Later, at home, she approached Jimmy. "Want to come to the track with me tomorrow?"

"Sure, why not. Is it a special day?"

Gerrie smiled. "You might say that. Have you heard about the Pick 6 at Churchill Downs?"

Jimmy nodded. "Yup, picking the six winners in the third through eighth." Gerrie's tone turned serious. "Just how are we going to do that?" Jimmy grimaced.

Gerrie looked at him astutely. "Come over here and I'll show you how."

Gerrie had the racing form. She and Jimmy studied it until Gerrie was satisfied that they had every possible combination. The next day Jimmy, Cindy, and Gerrie headed for the track. They bought tickets and combined their bets. After spending hundreds of dollars it finally happened—Gerrie and Jimmy pooled their choice of numbers and hit the Pick 6 for $120,000. "You cash it, Cindy," Gerrie said.

Dancing around, Cindy skipped over to the pay window and flashed the winning ticket. "Pay me," she said with a huge grin. Claiming the money as income, Cindy later reported it to the I.R.S.

"After that, I knew everything would be safe if I were ever caught," Gerrie said. "No one could touch her. I felt I could protect her through any audit by the I.R.S. And I resolved if I had to do time in jail, Cindy and I would have enough for a fresh start after I had served my time. I would need lawyers and bond money, but Cindy would be there for that. She loved me; we were happy. The money was ours. Cindy was my ace in the hole."

To split the $96,000, Gerrie took $40,000 off the top for herself and considered it a reimbursement for part of the money she had invested in the business. Then she divided $30,000 three ways among Cindy, Jimmy, and herself. A balance of $26,000 was used to pay bills.

The $120,000 ticket gave Cindy the means to explain the business being in her name. To her friends this would justify their heavy expenditures.

Jimmy, who prior to the race was only paid $200 a week to train and help groom the horses, changed after the Pick 6 win. He had never had so much money at one time. In Gerrie's opinion, it went to his head. "He thought he was a big shot." Jimmy started complaining about having too much work, saying he needed more help with the handling of the horses. "I'm a trainer," he told Gerrie, "I'm not supposed to be grooming horses." Gerrie groaned. Since they had only two horses, his argument was ridiculous to Gerrie.

But nothing would stop Jimmy. He wrote to his sister Kim, telling her how lucrative it was in Louisville working for Gerrie. He offered her a job as one of his grooms and wrote, "Gerrie will pay you."

However, there weren't enough horses to warrant another employee. Actually, there was not enough full-time work for Jimmy. In retrospect, Gerrie said, "Jimmy was playing the big-time trainer, but I was obligated to supply the money."

Traveling from track to track with a van full of horses,

Jimmy called his mother long distance several times a day to voice his discontent. At the same time he kept writing and calling his sister, asking her to come to Louisville to help him with the work.

Within a short time, Jimmy persuaded Kim to make the change. Leaving her two sons with their father until school closed for the summer, Kim arrived "bag and baggage" to live at the Chenoweth Run home with her mother and Gerrie. For Gerrie it was hardly an ideal set-up. As Gerrie later remarked, "They had never lived so well, and I was paying for everything." But, most important to Cindy, Kim was back in the nest again. Her mother had resented losing her to marriage in the first place. Now Cindy had what she wanted.

After Kim moved into the Chenoweth Run home, Gerrie was given the choice of supporting her or creating a job for her at the credit union. Since Kim would be furnished insurance and vacation benefits at Henry Vogt, Gerrie decided to give her a desk job at her office.

With his sister around, Jimmy became more belligerent. It was as though having Kim to back up his complaints, he complained more. He became difficult to control, causing friction between Gerrie and Cindy. Their entire relationship became filled with havoc.

On the pretense of gambling at the track, Gerrie was spending even more time away from the office. This added to the already heavy workload, and Pat was running two weeks behind in her posting. Gerrie requested all employees to stay two hours extra in the evening and work three Saturdays and one Sunday. All agreed except Pat. The relationship between Pat and Gerrie had long been strained. Realizing the cause for the overtime was due to Gerrie's absence, Pat voiced her resentment. "My flea market business will have to close if I spend my weekends here," she complained. As an alternative, she told Gerrie, "I'll work the extra two hours on Saturday morning from 6:00 A.M. to 8:00 A.M."

Gerrie couldn't risk having Pat in the office alone. She responded, "Look, Pat, you'll have to work the same hours as everyone else. All personnel is needed in the office simultaneously in order to assist one another."

Pat argued, "With the simple posting I'm doing, there's no reason why I can't work alone. Is there, Gerrie?" Her voice darkened. Gerrie flushed but didn't answer. Pat continued defying Gerrie and became more suspicious.

After the continuing defiance, Gerrie related the matter to Norman Smith, the balding, stocky president of the credit union. This was one of those small matters in which she allowed others to become involved. "Pat has no regard for authority," she told him. "No one else but a friend would have tolerated this insubordination." Smith nodded, running one hand over his glistening dome.

"If Pat refuses a direct order, she should be sent an immediate letter of termination of employment, Gerrie. Don't let your kindness interfere." He patted Gerrie on the back sympathetically. "It's unfortunate that sometimes people take advantage of those going out of their way to help them. But even as nice as you are to everyone, there has to be some reckoning."

Gerrie presented Pat with a second warning: "Either reverse your attitude and work when requested, or I'll have to issue a two-week notice of termination of employment, which will go into effect immediately." Pat altered her behavior, apologized to everyone, and worked all requested times. But it was the breaking point in her relationship with Gerrie.

From that moment on she was coolly polite, but every chance Pat had, she searched for evidence. Her once happy, effervescent personality changed, causing Jane Harden, one of her fellow part-time employees, to ask, "What's wrong, Pat? You're not yourself. Is something bothering you?"

"Yeah, there is, but . . ."

"What is it? Did I do something?"

"Oh, no! Not you! You didn't do anything. Look . . . I can't tell you now, because I don't have enough— . . . Well, I'll tell you when the time comes. Okay?" Pat turned away, obviously unwilling to continue the conversation.

"Okay," Jane sighed. But she later told Gerrie, "Maybe Pat's ill or something. I've never seen her like this."

Pat was not Gerrie's only problem person at the office. Office work had a negative effect on Kim, Cindy's daughter. She was not the type of person to be content behind a desk, because she loved being out of doors. After working six months she quit, taking her complaints and perhaps her suspicions home to her mother.

Moreover, people problems were not Gerrie's only worry. The amount of money Gerrie was siphoning had reached new heights. Gerrie worked evenings and Sundays on the books . . . juggling. The huge shortages were becoming more and more difficult to account for. She decided she had to hold off taking more for a while.

To Cindy's continued demand for money Gerrie said, "I don't have it now." In essence she was saying, *I can't take any more because the examiners are due any day.* However, Cindy increased the pressure, saying, "It's to pay another bill."

The constant hounding for money put Gerrie in a constant verbal confrontation with Cindy. Near the breaking point one day, Gerrie yelled, "Damn it, Cindy, I can't take any more money." As she yelled, Cindy put her fingers into her ears, like a child, shaking her hands to distort the sound and perhaps to keep from being told where the money came from. Cindy knew that when she asked for anything long enough, she received it; she simply didn't want to know anything else. But this time the request for more was not filled, because Gerrie was more frightened than usual.

A few days later, the examiners gave Gerrie a good report of a balanced audit. Her relief only lasted forty-eight hours. She had to continue tapping her "resources" to satisfy Cindy's demands.

Money from the credit union financed everything, but this didn't seem to matter. As long as the money was coming in, who cared where it came from?

There were constant new requests. Kim defended Jimmy's unreasonable demands and Cindy continued asking for more money to run the household and business.

A turning point came on Easter Sunday 1986. The four had just finished dinner when Jimmy announced to everyone that he was entering Gerrie's little filly, Virgil Lady, in a mile-and-sixteenth race. Because of Jimmy's lack of expertise in entering horses, Gerrie began defending her own decisions on when a horse was ready to race. Entering a horse in a long race before it has been properly trained to go the distance can be fatal to the animal.

Gerrie knew the filly could barely make the distance of a six-furlong race. Listening to his plans, she exploded, "You're crazy, that would kill her." The discussion heated to the boiling point.

"*I* make the decisions," Jimmy yelled.

"While I'm paying all the bills," Gerrie informed them, "I intend to have some input into what is being done."

Kim joined in, "You ought to listen to my brother. What do you know?"

Annoyed, Gerrie looked at Kim. "If you don't like the way things are run in this household, you can leave."

Kim screamed back, "This is my mother's house, and I don't have to leave."

Gerrie bit her lip. It hurt deeply, knowing she was risking her future to provide for Cindy and her family, and they were so ungrateful. In the heat of the quarrel, Cindy sided with her daughter. "Damn it, don't tell my daughter to leave."

Gerrie lashed back, "If you feel that way, then pay the bills." She stormed out of the room. Throwing a few things into her suitcase, Gerrie left the house and checked into the Holiday Inn, leaving Cindy with everything, including massive bills. She felt that one week without money would bring Cindy to her senses.

However, reality intervened sooner. After several days without income, Cindy was frantic and willing to cooperate in any way she could to get Gerrie to take over the finances again. At that point Gerrie called. "If I'm to come back, your daughter has to get out." Kim left the house, but Gerrie lived to regret the order.

When Gerrie came home, Cindy's demands increased. She wanted more money—faster than Gerrie could risk taking it from the company. Gerrie could no longer say she was winning at the track. There were not that many sure winners, and if there were, the pay-off on the favorite was small. Gerrie finally decided if she were going to keep up the pretense of being a successful gambler she had to upgrade her image and go to Las Vegas or Atlantic City. Moreover, she had to come home looking like a winner.

During the next weeks, Gerrie stole $15,000 in a combination of cash and money orders. Looking up travel agents in the yellow pages she selected one at random and called the number listed. "This is Gerrie Powell," she said when connected. "Let me have a first class ticket to Vegas for late Friday. I feel like this is going to be my lucky weekend." To further develop the image, Gerrie booked the best room at the Rio Grande. That Friday night, dressed in a green silk skirt with a cerulean mink stole, Gerrie hit the tables.

A suave French casino employee, who immediately noticed the pit of chips in front of her, introduced himself. "My name is Roberte," he said huskily and offered to teach her the game. With his guidance and a feeling of proficiency she attacked the dice. She won $5,000 in the first hour. "I think you've got a system," Roberte said. She continued to play. From then on it was downhill until she had lost two-thirds of the money she had come with. "Bad luck," Roberte smiled, "wait till next time." At home, Cindy was thrilled to receive the money Gerrie had left, money she said she had won.

Gerrie started going on gambling junkets to the casinos. She lost, yet, claiming to be a winner, she handed thousands of dollars in credit union money over to Cindy. Once again she was a hero. Gerrie rejoiced in the surging thrill she received from the grandiose treatment bestowed upon her at home and at the casinos. She became addicted to the high she felt from the praise and respect. The habitual desire for more importance became a hunger never completely satisfied but, once tasted, savored. Even when she lost she was treated royally, and it was this royal treatment for which she had such a hunger. Gerrie saw other addicted gamblers, young and old, entrenched at the slot machines in Vegas or rushing out to buy lottery tickets. The elderly ones cashed their Social Security checks and ran to the casinos to gamble. Gerrie lived for her weekends gambling, yet she believed she had no problem.

In that respect she was no different from the others. And like the others she didn't concern herself with the reality that the chances of winning are about twenty percent, which means they're going to lose the remaining eighty. However, the drive to beat the odds overrides all reason. That's why some people lose their jobs, embezzle, cheat, and have broken marriages. For them it is the same as a craving for alcohol or drugs. If gamblers have ever been lucky, they simply don't want to admit it's merely a game of chance. If they are winning, they keep playing to win more. If they are losing, they play to recoup their losses. Yet the habitual gamblers simply cannot win all the time because they can't beat the odds.

Despite this, the higher the stakes, the more action, the more they throw themselves into the game that engulfs them. Win or lose their adrenaline pumps and they become flushed with the thrill of the action. They feel all-powerful, caught up in the excitement. The "rush" causes them to lose their feelings of depression, their inner guides, and rational reasoning. The high is short-lived, however, and they lose everything while trying to reach a greater high. There are many suicides because of gambling losses.

Gerrie met many different types of gamblers. "I feel sorry for the addicted ones," she said wistfully. Late one night, gazing up at the mirrored ceiling of their hotel suite, Gerrie told Cindy, "A 21-year-old gambler jumped to his death from the top floor of the Casino. Witnessing that should have made the gamblers quit, but it didn't. Did you notice those people in torn clothes, tattered shoes, obviously poverty-stricken but putting their last quarters into a slot machine? They ought to give up, but they don't." The look of determination on the wrinkled face of an elderly person trying in vain to win was depressing to Gerrie. "I can't stand seeing them neatly fold the empty paper from a $10 roll of quarters, stuff it in their hanky pocket, and save it for the next time."

"But *you're* a gambler," Cindy said.

"I'm not one of the pitiful souls. I'm a winner."

Cindy smiled. Gerrie turned toward the wall, thinking she merely had to play the part of a winner. Then she could return to Louisville and talk about her trip to Vegas. She was losing money, but it created the cover, and she thoroughly enjoyed the "King of the Hill" lifestyle the cover furnished.

For Gerrie it was imperative that she was seen gambling everyday on anything and everything—ballgames, horses, whatever. She had to look the part. If people around her saw her or heard about her gambling constantly, she felt, it would account in their eyes for the hundreds of thousands of dollars she and Cindy were spending. She'd flash her winnings, or the company money, and hide her losses. Friends around her were told of her successes and believed she was a hell of a gambler. However, her losses were eighty percent greater.

By the end of Gerrie's first year, she had become a High Roller. That is a person who will gamble four hours a day, win or lose, in a casino of their choice, and have $1,000 or more on the table at all times. She was given a card stamped V.I.P. After that when she went to Las Vegas she was furnished with roundtrip air fares and a stretch limousine waiting to transport her and her guests to the hotel. She was made comfortable in a $500-a-night suite. Stepping from her limo, she would enter the casino with a confident gait, feeling like a big-time gambler.

Seeing Gerrie lose thousands of dollars at a time, however, Cindy soon refused to go with her. To friends who found it hard to believe a person would pass up such an exciting trip, Cindy covered the truth by saying, "I was bored to death. There was nothing to do but lie around all day. It made me sick."

Annoyed by Cindy's desertion, Gerrie started inviting another guest—a very special guest. They stayed in the

Monte Carlo Hotel's most luxurious suite. A private bar in the room was stocked with imported Dom Perignon, beluga caviar, an assortment of rare cheeses, and champagne. The tab was picked up by the casino. While Gerrie gambled, her guest was entitled to the use of Gerrie's V.I.P. card for room service, long-distance calls, lobster, caviar, or whatever else she desired.

Donna Bentman, Gerrie's new lady friend, was young, vibrant, and impressionable, someone who could enjoy any show in the city with a front-row seat. Dinner, more champagne, all the amenities—there was no limit to the luxuries she received, and the casino footed the bill. Nothing was omitted in assuring the comfort of their big-betting guests. Donna was awestuck. Seeing the girl experience luxuries she had only dreamed of thrilled Gerrie and gave her a feeling of power.

The couple enjoyed their time together. However, when she was ready to gamble, Gerrie told Donna, "I play alone. I'm here to do a job, and my job is to make money." It made her sound powerful and successful.

But, once Gerrie returned to her workweek the glamour and glitz were gone. Once she was at home, she sat thinking of her losses and the pit she had fallen into. . . . Alone in her bedroom, the real Gerrie surfaced as she sat consoling herself with a can of domestic beer and a hunk of American cheese.

CHAPTER 6

Added Pressures

As planned, after school closed for the summer Cindy's daughter Kim's two boys moved to Louisville. Kim's husband Martin was to join them when a buyer could be found for their home in Wisconsin. Kim's small paycheck didn't go very far after her sons arrived. The more Kim spoke of needing money, the more frustrated Cindy became. Although Cindy was funneling some of Gerrie's money to Kim, it wasn't coming fast enough.

Since Kim could no longer live with them, Cindy had to think of some other way to help her daughter. But first she had to wait for the opportune moment to get Gerrie in the right mood.

One evening as the two were alone talking, Cindy heard sadness in Gerrie's voice as she spoke of a little black dog she once had. The next day Cindy called several breeders throughout Kentucky until she found a six-week-old black toy poodle that had been bred from champions. Cindy and Kim hurried over to purchase the dog. "Gerrie will love him," Cindy said thoughtfully as they drove home. "She'll be really grateful," Kim said, gazing at her mother.

"My thoughts exactly," Cindy laughed.

Tootie, as the puppy was named, became the joy of their evenings alone. She was four inches wide, six inches long, six inches high, and a mass of tight, black curls.

One evening a week or so later Cindy watched as Gerrie played with the tiny puppy. "Tomorrow," Cindy said, "I'm going to help poor Kim find a different apartment. The children can't stay in that dreary little place she has now." Preoccupied with her new toy, Gerrie had no inclination of what was coming.

The following day while Gerrie was at work, mother and daughter went searching. That evening Cindy came home, all chipper and bubbly, and announced, "I've found the nicest little ten-acre farm for us. It has the most beautiful barn. I know you think you don't want it, but would you just look at it with me? It would be perfect for us, and it's only $87,000."

Gerrie was stunned. "I can't afford to buy a farm. I don't have the money," she told Cindy. "I'm happy here." It was the first time she had felt she had a home that was hers. They had just put in a new pool; it was comfortable. With a mortgage note of $259 a month and a $15,000 balance, to all outward appearances they were living within their means and capable of handling monthly payments easily on Gerrie's salary. This kept her at a safe level; moving was the last thing she wanted.

Cindy went on and on about the farm. Gerrie calmly but definitively stated, "I don't want to move. I love it here." Gerrie looked into Cindy's eyes, "This is also *my* home. I know you've put your money down, and I know it's in your name, but I have made all the payments and it's home to me."

Cindy moved about the room from place to place, flirting and continuing with the conversation. Cindy had a playful way about her that usually got what she wanted from Gerrie. But even this was having no effect. After an hour or so she became quiet, then she sat on the couch next to Gerrie and Tootie. Gerrie was reading Judith Krantz's novel *Scruples*.

The seductive stratagem wasn't working. Cindy was used to Gerrie's bullheadedness but wasn't accustomed to her approach failing. In a few minutes Cindy said, "I know why you're not going to see that property. You don't want me to have the horses, or the farm. I think you just want to hurt me." Cindy stormed out of the room and ran to her bedroom, slamming the door shut. Sobbing sounds disrupted Gerrie.

Sitting there trying to concentrate on her novel with the puppy snuggled close, Gerrie recalled the hours Cindy said she had spent looking for the perfect dog for her. "How can I be so selfish?" Gerrie murmured to herself. "The least I can do is take a look at the place. I don't want to seem uninterested in something she obviously feels is so important." After a few minutes she tapped on the bedroom door. The sounds of crying came from within. She opened the door and crept in.

Like putty in Cindy's hands, Gerrie went to see the farm. It was located on Taylorwood Road in Shelby County, a picturesque country setting. Cindy danced about, holding her partner's hand, and spoke of starting their own breeding business and maybe raising their own Derby winner. She had the look of a young girl in love with life. She threw her arms around Gerrie, and Gerrie melted. It sounded wonderful. The house needed a lot of work inside and out, but it had a good barn for the horses.

In hopes of preserving the happiness she saw in Cindy, Gerrie made an offer on the farm for $82,000. With credit union money orders and cash totaling $20,000, she made a down payment and put the farm in Cindy's name. Since the farm needed too many repairs to make it livable, they agreed not to sell the house on Chenoweth Run until the farm was renovated.

The bills mounted. Gerrie was pressured into figuring new ways to pay them, cover herself, cover Cindy, and not leave a trail. The amounts she needed were growing daily. To get it she became bolder. Switching methods of taking cash and money orders, she started writing credit union drafts to a selected member, forging the required two signatures of credit union officers and then cashing the drafts at the First National Bank. No entry was ever made against the member's account.

Meanwhile, Cindy's assets were multiplying. "I have two homes in my name," she reminded her daughter. The rest of the family was told the same story. But their friends knew the truth. Cindy was no gambler, nor was she an antique dealer. Whatever she was able to buy came from Gerrie. Gerrie would say, "I have everything in her name because, if something were to happen to me, Cindy would be without income or insurance. I want to make certain she is provided for without having to pay inheritance tax." Cindy's story was a bit different, and it involved someone she hardly knew. "To support the farm," she said, "I'm boarding horses for Russell Newlander." Some of her friends believed her . . . others felt certain that the business was a front and Russell was only in the picture to convince Kim that her mother was not gay.

Cindy had seen Russell on many occasions at the races. He was a big man, with dark hair man graying at the temples, and who wore expensive, flashy-looking clothes, which hung well on his tall straight frame, and a complexion made ruddy by the outdoors. Cindy didn't like his dominant masculine look, and she hated his voice— stern, with a strict delivery of words. Cindy had occasion to speak about Russell to her daughter several times as they worked together at the farm.

Daily they cleaned as remodeling continued inside and out on the four-bedroom home. Additions included new carpet, appliances, renovation of the barn, and fencing for the paddock.

To pay for all these Gerrie used the names of five employees and wrote a total of $35,499 in checks for the month. To cover her theft she spent every weekend in Las Vegas.

Cindy began moving items from one home to the other. She moved a bedroom suite and buffet to the farm while Gerrie was away. The farm house had large rooms that needed furniture. Cindy filtered things from Chenoweth Run to the farm. Piece by piece, articles made their way there. Then Cindy moved Kim and her family in. Perhaps to deny her relationship with Gerrie, Cindy began spending days and late evenings at the new farm. Then she started staying overnight.

Any inquires Gerrie made about the farm put Cindy on the defensive. Questions about horses, money, or the children increased the air of tension. Meanwhile Cindy pressured continuously for more money. In the following month, December 1986, Gerrie wrote eight credit union drafts totaling $60,061—nearly double the previous month's expenses.

One week later, after working hour after hour of overtime to get the books in order, Gerrie exhaustedly realized she couldn't take additional funds—the auditors were due. She had to stop. Because of this, many arguments followed.

Cindy announced, "If you don't get the money we need, I'm leaving you."

Gerrie sighed heavily. "Cindy, take what you need and move to the farm with Kim if that's what you want." Even when Gerrie told Cindy to go, she was praying she wouldn't.

Still, Gerrie realized things were escalating out of control. "We simply cannot live like this. There is no way I can support two homes and your family, and I can't keep going this way." For the present Cindy backed down.

One Monday morning several weeks afterward, after a miserable night of disagreement, Gerrie gave Cindy several thousand dollars to claim as stall rent. "It's not enough," Cindy said. Disgusted, Gerrie felt compelled to get away. The books had been examined, she was safe in planning a trip to Vegas—alone. That day at work she started forging checks under $10,000 and continued this until she had over $30,000 accumulated on Friday. At five she left the office. For security reasons she concealed her cash in her bra, $15,000 in each cup.

At the airport in Vegas, a limousine was waiting. Getting in, she settled back against the plush gray velvet seat and listened to the quiet sound that only a limo affords humming up the resplendent driveway to Caesar's Palace. She began to reminisce. "I've come a long way from gambling with a $2 bet," she murmured.

She vowed that this time nothing would stop her. This time she would play until she won. Like Gerrie all addicted gamblers think they can beat the system, and they have to keep going to prove themselves right. The high reached from winning is an instant fix. On the down side, the depths one can fall to when the losses come is unbearable. That Saturday night, after ten hours of playing, Gerrie had lost everything. She left the casino more depressed than when she had arrived. The next morning she flew back, saddened but still believing that the next time she would be a big winner.

She returned to the office on Monday. From her desk she had a clear view of the parking lot. It had become a habit of hers to watch for the auditors' cars even when they weren't due. Regardless of what she was doing she kept a constant lookout. Being so tuned in, she could almost feel their presence on the premises. As a general rule audits were conducted on Mondays, but then they could happen any day. "I had to keep a running balance at all times. Between the time I removed funds and totaled a running balance, I lived in Hell. In the pit of my stomach, a ball of fire rolled continuously. My ulcers ate at me, and the sickening feeling was enough to make me vomit. I remained that way until I could arrange time to stay alone all night and balance the books once more."

This Monday was like that. Gerrie had planned to remain at the company that evening. She had just arrived at her desk, looked over the parking lot . . . and there they were. All the pressure in her body rushed to her heart, and it pounded furiously. She was frantic. The books were out of balance by $30,000—the amount she had taken that previous weekend to spend in Las Vegas. There was no time to pull all the accounts she had "flagged" earlier. She heard the men in the hallway outside the door. As the examiners walked in, she grabbed a handful of account cards from the office file, praying to God they hadn't seen what she was doing. After placing the cards in her private file Gerrie greeted them with a cheery "Hi-do!" As the words came out, fear ran through her body and she began trembling, clammy cold.

Still shaking, she put the work in front of them on the desk and gave them the books. While trying to answer questions, she could only think of what to do when they confronted her with the shortage. After two hours she saw the auditors checking their tape . . . then . . . rechecking it.

The uniform stroking sound of the calculator marking the totals was for her a toll of doom. They moved slowly, carefully verifying their own figures. Sweat rolled down her sides, soaking her underclothes. Gerrie listened to the rotating cams of the adding machines and tried unsuccessfully to carry on with the business of waiting on members.

That day there were more customers than usual, because government-backed mortgage companies such as Guaranteed and American were recalling G.N.M.A.s and returning the principal to the investors. Company employees were choosing to put their money in the credit union. Staying busy assisting members, Gerrie watched the expressions on the auditors' faces to detect something that would convey their thoughts or suspicions. But they were like the poker faces she saw on the men in the card games her father played when she was a child. She sweated it out; several times she choked on the lump in her throat as she tried to swallow. Positive they had discovered her, she began putting her personal belongings into a box; she wanted to get it over with . . . get out . . . and run . . . like . . . hell.

Finally one of the examiners pushed his chair away from the desk and turned to look at Gerrie . . . in a time frame that seemed an eternity. Finally he said, "We're way out. . . . We're going to break for lunch; we'll be back in a half hour."

She watched them leave. Then, pushing aside chairs, paper-baskets and anything in front of her, she rushed to the window and watched as they drove off. Moving as quickly as possible, she hurried to her office. She grabbed a handful of accounts from her personal file in her office and replaced them in the main office's file cabinet. Checking the clock on the wall at intervals Gerrie saw the minutes pass . . . ten minutes, fifteen, twenty. . . . Working in alphabetical order, she removed from the file the previously flagged accounts that would total the amount she had taken. Thirty minutes had now passed . . . thirty-five. . . . She had all the accounts in her hands. She slammed the drawer to the file with her hip . . . and the auditors walked in.

"Hi-do!" she said, half-grinning, half-grimacing, as she moved towards her office. Her hand shaking, she hid the accounts in her secret file. She waited and thought of the times she had come to work in the morning, edgy and trembling, knowing she had to get more money to satisfy Cindy, how Cindy came home twice a week just to get more money, and how she was beginning to hate going home when Cindy was there.

Listening to the rhythm of the auditors' electric machines stop and start, Gerrie felt they mimicked the irate sounds of her own heart.

After several hours the calculators stopped completely. The silence was deafening. She heard conversation between the two auditors that indicated that they were finished. Unable to look them in the eye, she turned her back . . . and froze.

She was ready to grab her box of personal things when she heard, "Gerrie, it's okay, we must have made a mistake earlier. Everything's fine, see you next time." For the first time since she had seen them in the parking lot that morning, she breathed normally. Gerrie wanted to shout for joy, but she was too drained and relieved of tension to do so. Sinking into the chair, she fell limp. She sat dazed in her chair for the rest of the afternoon.

It was one hour until quitting time when Harry Roth, a union member, came to the window to add $15,000 to his account. He placed the money in front of her. As soon as he was gone, she placed it in her bra. She left the office early and hurried to her car. Stopping first at the credit union bank, she went to see her new friend Donna. They made plans to go to Las Vegas the following weekend.

The week inched by. Finally it was Friday. They flew to Vegas. A huge white Cadillac limousine waited as they came out of the airport entrance. They headed for it and got in. Dressed in silk and furs, Gerrie sat with her lady companion in the chauffeur-driven stretch limousine. As they drove through the city, the fairy-tale twinkling lights of billboards and hotels beckoned. They headed for the brightest. The driveway, flanked by tall pines and free-form bodies of water with lighted fountains, led them to an impressive entrance. Stately white marble pillars topped with gold Corinthian capitals seemed to dwarf the surrounding world. "It was more beautiful than I ever imagined," Donna exclaimed. In the mirror Gerrie caught a glance of her own awestruck face. She smiled at the reflection.

Once inside Caesar's Palace, the lavish hotel to which they'd been invited, they were escorted to their suite where fresh purple and green orchids, a basket of exotic fruit, and chilled Mumms champagne awaited them. In the center of the room was an elevated, circular king-size bed with glistening mirrors on the ceiling framed by tiny bulbs of light and purple velvet drapes for privacy. Adjacent to the bedroom was a luxurious Italian black marble bath. Gerrie sighed. For such elegance she was willing to sell her soul. At the end of the weekend Gerrie told Donna, "I want to be with you all the time."

Donna replied, "I have to be certain that your relationship with Cindy is actually over before I make a commitment." Running a hand through her red hair, Donna added, "I find it hard to believe that a woman such as Cindy, having been handed the world, so to speak, could behave so self-ishly." Gerrie sighed. Donna admitted, "She's the luckiest woman around. I envy her. No one could have given her more." Donna's thoughtfulness and caring made Gerrie feel alive again. The difference between Donna and Cindy was becoming obvious.

By the time Gerrie returned home she had decided to make a final break with Cindy. Gerrie offered to give Cindy the farm and the payments, but Cindy wouldn't agree to set-tle. She wanted both places. Gerrie said, "Look, Cindy, I want to be fair, but you have to be fair also." Cindy was livid. She went to Chenoweth Run and took more items from the house while Gerrie was at work.

Finally, Gerrie went to her attorney, Jack Muldoon. The attorney gave Cindy an ultimatum: She was to keep the farm and its mortgage and sign over Chenoweth Run plus $50,000. Gerrie had the locks changed. This infuriated Cindy, but she had no choice but to accept the deal. Still, Cindy wasn't about to fade away. She frequented the track, where she could be seen turning all her attention toward Russell Newlander. Russell was flattered. Cindy was attractive and classy. She knew the business of the horse industry, and she looked financially secure, clothed in furs and diamonds.

After Gerrie heard rumors about the new couple, she stopped giving money to Cindy and refused to meet the mortgage note on the farm.

Going their separate ways with their new partners in the same surroundings, the two couples—Cindy and Russell, Gerrie and Donna—found themselves meeting accidentally at the racetrack.

Donna dreaded seeing Cindy at the track. "She became vicious when she saw me with Gerrie. She could blow in an instant, and you'd never know when it was coming." Cindy soon resorted to a childish game of hang-up phone calls. She'd scream threats of violence through the phone. Cindy's irrational, self-destructive statements confused Gerrie. "What does she want?" Gerrie asked, trying to understand. "Is she straight, gay, or what? After all, she has a man, isn't that enough for her?" Never once did she see Cindy as desperate and willing to do anything for security. The screaming over the phone tore Gerrie apart. She never saw Cindy the actress, Cindy the user—she only saw the fragile little girl she once loved.

During these rough times Cindy drank heavily. Her friends remarked, "When Cindy walks in, she walks in with a drink and never puts it down; she just keeps refilling." After many drinks she would pull into the driveway at Chenoweth Run and sit in her car with the engine idling. From inside the house Gerrie could hear the screaming, "I don't want to live! I'm going to kill myself!" After these outbursts, Cindy would leave the area with the automobile tires screeching. Gerrie was stunned. She had a horrible realization that if Cindy were killed in an accident, everything would go to her children.

Finally, on the fifth month of the separation Gerrie received a friendly call from Cindy. She spoke of her relationship with Russell as platonic. "There is nothing to it. Oh, there's more feeling on his part," she laughed. "He wants me." The calls continued . . . and as they continued, Gerrie was softening.

Meanwhile, unknown to Gerrie, Cindy told a friend, "I'll be damned if I will just walk out and let that bitch Donna have it all. And that's what she's after—Gerrie's money. You think I don't know?" Cindy was not about to let it happen. She had to get Gerrie back or lose everything.

Not long afterward, Cindy called Gerrie, crying, "I want to come home," she repeated over and over. And Gerrie, partially out of compassion and partially out of self-preservation, let her.

CHAPTER 7

Respites and Rumblings

Cindy moved back to Chenoweth Run. "I promise I'll stay with you always unless I'm needed for some emergency at the farm," she said passionately.

Her words had a reassuring effect on Gerrie. "She left Russell, because she can't stand a man. I know her," Gerrie boasted to friends triumphantly. Then, recalling some of the self-destructing messages on her recorder, Gerrie added, "I was making plans for a life with Donna, but I felt I had to take Cindy back; she would have killed herself and I would have lost everything."

The reconstituted relationship was not the same as the one Gerrie and Cindy had shared earlier. Gerrie tried to explain her decision to Donna. It saddened her to end their affair, but self-preservation prevailed. However, in no way did it completely remove Donna from Gerrie's mind.

Cindy and Gerrie resumed their life as a couple. They invited friends over and began throwing parties at the Chenoweth Run house again, but an air of tension prevailed. Sensing it, Cindy clung to her closest friend, Karen. Karen was a social worker, but other than that their lives were strangely parallel. Both had been married at the same age to men who worked in similar jobs. Both had two children of the same ages. Both were living with women. They formed a warm kind of sisterly friendship. Karen, who was both sensitive and empathetic, tried to help patch up Cindy's relations with Gerrie, suggesting ways to get around an argument, or how to mend an existing breach. Karen never turned a deaf ear to Cindy's request for help in understanding Gerrie, nor did she ever cease her tolerance of Cindy's constant complaining.

"She will never do this to me again," Cindy told Karen, "and I will never leave Gerrie again. If I do, that damn bitch Donna would come in here and I'd lose everything." As a mediator for the couple, Karen tried to help solve their problems by having them come to a mutual understanding of each other's needs. However, as soon as Cindy was comfortably settled, she turned to more material considerations. Cindy had learned the hard way. She couldn't have two pieces of property that someone else was buying for her and keep them both in the event of a break-up. She had to consolidate. Immediately, she began talking about buying a larger farm, a place for just her and Gerrie.

Daily, Cindy looked at real estate listings to find a place where they could keep the horses on the property. No separate house, only one big beautiful home with lots of acreage where they could live and care for the animals. That was all Cindy talked about. She even seemed to be more cautious with her spending. By holding down household expenses, Gerrie was able to keep the $20,000 from the "Pick 6" win in the bank and accruing interest. To outsiders it looked as though she was making it on her salary.

Meanwhile Cindy tried to solidify her relationship with Gerrie. Cindy would go to Gerrie and ask to be held. They were sharing the same bedroom, just as before. Gerrie understood Cindy's reason for wanting to move. She saw how difficult it was for her to go from their home to work at the farm and also build the business. She asked herself, "Why *not* consolidate the money from both the homes into one place where the horses would live on the property?" Cindy desired a more modern house. She told Gerrie the type of place she wanted. Every week Cindy picked up a *Homes* magazine, and every evening they looked at the pictures and read descriptions. After several weeks they saw a farm that even to Gerrie sounded very special and Gerrie agreed to take a look at it.

They drove onto a long, winding drive flanked by stately pines that led past a large aquamarine pond on which white swans swam amid weeping willows. In front of them was a cedar and stone home surrounded by fifteen acres of farmland. The setting was indeed impressive. The entrance of the house opened into a two-story living room with an atrium filled with exotic plants and flowers. Entranced, Gerrie couldn't help saying, "This is the home I wanted all my life." It exuded warmth and individuality.

"It's contemporary, yet classic," Cindy said excitedly.

They both fell for it instantly. "It's perfect," Gerrie exclaimed.

"It has a loft upstairs where Gerrie can have her office," Cindy later told Karen enthusiastically. Gerrie loved what they called the Florida room. It was adjacent to the open living room, which gave the effect of an enormous combination of living/dining room and kitchen. It was different, even unique. Outside, off the sunporch, a cedar gazebo with sun deck was reflected in a fern-encrusted pond. Low, rolling hills sprinkled with tall evergreens at the back of the acreage was the background for a large barn. The barn was in need of repair but would suffice until the business afforded a new one.

There was no need for them to look further. With more stolen money from the credit union a down payment was made, and the papers were signed to bind the deal until the two properties in Cindy's name could be sold.

Immediately Cindy began talking about breeding more horses. From a racing form they learned that a mare and a stallion were being entered in claiming races at Keenland. They saw their chance. "I need $15,000 to claim our two horses," Cindy said excitedly. It was Saturday; Gerrie's office was closed.

They drove to the Henry Vogt credit union office together. The two walked stealthily past the guardhouse and into the office. Gerrie made out fifteen $1,000 money orders to herself. The money orders were cashed by a friend. Jimmy went to Keenland to claim the horses.

After the purchase the sleek animals were brought to the farm. "They're so beautiful," Cindy said, stroking their manes. At last Cindy had what she wanted.

"The barn, however, is in such need of repair it's actually unsafe for the horses," Gerrie said philosophically. They decided to build a new barn along with the paddocks.

Gerrie drew up plans for the new paddocks and barn. Then Gerrie phoned Lou Moseley, a contractor she knew. "Can you build the barn at a price of about $42,000?" Moseley agreed. Gerrie needed a $10,000 deposit before construction could begin, but the auditors were due at any time. At the office she took $1,500 from the cash drawer but felt it was unsafe to write the balance in money orders because of the $15,000 she had written earlier. Devising a less traceable method, Gerrie selected a member's name and wrote a check against his account for $8,752.50, without charging it against his account. She placed $10,000 down on the project and financed the balance. This brought the total of the house, barn, and paddocks to $233,500, with quarterly payments of $3,500.

Gerrie knew she would need someone to help with the horses. He or she had to be paid in cash, so she needed someone she could trust. "What about my daughter?" Cindy asked coyly. Gerrie agreed to bring Cindy's daughter Kim back as farm manager.

"But," warned Gerrie, "she's not to interfere with our decisions in the business or our private lives." Cindy resented the unfavorable insinuations toward her daughter, but she was willing to agree to anything for this new venture.

Once again Kim's children were underfoot. Although Cindy enjoyed eating with the children, the chatter at the table was not Gerrie's idea of a peaceful meal at home. Aside from that, Cindy was being wonderful, and Gerrie tried to keep from making waves.

After Gerrie had finished the plans for the barn she called Lou Moseley to arrange a starting date on the building. The day he arrived with his equipment Gerrie was at work. Cindy, overseeing the job, asked her daughter for advice. That evening when Gerrie returned from the office, she found that her plans for the building had been radically changed. Gerrie wasn't happy with the new plans—or the new prices—but once again she said nothing.

Kim arrived each morning with her two boys and the family dog. Gerrie could hardly believe what was happening. Her thoughts of living quietly with Cindy were quickly being shattered. "Every day, Kim and her brood were underfoot and completely out of control. Between the kids and the dog running about with no supervision, bedlam prevailed." To worsen the situation, Cindy became enraged whenever Gerrie voiced her discontent. Gerrie's hope of a beautiful life with Cindy was fast evaporating. A few months later it vanished completely. But the move had been made and Gerrie reluctantly shouldered the disappointment. Cindy was once again completely occupied by activities with her daughter, her horses, and her ambition. Gerrie was merely the check writer who slept there and brought home more money when it was demanded—and the demands were constant.

Not only Cindy but Jimmy continued to ask for more money, and Gerrie felt that he was overpaid as it was. In one discussion, Gerrie said, "As much as I pay him to do a good job, he still can't get a win. I believe he is mishandling the horses."

While at River Downs in April, Gerrie decided to give several of the horses to Tim Johns, another trainer, as a test. If they had been losing because of Jimmy's lack of expertise as a trainer, the horses would improve. Gerrie had to find out.

After one week with Tim one horse named Chicago Blues began to run better, but they discovered he was having a breathing problem caused by the flap in his throat. Tim told her, "Jimmy should have found that, Gerrie, in the way the horse holds his head after a short run. See, it's down, which means he's having trouble breathing."

Another horse, Windy, a little filly that burned up the track in the morning workouts, had never won a race.

"What do you think is wrong, Tim?" Gerrie asked.

Tim examined the horse. "Windy has bad ankles and leg problems. She ought to never race again." Gerrie swallowed still another disappointment. Both horses were sent back home to Louisville, leaving Jimmy with only two horses to train. Since he had failed to detect either problem with the horses, Gerrie was incensed. The mistakes added further fuel to the fire ignited between the two women.

Gerrie waited as bills for entry fees, stall rent, and salaries mounted without income from a win. Instead of Jimmy entering the two horses he had left in a race with horses of the same value, he entered them with better horses. "Jimmy, Ivy Vine, the $5,000 horse, was entered in a $10,000 race. He didn't have a chance to win against those superior horses," Gerrie said.

"I need better horses," Jimmy said.

"That's not all you need," Gerrie turned away from him disgustedly. Hearing Jimmy's request, Cindy began looking at upgrading their stock. She found one horse she particularly liked and began pressing Gerrie to buy it.

"There's always something she wants," Gerrie told a friend. On March 8, 1988, Gerrie gave Cindy $6,057.92 for a $5,000 down payment on a horse named Four Digits. The total cost was about $10,000. Ten days later they made the down payment, leaving a balance of $5,000. An informal receipt was scribbled on a pad from Ceasar's Atlantic City and signed by the seller, Bill Gretsch. Both women were listed as owners of the horse. On March 23, Gerrie paid the remaining $5,000 from a forged check using a union member's name. The checks Gerrie had written in only fifteen days totaled $15,953.92.

It was an impossible situation that was rapidly worsening, causing the arguments to multiply. Every time Gerrie wanted to cut back, Cindy fought her every inch of the way, and Gerrie knew she was fighting a losing battle. With Kim and Jimmy as groom and trainer, the whole family was united in their demands on her.

Cindy started running up bills faster than Gerrie could pay them. Newly issued charge cards were taken to the limit,

and Jimmy and Kim were over-ordering: fancy western sad-
dles, mouth bits, plus hundreds of dollars a month in long-
distance calls between the family members when any of them
were out of town. Gerrie felt herself going under. There was
no stopping them. Every day something new was ordered or
arrived C.O.D.

The money was going out like water through a sieve
. . . $20,000 . . . $25,000 at a time. Nothing was ever
enough. Cindy was relentless.

Gerrie's investment in the farm was now over $500,000,
not including cash payouts that couldn't be traced: appliances, farm equipment, furniture, food, and salaries. She
used three different banks to camouflage the total amounts of
checks she had written to herself and deposited into her account. On several occasions she would be standing in line
with other bank customers and pray that she wouldn't get
the same teller who had served her the day before; each time
she cashed checks just under $9,000 that she had endorsed.

She couldn't use stolen cash to make the house payments, or to pay any invoices that left a paper trail to her;
however, dining out, traveling expenses, home repairs, and
some vet bills would be hard to trace. She felt herself going
down for the last time. Frantically she began gambling in
larger amounts to explain her huge cash flow.

Gerrie was stealing money daily; she spent endless
nights praying the thefts wouldn't be discovered. She knew
that if she were ever caught it would kill her mother. At night
she'd cry herself to sleep. Dawn found her in a cold sweat,
her mind flashing the same thought, *Would this be the day?*

An unbearable tension besieged her body and remained
each morning until 9:30 A.M. By that hour, if the auditors
hadn't come, they wouldn't, and she knew she would have
another day of freedom.

She worked hours into the night if she had a "sure-fire hunch" they were arriving, and many times they did. When they didn't find her theft because she had hidden it so well, she could breathe again until the following audit.

"Every time they left without finding a shortage, I took a week off with Cindy. Happy! Happy! Happy!" They went on cruises to the Islands and to Mexico on stolen money. In those short intervals Gerrie's tense body relaxed; she was free. However, in her mind, she was never free. Even in the good times she only had a few months to breathe easily, then it was time to look for the examiners again. And yet despite the pressure Gerrie stole more.

"Cindy had me trained. Whenever she wanted anything she pushed a button. Sometimes it was her delicate look of helplessness that made me want to keep giving to make her happy. And she was happy for a short while. Then, she could become so sad when she needed something—so sad she would have to push the button again. She'd push a button. . . . I would be gentle, push another. . . . I would be giving; and Cindy always knew which button to push. I was programmed very well."

In an upbeat mood one day, Gerrie decided to take Cindy to Turfway Park. "We'll make it a banner day and win big," Gerrie said. Turfway was a luxurious raceway. On April 9, 1986, Jerry Carroll and his associates had purchased a racetrack that had one hundred years of American racing history recorded. The track in Florence, Kentucky, had been called Latonia and was renamed Turfway Park. Carroll promoted a massive renovation costing $12 million, giving the track a new, beautiful look.

Although modern was the image, tradition was the key in thoroughbred racing. The $500,000 Jim Beam Stakes at Turfway had grown from a race of regional interest to one of national significance. This important event brought nation-wide attention and top three-year-old Kentucky Derby contenders to Northern Kentucky by becoming one of the most viewed thoroughbred races in the nation. The next Stakes Race was coming up on April 2, 1988.

Ten days before the race, when the auditors had come and gone, Gerrie forged one check for $3,500—a "loan" to herself for the April 10 house payment. Then selecting a member's name, she forged and issued a check for $6,396.75.

That first Saturday in April 1988 was a dreary, hot day; however, Gerrie was happy and feeling top-drawer. She had just been awarded four "on-ground" horse stalls, which were hard to come by.

Cindy and Gerrie arrived at the track a half-hour before post time and went to the lavish dining room. They paused on the stairway—an impressive sight with walnut banisters around every tier. Queen-like Cindy walked to their table and sat down, enjoying the ambiance and attention, but Gerrie could not sit still.

After they had made several trips to the parimutuel windows that day it was 6:10 P.M.—time for the eleventh race, the Jim Beam Stakes. Gerrie liked the favorite, but she bet a couple of hundred "across the board" on a longshot, Kingpost. "I feel daring," she said to Cindy. The examiners had come and gone, and things were temporarily running well. Gerrie was flushed with even more excitement as she watched the race. She stood cheering as Kingpost won the one-and-one-eighth-mile race, paying $44.40, $12.60, and $6.00. That mini win made her euphoric; it was like a reprieve.

Thereafter, she stayed busy every weekend, driving to Turfway Park. When River Downs opened, the drive continued to Cincinnati. Cindy and Gerrie joined the Turf Club at

River Downs; there was no charge for the membership, which entitled them to privileges at the track, free admission passes, and newsletters with information on coming events. As members they would receive points for attending special functions. For example, points were acquired for patronizing the second-floor dining room overlooking the track. The points were then used toward obtaining memorabilia of the history and special events concerning River Downs. Cindy swelled with pride as she told acquaintances of their membership.

Because of Cindy's preoccupation with her children, Gerrie had time to visit with her mother several times a week. Stella lived for these visits with her daughter. She would talk for hours about her life with her husband, Bill. "For years after the big flood of '37, he was feeling bad," she said as she reminisced. "He had chest pains he didn't want to talk about, and he always passed it off as something he had eaten." Bill pulled through a heart attack in 1947, but the illness left him unable to work. "And I was so thankful for you, Gerrie," she continued rambling on while patting Gerrie's hand. "You picked up extra jobs to help out. At least he got to see you graduate from high school." Bill had the second heart attack on the day Gerrie graduated, and he died a few months later. As Stella spoke of the past, Gerrie could see her health failing, and with each visit, the past became more her reality. Gerrie wanted to keep in close touch, but Cindy became suspicious of Gerrie's reasons for not coming home. She would call Stella's house several times while Gerrie was away until the phone calls became upsetting to the elderly lady.

On every visit, Stella would say, "I pray for you all the time Gerrie. I pray that God will keep you safe." Many times it was too much for Gerrie to hear, so she would leave, making excuses and trying to get away from her guilt.

One day Gerrie called from work. "Cindy, I'm going to visit mother and then on the way home have dinner at Grisanti's." Cindy was noncommittal, but when she hung up she realized the restaurant was close to Gerrie's old girlfriend Donna's home. As Cindy's suspicions grew, her beliefs about Gerrie meeting Donna mounted. She fixed herself a scotch and water. Cindy felt positive that the two women were together. Again, thoughts of her security being in jeopardy panicked her. She drove to Donna's home, thinking she would find Gerrie's car close by. The place was dark. Only Donna's car was in the drive. Cindy was certain Gerrie was with her. At a nearby pay-phone she called the house, letting the phone ring for nearly a half-hour. When no one answered, Cindy returned home. As she envisioned Gerrie and Donna together, she took out the bottle of scotch and she began drinking heavily. Soon she was quite drunk and set out to find them. She had to see for herself.

Gerrie was sipping a martini at Grisanti's in Jeffersontown. She relaxed, eating alone. It afforded her the quiet leisure time she needed so desperately to bring her thoughts together.

Her thoughts were interrupted by the ringing of the restaurant phone. The host approached her table. "You have a telephone call, Miss Powell," he said in a serious tone. Her heart jumped. She picked up the phone. It was the Jeffersontown Police. Cindy was found in her car parked along Taylorsville Road, slumped on the horn and screaming at the top of her voice. However, she was coherent enough to tell the police where to find Gerrie. The officers drove Cindy to Grisanti's parking lot, and Gerrie was summoned. They couldn't give any further information other than to say they believed Cindy was in shock. Gerrie said, "I will take care of the situation, I'll take her home." Gently reaching for Cindy in the back of the police car, Gerrie coaxed her out, telling the officers, "She has control as long as she doesn't drink, and I'm sure she has been drinking at home."

Cindy screamed, "I don't want to live!" The officers were about to take her to the hospital when Gerrie reassured them that she could handle her. The transfer to Gerrie's car was touchy. Gerrie had no idea what Cindy was capable of doing or saying in front of the police. Eventually, Cindy calmed down. Gerrie thanked the officers and started home. There, Cindy resumed her tantrum, storming through the house and destroying everything in her path as the puppy, Tootie, took her place behind the toilet. Using the bedroom phone, Gerrie called Kim. "Your mother has been drinking, I think you'd better come here," Gerrie said. Cindy remained hysterical until Kim appeared at the house twenty minutes later. The moment she arrived the tantrum stopped, but soon Cindy exploded in anger when she realized her daughter had been called.

"Why is she here?" she demanded to know. With complete disgust, Gerrie answered, "Because I need to have someone else see what you're doing to yourself."

"Our problem is you, Gerrie," Cindy shouted. "You need a psychiatrist." Kim walked quietly toward Gerrie. "To put it in a nutshell, you have to say no to my mother. Please help her help herself." Gerrie listened as Kim took control and firmly told Cindy, "I'm going to make an appointment for you with a therapist."

Cindy said nothing. She merely sat, childlike and pouting. Shivering from the outburst, Tootie came from her hiding place in the bathroom and ran to Gerrie.

"I'll find a therapist for Mother tomorrow," Kim added,

thanking Gerrie profoundly as she was leaving. The following week Cindy kept the appointment made for her with Dr. Joyce Randolph at the cost of $50 a session with two sessions a week to be paid for by Gerrie.

Months passed, but Cindy did not seem to improve. Cindy suggested to the therapist that perhaps the problem was her mate. She scheduled a meeting for Gerrie to see her doctor.

Willing to do anything to help the situation, Gerrie kept the appointment. "Ten minutes into the meeting, the doctor realized that she was hearing only a small part of the story from each of us," Gerrie recalled, "and she suggested that we start coming to meetings for married couples."

Gerrie felt the real cause of Cindy's problem was money. In associating with the affluent couples in the 500 Club, she kept wanting more. To her, possessions were a symbol of security. She wanted to buy things to have the same feeling of security she saw in her friends and her father.

Gerrie felt she had reached the bottom of the well and couldn't spend anymore. Complaining first to Dr. Randolph and then to others, Cindy called Karen. "I'm pissed," she said. "I can hardly stand it anymore. Gerrie watches every goddamn thing I do. I saw a little handbag that I liked in a catalogue. She threw a fit. 'No,' she yelled, 'you *cannot buy* anymore.' It was only $200—do you believe that?"

It was unfair, in Cindy's mind, to be denied anything. Dr. Randolph listened to similar complaints in several sessions and finally suggested that Cindy find a hobby to have the satisfaction of accomplishments.

Cindy's ex-sister-in-law owned a franchised Fred Astaire Dance Studio, and Cindy had been interested in studying dancing since she had heard Gerrie speak of the dance conventions during her life with Lucy. But more recently, she had seen Karen and a dance partner clear the floor at the Carriage House while dancing to everything from country-western and rock to fox-trot and swing. "Oh!" Cindy remarked to Karen during a break, "I wish I could do that."

"But you can, Cindy. You can learn," Karen replied.

Cindy enrolled at the Fred Astaire Studio. She could hardly wait to tell Gerrie what she had done . . . because "it was doctor's orders."

Gerrie agreed to pay the initial fee of $500 for the introductory offer. The next session for $2,000 was paid in cash. Cindy was happy again, receiving compliments continuously at the studio. After each session she purchased more lessons. The lessons helped. She seemed better able to cope. Seeing this, Gerrie continued to pay for the lessons. This plus $100 a week to the therapist compounded Gerrie's financial burdens. "I needed $1,000 a day to finance the entire budget. Cindy kept wanting more lessons," she said, "and each time I tried to stop because the books were in order and the examiners were due to arrive, Cindy's demands became greater." Soon Cindy enrolled Kim for dance lessons.

Several months into Cindy's lessons, the dancers were planning a trip to Columbus, Ohio, for a dance competition, and Cindy wanted to go. At intervals, she began talking to Gerrie about exhibition dancing for beginners. Hoping to catch Gerrie in a good mood, she casually remarked, "The cost is $1,500 for a weekend."

"I can't handle it, Cindy," Gerrie said. "You know I'm having trouble paying the bills we have."

"I didn't say I was going, I was just telling you." Cindy was like a child hinting for a trip to Disney World. "But, sometime I would like to go," she said, adding, "It would do a lot for me."

The noose around Gerrie's neck was slowly tightening.

It was the end of the year, a slow period at the Henry Vogt credit union. There were few new members and very little money being added to established accounts. Consequently, Gerrie had to guard against taking large amounts of money. Due to the holidays, there were more withdrawals than deposits. She could only risk taking a few hundred a day. For the first time Gerrie was unable to meet the obligations of the farm, Cindy's credit cards, and the other expenses on the amount of money she could safely take. Gerrie worried constantly. She became more and more withdrawn.

Finally Gerrie decided she had to confide in someone. Careful to avoid anyone who was a confidant of Cindy's, she chose Jan, an old friend she hadn't seen much of in recent years. They had met when Gerrie and Lucy were together. Jan, who had once been an entertainer and America's first female bullfighter, was aware of Gerrie's extravagant lifestyle being a bit too grand for the manager of a small credit union. At the time, Jan held a middle management position at Brown and Williamson Tobacco Company; this was her leverage for comparison and suspicions. Still, Jan liked Gerrie and kept her suspicions to herself.

Approaching Jan to discuss the issue, Gerrie decided to only reveal the surface of her problem with Cindy—more would be dangerous.

"The bills for clothing and jewelry keep piling up, and Cindy doesn't want to hear about money problems," Gerrie told her. "To her, it's as though they don't exist."

With sober realization, Gerrie said, "Cindy keeps telling me to slow down, but it's because of her that I have to keep going. I think she is trying to push me toward a heart attack." Of course, Jan disagreed. Viewing the situation from a different perspective, she thought, "The last thing Cindy wants is to lose her supply of cash."

During their talk, Gerrie revealed that she was so miserable at home, she was unable to concentrate on work, the business, or gambling. She hesitated and added, "And that's the way I make my money." Jan, who had heard rumors of Cindy's demanding ways, noticed Gerrie's extreme anxiety and felt sorry for her but could only act as a sounding board. "I have given her everything; it's never enough." This was no surprise to Jan, who said, "That's because her 'needs' are based on the possessions of others, Gerrie." Jan had been skeptical for years, and without making accusations, she could only say, "Girl, if it were me, I'd get out. Give her the goddamn house and leave."

The talks helped, but at home, the arguments continued escalating. During one of them, Gerrie forlornly cried, "Cindy, we have no more money!"

Desperate now, Gerrie was making cash loans to anyone who wanted them, and upon repayment of the loan by check, the money was given to Cindy. However, Gerrie couldn't launder the money fast enough. As much as she studied the speed ratings of the horses, she couldn't win all that was needed.

At home the tension was constant. A verbal conflict started every morning. The arguments were always the same. "If Cindy didn't need money, her kids did."

Jimmy and Kim were paid in cash for working at the farm. It was up to them to claim their salary as income; Gerrie never withheld anything. Jimmy picked up the pay for himself and his grooms. The total amount each week grew until it was between $600 and $800 in cash. Cindy's salary was several hundred daily. Gerrie didn't ask her where the money was going any longer. She had enough worries just getting it.

Gerrie felt she had nothing to live for. She began thinking of suicide and searching for ways to do it . . . maybe the hose from the car exhaust. This was followed by a horrifying thought: If she were dead, the missing money would be discovered and her mother would be disgraced. She couldn't even kill herself! Cindy had her caught financially, but because of Stella, Gerrie had to live with it. She remained the devoted daughter and checked on her mother daily by phone when she could not see her.

During this time she made plans for her office Christmas party. It was to take place on December 22. Her menu included a delectable array of food and drinks that she would prepare the night before.

She also arranged to surprise Cindy with a family affair for her birthday, on December 28. Gerrie prepared for Cindy's big day during the month of December. Kim helped with the guest list and sent out invitations to relatives and friends. Cindy's step-mother, father, and many of her straight friends, including Russell Newlander, were invited.

Gerrie bought the party supplies and made arrangements to reserve a "party room" at Grisanti's. The restaurant was to cater the affair with its special hors d'oeuvres and an open bar. Gerrie purchased matching balloons, banners, napkins, and plates that were sent to Grisanti's. She arranged to have guests with cameras ready to flash pictures on Cindy's arrival, celebrity-style.

One week before Cindy's party and the night before the office party, Gerrie worked in the kitchen until 1:00 A.M. making hors d'oeuvres for the people at work. The next morning, on December 22, 1988, she listened to Cindy rave on about needing more money for extra Christmas gifts. Loading her car with trays of food for the credit union Christmas party, Gerrie felt ready to explode from pressure.

As Gerrie hurried into the house for the last time to get a

punch bowl that had been stored in the basement, Cindy met her at the doorway. "You have to get more money. You just have to." Gerrie rushed up the stairs, trying to get away from the madhouse. Her chest pounded. Cindy's words came in quick, shrill spurts penetrating Gerrie's head until it was spinning.

Turning toward the stairwell, she reached for the side wall to steady herself; a banister had never been installed. The combined sound of Cindy's voice and her own frantic pace caused her to lose her balance, and she fell head-first, twisting herself from side to side. Grabbing frantically at the slick cement walls, she rotated downward . . . bumping . . . pounding . . . jolting with each violent impact. She grabbed at the wall as her limbs hit the sharp edges of the steps. She came to an abrupt stop as her head hit the concrete of the basement floor.

Lying in a heap, face down, she remained motionless, afraid to move. She lay there in pain, moaning until the medics arrived. Her only thought was *My God, how will I get to the money?*

CHAPTER 8

Broken

"Hey, easy putting her on that stretcher. She's badly bruised and that right arm looks broken," the blond, boyish looking medic called in a southern drawl.

"Please," Gerrie begged, trying to get up, "I don't want to go to the hospital. I'll be fine."

The medic looked sympathetically at her but used his arm as a brace to push her back down. His voice was firm, "Ma'am, you're hurt, maybe badly. I wouldn't do anything foolish if I were you."

Gerrie didn't know whether to laugh or cry. "Foolish," she murmured, "describes me to a T."

He chuckled.

"It hurts too much to laugh," Gerrie said as they adroitly lifted the stretcher with her on it into the ambulance.

In shock, Gerrie heard the siren blaring as if from a distance. In the emergency room doctors examined her. Gerrie was bruised over her entire body. Her left elbow was broken. Three large clots had formed on her leg, back, and head. One of the clots was the size of her fist. "We'll have to operate right away to remove the clots," the balding resident surgeon informed her.

Gerrie nodded, stoic by this time. Despite her discomfort she hardly spoke as they prepped her for the operation. During the surgery doctors removed the clots, did a skin graft, and placed two pins in her elbow.

After the surgery, white-clad nurses flitted in and out of her room, administering shots and pills to make the pain subside. After forty-eight hours, as her pain diminished, the agony of her reality returned. She racked her brain trying to figure out how she could still get money when she was immobilized in a hospital.

Frantic, she called the credit union to ask for a loan and reached her old supervisor. "This is Gerrie Powell. I guess you've heard about my accident," she said, trying to keep her voice from trembling.

"We've all been worried as hell about you, Gerrie. How can we help?"

She swallowed hard. "I need a loan."

"Whatever you need, Gerrie, we'll take care of it. How much?"

"$15,000," she muttered.

"Gerrie, speak up. I can hardly hear you."

Her heart quickened. Was he suspicious? Her mouth was dry. She coughed several times to clear her throat. "I need $15,000," she said.

A second or two passed. To Gerrie it felt like hours. Finally he spoke, "I'm sure it won't be a problem, but that's a large amount. Let me check it with my superiors and call you right back."

Gerrie thanked him and lay back exhausted.

CHAPTER 9

Slip Sliding Away

She was thankful it was December; she could forget about auditors until the end of January. The last thing she needed was to worry about the examiners. She called Cindy's daughter and tied up the loose ends for Cindy's birthday party, which was to take place three days after Christmas. She knew Kim would pitch in.

When the magic moment arrived, Kim, on the pretense of taking her mother to dinner at Grisanti's, walked with her into the party room. As usual, Cindy looked beautiful. She was wearing her full-length fox coat with many gold chains. Deeply touched with excitement, Cindy started to cry. Her family and a host of other straight friends, including Russell Newlander, had made it a happy occasion. If she missed Gerrie, she kept the feeling to herself.

Although Gerrie was pleased that the party went well, her main concern was her mother. Stella, now eighty-seven, had become more fragile and could not get out. All she had to look forward to were the phone calls and visits from Gerrie. When she heard that her daughter was in the hospital from a fall, she believed the family was keeping the truth from her.

"Gerrie's condition is more serous, isn't it?" she kept saying. Her health started to deteriorate as soon as she was told. Five days later she became critically ill.

Gerrie's sister Bridget was summoned to Louisville from Pittsburgh to care for her mother. On January 2, Bridget was alone with her mother as Stella lay quietly reminiscing about the wonderful times she had in Florida. "Gerrie isn't calling me very much. I think she's much sicker than I've been told. I don't believe Gerrie will recover."

"No, Mom, really. She's going to be fine," Bridget said.

Unbelieving, Stella shook her head. As she turned toward a window facing the street, Stella talked to Bridget about the view she remembered of the ocean while she was in Florida. After some time she whispered, "Gerrie, look at the beautiful sunset." Smiling, she said, "Gerrie, isn't that the most beautiful sunset you've ever seen?"

Bridget answered, "Yes, Mother, it's beautiful."

Then Stella closed her eyes.

Throughout her mother's life, Gerrie had given her everything she wanted—she had kept her promise. But the fact that she couldn't see her mother or even go to her funeral was totally devastating to Gerrie.

After Stella's death, Gerrie began brooding about the future. "With her gone I knew they would get me. It was only a matter of time. There was no one left to protect me." She felt spiritless and saddened; meanwhile the bills kept mounting.

During one of the visits to the hospital, Gerrie told Cindy, "We are going to have to sell the farm, Cindy, and we're going to get a smaller house. The dance lessons have to stop, and I'm going to destroy all our credit cards."

"Why, Gerrie? I can't handle that," Cindy objected.

Gerrie continued, "And instead of buying clothes with labels from Karen's or Gidding-Jenny's, you'll have to shop at a moderately priced shop like Penney's or Sears, because we cannot go on as we have been."

Cindy was shocked. She listened and could only say, "Gerrie, you don't mean that! You can't be serious! What will our friends say?"

Gerrie looked at her appraisingly. "To quote a famous Southern gentleman, I don't give a damn. I want Jimmy to put the horses in claiming races in order to sell them. And that's the first step to liquidating everything."

"Cindy became quiet," Gerrie recalled. "There was no argument or discussion, and after a few minutes she left. The next day Cindy opened new accounts to buy clothes. She ran her charge accounts to the limit, knowing positively that I would get the money to pay them off. Cindy also needed cash, lots of it, as much as she could get her hands on. I knew she would start putting pressure on me again."

By now Gerrie had been in the hospital for more than a month. She had no idea when she would be able to return to work. Her doctor said she needed a second skin graft. She called Cindy at home to tell her that she needed another operation. "I'm sorry this has to fall back on you, but please handle it, Cindy." The other end of the conversation was short and abrupt. Cindy hadn't visited Gerrie that day. Assuming she would be coming the following day, Gerrie asked that she bring a few personal things from home.

Cindy snapped, "I'm being run ragged as it is, Gerrie, trying to handle everything alone; I cannot come to the hospital every day."

As Cindy was talking, Gerrie wondered, "How could she be so busy? She has a maid, a farm manager, a gardener, a groom for the horses, and she only has to cook for herself." But, once again, seeing Cindy as one in need of protection, Gerrie justified the outburst by telling herself, "Cindy's only frightened. If something were to happen to me, she would have no one."

Two more weeks passed. People from the office called daily. Friends from Louisville and Lexington flooded Gerrie's hospital room with cards and flowers. At any other time the attention would have comforted her, but now she could not relax. She had to get back to the credit union, to her "resources." Gerrie was instructed by her doctor that to be released from the hospital, she would have to stay at home and keep her leg elevated. After she promised she would, he finally allowed her to go home.

Without Gerrie at work for the entire month of January 1989, the crew at the credit union worked overtime until everything was up to date. The following month the supervisory committee chairman came in and helped prepare the statements; however, the books were two and a half months behind.

Communicating by phone, Gerrie taught the women how to operate the computer to figure dividends and print the 1099 forms. Pat took charge as manager. She was efficient, considering the fact that she had very little experience in bookkeeping.

For the first time in years, Gerrie was away from daily pressure. She fanaticized about what it would be like to be free, to stop.

Then, frantically switching thoughts back into the pitfall of the present, she became depressed over losing her mother and feeling that she was soon going to be caught.

It was a dreary, cold February and she was still unable to get up. The extent of her activity was television, therapy, and the doctor. The $15,000 loan made from the credit union two months earlier was gone. There was no money to pay bills. Although the phone rang constantly with calls from well wishers, fellow employees, friends, and family, never did it relieve even for one moment the agonizing hell she was going through mentally. Immobile in her wheelchair, she stared at the polished planks in the floor leading to the atrium. There, dried ferns drooped from baskets hanging on wrought iron hooks. Lining the brick floor, flowers and greenery wilted from lack of care. The sight of them was merely a reminder of other things she could not save.

Her need for money had become critical. She was ready to risk anything. With a touch of her old confidence, she figured that the shorter the length of time a forged check would be out of her hand, the less likely it would be discovered. On the verge of bankruptcy, she was trapped with no way out and no means of getting to the cash. The two audit-free months were over. Not only was another quarterly check of the books impending from the supervisory committee, but she had to wait to the end of February before disturbing any funds. If she could hold out until the first Monday in March, it would be safer. She sat waiting, and listened to Cindy reciting like a litany the balances of bills to be paid: $350 stall rent, $1,700 vet charges, $920 van repairs, $850 salaries, psychiatrist fees, . . . and Gerrie sweated it out.

Finally, desperate for money, Gerrie called Pat Salzman. "Would you bring the past day's work, plus the credit union checkbook to the house?" Gerrie asked.

On previous occasions Gerrie had written large checks using members' names and then adjusted the books in the office. Now she had to change her method, using her own name.

On February 7, Gerrie wrote a company check for $9,877.25, payable to herself. She forged credit union officers' names. Cindy drove Gerrie to the First National Bank in Jeffersontown, where Gerrie endorsed and cashed the check. They knew her at the bank; there was no problem.

After cashing the checks, Gerrie gave the money to Cindy, who paid their bills. Continuing in this manner, Gerrie had no problem cashing the checks. Two days later she wrote an additional one for $5,500, to herself, and again Cindy drove her to the bank to cash the check. Then on February 24, still another check for $5,000 was made payable to herself. Each time Cindy drove Gerrie to the bank, struggling to manipulate the wheelchair and cast safely to avoid causing further injury to Gerrie. Again she took the money Gerrie gave her and paid the bills.

It was the last of the month, five weeks after Gerrie was released from the hospital and eight weeks after her mother died. The office workers were aware that all office mail was "off limits." Bank statements arrived on the fifth or sixth of the month, so to be safe, Gerrie had to be in the office to pull the forged checks from the statements. Facing Gerrie was debt and problems—problems with Jimmy, problems with the horses. Cindy argued constantly over the farm, her children, and everything Gerrie said or did. Gerrie didn't care about her life any longer; the pleasure was gone. She thought of buying a van and running as soon as she was back on her feet, but she couldn't leave Cindy and knew that Cindy wouldn't go. Besides, Gerrie knew that if she didn't do something soon the theft would be discovered. She had to keep working to hide the shortage.

The doctor ordered her to limit her exercise and keep her leg elevated, but at that moment the leg was the least of her worries. She wanted to get to the racetrack, too, not only to keep up the pretense but to try desperately to win. On March 3, while Cindy was away, Gerrie wrote a check for

$8,127.35. She had a friend drive her to the bank and, against doctors orders, went to Louisville Downs. She bet on races being televised from Turfway Park. Wheeling every horse in an Exacta, she won $2,300—to be applied to the next house payment. With the balance of the $8,127.35 check, she paid cash for services for the farm, thereby eliminating a paper trail.

Some officials and office workers saw her at the track, called and asked when she was coming back. "The members are upset, thinking you aren't going to return. To them, you *are* the credit union," they said.

Gerrie murmured a meaningless reply. She dreaded going back because she couldn't stand the pressure, the temptation, the guilt, and the hell.

On March 6, she asked Cindy to take her to the office— the bank statements were to arrive that day. They argued, and Cindy stormed from the house. Gerrie sat slumped in her wheelchair, looking at the leg that was supposed to have been kept elevated; it was beginning to swell. She knew that the forged checks would be easily recognized as such by a person doing the posting if they saw how they were endorsed. She thought, "It's possible that Pat won't open the statement for February because I warned her against it."

March 6 passed. Gerrie's foot and upper leg were throbbing. Again, she was taken to the emergency room, where the cast was removed. She was told to stay off her leg, or she might lose it. For five days her leg throbbed. She had to keep it elevated for two more weeks. Sweating out the time at home, worried to death and extending herself in all directions to keep things going, Gerrie was beginning to break.

March 14, she wrote a credit union check for $8,787.88 to herself, and again ten days later, one for $4,757.88. Both times Cindy drove her to the bank to cash the checks.

Gerrie had been living on the edge for so long she now felt herself slipping into a stupor. Her arm was healing, but not well enough to push the wheelchair, so she stayed wherever Cindy put her in the morning until Cindy returned to move her again. She sat . . . and waited . . . thinking of the disastrous turn her life had taken. The weeks passed, and finally her leg started to heal. She counted the days until her doctor allowed her to return to work.

Finally the day came. Waiting for her at the office when she arrived were two stacks of mail eighteen inches high. Quickly shuffling through the assorted letters and notices, Gerrie saw with a sinking heart that the February bank statement had been opened. Trembling, she turned toward Pat. They looked at one another for a moment that seemed endless.

Pat stammered, "I was trying to find an amount on someone's cold check. I had to open it . . . sorry!" She turned away.

For too many years Gerrie had agonized when the bank examiners came for the audits. This time she fell into quiet desperation, seeing no light at the end of the tunnel.

After Pat left the room, Gerrie spread the checks and statements on her desk. There were the forged signatures amounting to more than $20,000. Her thoughts came in spurts, each one more frightening than the last. She was terrified at the thought of being caught. *What if Pat saw them . . . could she have? Maybe she missed them. . . . She had been looking for something else.* Gerrie's mind ran rampant. Yet nothing happened.

Days passed. . . . The first week back at the office was over. Still nothing had happened. Not a sign. Not a word. The immediacy of Gerrie's fear passed, and she felt safe. "Pat missed it!" she said leaving the office.

The expression of guilt on Gerrie's face when she saw the bank statement had been opened must have deeply embedded itself in Pat's mind. Pat had long been suspicious, but never had her suspicions been confirmed. Now she knew where to look.

Gerrie felt she was being watched constantly. She found that personal things on her desk were rearranged when she returned from lunch and drawers on the file cabinet were left open. She grew more frightened and more cautious. She still needed money desperately, but now she agonized and waited till Pat was out of the office. On March 31, she could wait no longer. She drew a check for $5,875 made payable to a member and endorsed by Gerrie after forging the member's name.

"Kim was asking for more money. There were arguments over Jimmy's lack of knowledge with the horses and over Cindy wanting to pay her daughter more money for the four hours a day she worked at the farm."

Gerrie countered each request with "No! I will spend no more money!" She said, "Kim isn't worth the amount she is being paid. Jimmy has failed as a trainer, so I will give him two weeks to place the horses in races they can win at River Downs or send them home!"

It came as a surprise to Gerrie the way her refusals were received: No one objected. Cindy suddenly became more engrossed in her dance lessons and was unwilling to disagree on anything. Happy with her accomplishments, mastering all the basic steps in the fox trot, waltz, and swing, she said, "Some steps are a little more difficult, but I'm determined to learn." This was all she talked about. She came home thrilled when she learned of another competition in Louisville at the Galt House.

"At last, I can put myself on a level with Lucy and Karen." She added, "It's for two days and it's only $1,000!"

Gerrie listened to the ridiculous request. With total disgust she replied, "Look, we have just agreed that the horses at River Downs were coming home if they continued to lose." Snuggling close to Gerrie on the couch, Cindy apologized, saying, "Ohhhh, I'm sorry. I keep forgetting."

Two more weeks passed without Jimmy getting a win on horses he had trained. As he had been instructed, he sent the horses back to Louisville. It was apparent to Gerrie that his training skills "were mediocre and would remain that way." Cindy accepted the decision without further discussion.

As Gerrie returned from work one evening, Cindy greeted her. She was happy, smiling. She had prepared a mouth-watering dinner of steaks Morteur with a picture-perfect cherry mousse. They were well into finishing their feast when Cindy said softly, "If there is any way that I could go to just one dance convention, I promise I will be forever grateful and never ask for anything big again."

Gerrie looked at her mate affectionately, the way she looked at her when they were first together.

Cindy smiled radiantly. "I promise I won't spend money for anything except food and the trip. I won't have to buy shoes or a costume; I won't need one thing."

Perhaps Gerrie felt it was better to give her money to go on one trip than to listen to the same plea over again. And perhaps Gerrie believed her because, more than anything, she wanted to believe.

"Alright, darling," she responded. "Let me know when the next one comes up." Excitedly, Cindy jumped up, whipped around the table, and hugged Gerrie, "There is one, a trip to Florida for the week of April 18." She had it all figured out. "The horses are coming back, and we've got a buyer for Windy!" She wasn't about to fail at convincing Gerrie this time.

"How much?" Gerrie asked defeatedly.

"The cost of the trip is $5,000." Cindy looked at a spot on the ceiling.

Gerrie flushed and grew noticeably upset at hearing this. "Cindy, we spent less than that amount for ten days in Acapulco."

"Please, Gerrie," Cindy begged. "My teacher told me I could win."

Gerrie grimaced. She knew from her involvement with Lucy that the more students a teacher had attending an event, the more a teacher had to gain in cash, trophies, or a reduction in the teacher's fees. But Gerrie was not ready for another argument. After a while, Cindy heard the words she had been working so hard to hear.

"If you *promise* not to ask again, I'll get you the money."

Of course, she promised not only to be satisfied with just that one trip to Florida, but also to give up the dance lessons they couldn't afford, after she returned.

The next morning Gerrie tapped her "resources" once again to get the money for Cindy's trip. Using a member's name, Gerrie wrote a check for $6,800, cashed it, and gave the money to Cindy.

By April, Gerrie had written $22,505 in checks and taken $15,000 cash. At the end of the month she went to Vegas for a weekend. Troubled and depressed, she felt emotionally drained. After eight hours of gambling she had lost $5,000. She returned home with $32,000, still convinced that everyone believed she was a winner.

The following morning, Gerrie set out to perform the most important task of the day—to pay Cindy's charge cards and the numerous other bills that were due. Dejectedly Gerrie sat at the dining room table, writing out check after check.

She felt she was signing them in her blood. Finally she was finished; she started to get up when Cindy walked over.

"All done?" she smiled.

Grimly Gerrie nodded.

"Guess what," Cindy said.

"What?" Gerrie asked in a monotone voice.

"I really could use just one itsy dance outfit."

Caught by surprise, Gerrie demanded to know, "What outfit? Cindy, you promised you wouldn't need anything!"

Enraged, Cindy began yelling, "Look, I only need a measly $3,000. All right, forget it. I'll keep the damn promise!" Marching to the bedroom, Cindy gouged her spike heels into the plank floors with each step.

Gerrie couldn't stand another scene. She had to have some peace somewhere, somehow.

Gerrie felt as though she were standing alone waiting silently for pressured energy to release with sudden violence like dynamite at the touch of an electric fuse.

It was Friday. She left work early with the $3,000 that Cindy had requested. Cindy was sitting at the desk, just outside the doorway to the kitchen, when Gerrie came in. After closing the back door, Gerrie pulled thirty $100 bills from her purse and placed them on Cindy's lap.

"Oh!" Cindy said. "Where'd you get this?"

With combined humility and disgust, Gerrie answered, "The same place I got all the others!"

Motionless, Cindy held the bills. After a moment, she said with shock and innocence, "Gerrie, you're not stealing, are you?"

"Well, Cindy," Gerrie said, "you cash my paychecks—where do you think I'm getting all this money?"

Cindy said nothing. She thumbed through the bills,

waited until Gerrie walked away, then she calmly left the room and took a shower.

In Gerrie's opinion, "Cindy didn't care where the money came from, as long as it kept coming." She told her friend, "That next week I saw three charges totaling $15,000 that Cindy had created, and the house note of $3,500 was coming due in two weeks." She needed to talk to someone. She called Jan.

"Jan, everything is out of hand," she said. "You know, I've had bad luck at the track lately, and if we keep going as we are we will be broke very shortly. And we are blaming each other!" Jan asked if she could be of help.

"Yes! Cindy may listen to you or Karen." Gerrie admitted, "We need to discuss our problems in front of someone. Would the two of you act as counselors?" They agreed, and the four friends met the next evening.

A half hour into the discussion Gerrie responded to Cindy's request for more money. "See? See what I mean, Jan? I haven't had a decent win since I won the $125,000 Pick 6." In a state of frenzy, Gerrie demanded, "We have to stop spending. If we continue as we are, we're headed for financial destruction! We have to stop!"

Cindy sat with her chin in the air for a second or two, then finally asked, "Does that mean I can't go to Miami?"

"No, but you said the dance competition in Miami was costing $5,000 plus! How much 'plus'?"

"I'll need a gown to dance in . . . and shoes."

With a tone of defeat, Gerrie asked, "How much will that be?"

"Oh . . . a couple hundred."

"Fine, but after that we have to stop spending. We cannot afford it!"

Resenting the reprimand, Cindy reminded her of the

thousands of dollars she had lost to gambling. "You spend money going on your junkets," Cindy retorted with a look of bitter innocence, "why can't I?"

Gerrie quickly gave a furtive glance to all present.

"When I go," she informed them, "I go to make money, not spend it!"

Cindy's expression changed—a look of hatred covered her face.

In defeat, Gerrie turned to Jan and sank deeper into the couch. Karen, who had seen Cindy's look, snapped back in Gerrie's defense, "Cindy, didn't you hear her say, 'financial destruction'?"

Cindy stood and quickly marched toward the door, as her voice changed to a cry, "You are all against me! I'm leaving!" She was indignant, and nothing could appease her.

She called Karen a day later, trying to explain the outburst.

"But nobody understands what I go through; now she wants me to give up my dancing."

Still trying to give counsel, Karen justified Gerrie's actions. "She is terribly worried about all the expenses, Cindy!"

"Expenses? She spends money on strangers. Besides, everyone else takes advantage of her, why shouldn't I?"

"Well, Cindy, she said she doesn't have it . . . and I'm going on that."

"Oh, she had the money!" Cindy lashed back. "She has the money all right, or she can get it!"

"Well, I don't know how."

With a harsh burst of words, Cindy spurted out, "She can get it from her company when she wants to go on a goddamn junket! And if she can get it for herself, she can get it for me!"

Within days, Cindy was sorting her clothes, preparing

for her trip to Miami. While packing, she told Gerrie, "I've found a costume for $200."

Gerrie saw the waltz-length melon chiffon dress with a fitted bodice. Coming from the straps on the shoulders were chiffon leaves outlined with rhinestones. The leaf design was carried onto the shoulders, neck, and back. Rhinestones studded the layers of many chiffon skirts. Gerrie knew it was expensive. Her first estimate was in the thousands. She had been buying clothes too long to believe it was a $200 gown. Gerrie opened the zippered shoe bag and held up a pair of melon silk slippers with rhinestone straps and heels.

"Oh, I see . . . two hundred, huh? Tell me, Cindy, how much was the dress really?

Cindy hesitated a bit, then spit out the words, "I had to have it made. The dress cost $2,000."

Gerrie turned to stare at Cindy, and with complete candor she said, "Well, Cindy . . . I guess I'll just have to steal some more money."

Cindy clutched the melon chiffon dress to her chest, lovingly fingering it as if not hearing.

Gerrie lowered her head and went to her room.

The trip to Florida cost nearly $9,000. Remembering when James Kelly had to file bankruptcy, Gerrie murmured, "No average-salaried man could keep Cindy supplied."

Though she had begun to hear rumors about Cindy and Russell Newlander, she angrily dismissed them. "Who on this earth could support Cindy in the way she has been supported?" she asked herself. "Damn few." And she admitted, "That's why she's with me!"

It was the last week in April that Gerrie started hitting the till and didn't give a damn. She continued her trips to Louisville Downs daily, having one good day and two bad ones, but that didn't matter. Bills were pouring in; company money was covering them at the rate of $9,000 a week.

Havoc prevailed. "It was an on-going occurrence," Gerrie recalled. "No harmony, no peace, or understanding, only giving on my part and constant complaining and taking on Cindy's. At home I felt totally defeated. Regardless of how much I won, or how much I took, when I gave to Cindy it was never enough."

It was almost impossible now to get her mind off her problems. Gerrie's only momentary relief was immersing herself in the excitement at the track, and although she was betting heavily to get a win, trying to recover, she was losing . . . losing. . . . There was no peace anywhere. The debts at home were growing faster than credit union money could be taken. Gerrie knew that cash spent on clothes, food, dance lessons, or salaries wouldn't be easily traced, but checks written to pay on the house, cars, horses, and credit cards could easily be traced to Cindy—but she had long since stopped caring.

Because of the growing amount of money they were spending—more than her salary, her winnings, and her stealing—Gerrie couldn't keep up.

"Cindy needs $3,000 or $4,000 a day—for her family, her business, and herself," Gerrie confessed to Jan.

"One evening Cindy announced, 'I need money for bills!' I snapped around to look at her and asked, 'What happened to the five thousand I gave you yesterday?' She stammered a bit and answered with jibber-jabber about things she had paid for. So I started pinning her down. 'I know what it went for,' Cindy said finally. 'It was the vet bill, remember? I paid that!' Jan, I had paid the vet bill with a check, plus I gave her five thousand in cash." Gerrie quickly lowered her eyes and added, "The money was from, uh, my winnings." To

Jan, it seemed that Gerrie wanted to keep talking, so she listened as Gerrie continued. "I just stopped questioning her after a while because my nerves couldn't stand the hell! When Cindy said she needed more, I'd, uh, start betting heavier and gave it to her. I had no idea where the money went, but it kept Cindy happy, and that was the only thing that did."

To keep the supply coming, each afternoon Gerrie left the office with cash and checks, telling Pat she was going to the track. However, the next morning after being away from the office, Gerrie constantly found that her desk and files had been disturbed, as though someone had been searching her office. Like an ostrich she tried to bury her head and ignore the signs of impending doom. Rather then trying to escape she checked and rechecked the bank statements for April against the forged checks. In May she was stealing at least $3,000 a day using any means available: money orders, cash from the petty cash drawer, and members' bank checks that she endorsed over to herself. Knowing the statements would not arrive until June 5 or 6, she rationalized that she had the entire month of May to write her "own" checks, but she was scared all the time now.

CHAPTER 10

In Search of a Silver Chalice

The Kentucky Derby was coming up the first Saturday in May. Gerrie's fervent desire to raise her own Derby winner had, in desperation, changed to merely wanting to have the ticket on the first horse to cross the finish line in "the Race."

Kentucky was abuzz with Derby rumors. Some of the most talked-about horses in the spring of 1989 were Easy Goer, Awe Inspiring, Sunday Silence, Triple Buck, and Houston. Many gamblers were putting their money on the favorite, Easy Goer. Gerrie knew the payoff would be small, but she felt almost obsessed to win anyway, as if this one win could obliterate all she stood to lose at any time.

And everywhere she turned, she heard, "Easy Goer's a shoe-in." He was fast and beautiful; he had everyone's attention. The general consensus was that no one could beat him. None of the other three-year-old entries had his track record. In fact, he was thought to be the best horse since Secretariat. "Here's my chance at a possible $40,000 in clean money on each race," Gerrie kept murmuring.

Gerrie started accumulating money from the credit union to bet. She had three races before her: the Derby, the

Preakness two weeks later, and the Belmont three weeks after that. Side bets were made on Easy Goer's capabilities of taking all three races and becoming the next Triple Crown winner. This amazing feat requires a thoroughbred of unique speed, heart, and maturity. Certainly Ogden Pfipps, owner of Easy Goer, had dreams of being presented the sterling silver Cartier-designed Triple Crown vase, the most elusive prize in all of sports. Displayed for the first time in 1949, it had been taken from its case again in 1989 and splendidly polished in anticipation of another champion, and Easy Goer was said to be that superhorse.

An accomplishment of a lifetime and every owner's dream is having the three-year-old that is blanketed with the Kentucky Derby roses, the Preakness Stakes black-eyed Susans, and the Belmont Stakes white carnations in one single flowering year. Historically, the probability of this triumph is estimated at 100,000 to 1. Since Affirmed had won ten years earlier, many prophets of doom were saying that the odds of having a Triple Crown winner in the spring of 1989 was 400,000 to 1 because of the increased annual foal crop. With more eligible three-year-olds there were more horses trying for the prize.

Optimists argued that the Triple Crown is a surer bet than the New York State Lottery, with its odds of hitting at about 13 million to 1. For the 1989 Derby, the chance of having the winning horse was more of a reality, the odds are around 43,000 to 1.

In Louisville, Kentucky, on Derby Day, May 6, 1989, everyone was celebrating. It was hard to find a place without a party. To Gerrie's surprise, however, Cindy now refused to be in public around gay people. In years past there had always been a big crowd at the Powell/Whitehall house on Derby Day. Pat acted as a bookie, taking bets throughout the day, as guests studied Derby programs and racing forms that had been furnished as party favors. There was lavish spreads of every type of food, each dish more mouth watering than the other. Television sets tuned to the event were in every room, including a 5" set in each bathroom. In 1989, however, because of Cindy feeling as she did, they decided against having a party.

Visitors drove to the Derby from other states, seeing a countryside uncluttered with commercial billboards. Long ribbon-like strips of highway are neatly cut through low hills of limestone. Every few hundred feet, crystal clear water from natural springs trickles through the rock walls that parallel the roads. And as far as the eye can see, groves of wild cedars magnificently dot the grassy acreage. Louisville is most beautiful at Derby time. Clusters of yellow forsythia, flowering almonds, peaches, and quinces spot the bluegrass in front of homes. Residents plant purple tinted pansies and tulips in every color around their meticulously manicured lawns. Each property owner is vying for the "First Place" plaque displayed at the front of the home with the most beautiful landscaping.

The magical sounds of the calliope from the *Belle of Louisville* filled the air on River Road at the waterfront. There the city's emblem, the fleur-de-lis, depicted in the form of an eighty-foot water fountain, captures the attention of passersby. Gaiety is everywhere. The week of events leading up to Derby Day set the pace for the "Run for the Roses." One main event is a balloon race, where leading companies sport their logos on rainbow-colored balloons and race to toss a bag of bluegrass seeds closest to a spot designated by the hare balloon. Two famed steamboats, the *Delta Queen* and *Belle of Louisville*, race on the Ohio River. The prize awarded to the winner is a pair of golden antlers to be displayed on the bow of the boat for one year.

However, not everyone's mind was on the celebration. In previous years, Pat had devoted her entire time to studying the entrants in the Derby. In 1989, she was preoccupied, running tapes of the accounts in Gerrie's personal file, along with the accounts in the office files, trying to find the illusive evidence to prove fraud.

While she searched, Derby day traffic grew heavy, but despite it every able-bodied person scurried around either the track or a party in progress. Those who had waited until Derby Day to find a hotel room had to journey to another city—even another state—to bed down.

However, Cindy didn't want to go. She announced to Gerrie that she wanted to stay home and take care of her horses, but actually she had other plans. Distressed, Gerrie went to the track with friends.

That year it rained all day, catching Derby regulars by surprise. "It's even snowing a little," complained one indignant bettor, glancing skyward. "Doesn't He know it's Derby Day?" The cold, unpleasant weather for the race broke records.

Merriment persevered regardless. The big item on Derby Day is the mint julep. Some 250 vendors sell 80,000 juleps in glasses specially redesigned each year. This simple concoction includes $2^1/2$ ounces of straight Kentucky bourbon whiskey over a glass filled with crushed ice, powdered sugar, five sprigs of mint, and a short straw. The mint is intended for aroma rather than taste; the short straw is necessary to bury the nose in the mint as you sip.

At the beginning of the day Gerrie sipped several mint juleps, won a few races, and lost a few. Then refocusing concentration, she checked her choice for the winner of the eighth, the Derby—Easy Goer.

There is no moment more stirring for a horse-loving Kentuckian than the eighth race on Derby Day. For Louisvillians who are proud of their heritage, it is an awesome occasion.

Gerrie waited for the call to the post, a single brass horn in the Churchill Downs presentation stand. The blaring sound had a quieting effect on the crowd. And then from that silence grew an unmistakable roar of tension as the courageous horses entered proudly through the darkened tunnel, into the light, and onto the track. They paraded to the post in full view of the thousands of spectators, who sang Stephen Foster's "My Old Kentucky Home." Many eyes welled up with tears. The pride of the people merged with the gallant hearts of the most select horses as they faced the challenge to make an indelible mark in history.

The moment, electric in its presentation, was breathtaking and unforgettable. The excited voices of first-time touters shouted last-minute tips. Half of the people shuffled along slowly, eyes glued to their program, while the other half tried to elbow their way around them. Each one hurriedly checking their racing form for one last feel of assurance before taking the risk.

Elbowing her way through the mass, Gerrie stepped up to the end of a string of people and took her place in line. There was no hesitation or second thought when Gerrie placed her bets: $5,000 to win and $5,000 to place on Easy Goer and $5,000 on Easy Goer and Sunday Silence in an Exacta. It was a double entry of Easy Goer and Awe Inspiring with odds of four to five. She noted that the jockey on Easy Goer, Pat Day, had won the last five races. "That could be a good sign if his luck doesn't run out by the time he gets to the eighth race," she told herself.

Her heart pounded as she watched the horses loaded into the starting gate. And . . . the gates sprung open. Sunday Silence came out like a shot, only to bump Triple Buck seconds later. Houston was in front from the beginning and Easy Goer was fourth. Sunday Silence was running in a staggering line, weaving from right to left until he was in fifth place. A few moments later he put on the pressure, passing Easy Goer and challenging the frontrunner, Houston.

Like the wind . . . no one could catch him for the last quarter mile of the race. . . . Sunday Silence was out in front to win! Easy Goer came in with his stablemate, Awe Inspiring, to capture place and show. Gerrie sat slumped in her seat, crushed—she had lost $8,500. She didn't know what to do next. She didn't want to go home to be reminded of another loss; she needed to be around people. Having been invited to several Derby parties that day, she left the track and stopped at one of them. For a fleeting hour or two she forgot her problems.

Somehow she got through the rest of the weekend. On Monday she went to work as usual. In private she endorsed and forged thousands of dollars in checks while in public she and Pat carried on business as usual.

Despite her disappointment, Gerrie kept her thoughts on the next race—her chance to catch up. The second leg of the Triple Crown was coming up in two weeks. Only one horse would cross the finish line first. The owner would be presented with what is called "the most valuable trophy in American sports," the Woodlawn Vase. Appraised in 1983 at $1 million, the work of art was created by Tiffany & Co. in 1860. It is sterling silver and weighs nearly thirty pounds. Racing buffs in the know were saying Easy Goer was still the best horse, he had just had a bad race—"He was held back a little too long!" Gerrie, like many others using past records, could see that he should have won. They were saying, "Perhaps Pat Day should have been more aggressive; he certainly had enough horse under him!"

Always hopeful and always trying to recover, Gerrie did her homework for the Preakness. She read all the reasons Easy Goer lost the race and all the reasons he'd win the next. She wasn't alone; Easy Goer was still the heavy favorite, although no longer a contender for the Triple Crown.

When the big day came, she sat for a while in the dining room at Churchill Downs, waiting for the race at Pimlico Park to be shown on the monitor. Then she made her way back to the bettors' window and placed the same bet as before. "I can't be wrong on this one. He's got it; I know he's gonna win," she told herself over again as she clenched the bills in her hand determinedly.

In the Preakness, Gerrie bet $5,000 on Easy Goer to win, and $5,000 on Sunday Silence to place, then she bet $5,000 on an Exacta with Easy Goer to win and Sunday Silence to place.

She wasn't too interested in any race at Churchill; as a matter of fact, she wasn't really interested in anything. She could only think of the thousands she had taken that week. With these desperate thoughts spinning about in her mind, Gerrie ordered a bourbon and water and watched the closed-circuit TV for the beginning of the Preakness.

On her pocket calculator she figured her possible winnings as she waited. They came to $40,500. That would cover her house note, pay off the charges, and clear her of debt with clean money. The only thing remaining would be to force Cindy to sell the house and the horses, split the money, and get out from under the pressure.

The race was about to begin. The horses were at the starting gate waiting for what was destined to be one of the most exciting races of all time.

The buzzer sounded. The gates opened. Eight magnificent thoroughbreds began their battle to capture the highest spot in the record books. As the viewers yelled encouragement, each horse challenged the other. They were neck in neck until the stretch; from then on it was a two-horse race— Easy Goer on the inside by the rail, and Sunday Silence to his right. The two were eye to eye thundering down the stretch. Both champions charged in perfect unison and continued with precise and flawless rhythm . . . two animals extending at full length, covering ground equally . . . to a finish that could be captured only by the sharp lens of a camera.

Trembling with excitement, Gerrie waited . . . minutes passed . . . the results came in. Easy Goer placed once more and Sunday Silence had won the second leg of the Triple Crown by the shine on his nose. Like many others, Gerrie had the wrong horse. She had lost again.

Depression engulfed Gerrie as she slowly walked from the racetrack. Once again she told herself she could recover by winning the next race. She went home. The days inched by; she concentrated on the upcoming race. She could taste the excitement.

On June 6, she worked a few hours and was ready to leave the office for Churchill downs when the mail was delivered along with May's bank statements. Turning quickly and opening the envelope, she thumbed through the checks and placed the envelope in her file.

Gerrie had one thought in mind: She had one more chance to win on a sure thing . . . this time she was going with the new favorite, Sunday Silence.

On Friday, June 9, a big weekend for all who love horse

racing, Gerrie rose early. At the office Gerrie noticed Pat seemed preoccupied; she hardly spoke to Gerrie and seemed uninterested in the race that was coming up. Pat left at 3:30 to run an errand. Gerrie quickly and expertly secured her "resources." With calculating calmness Gerrie walked out of the office with forged documents and cash totaling $23,000.

The time had come for the Belmont Stakes. Gerrie reserved a table for a party at Churchill Downs. She had invited her brother and his friend along with two other friends. Once again, Cindy refused to go. This time Gerrie hardly noticed or cared. Her only thought now was of the race—of winning.

Gerrie had given up on Easy Goer. Like many people who play the horses, she was wishing for another Triple Crown winner. There had only been eleven in the history of racing, and most people familiar with the event felt Sunday Silence had a good shot. Gerrie had an internal analytical fight as she tried to decide how to bet. The Belmont was the longest of the three races. After having run the mile-and-a-quarter in the Derby and having shown the agility to handle the tight first turn at the Preakness, only eleven horses ever had enough fight and stamina left to win the mile-and-a-half in the Belmont. Gerrie knew Pat Day would be out on the track racing with a vengeance. But who could turn their back on Sunday Silence? He had proven himself twice. All of these thoughts buzzed through her mind as she looked at the odds on the Tote board. She was trying to figure a way to cover herself, perhaps with another Exacta.

Inside her head her thoughts went back and forth. This was to be the most grueling race of all, and no one could discount Sunday Silence's performance in the mile-and-a-quarter Derby. People were saying, "Sunday Silence was all over the track at Churchill Downs. Imagine what he could do if he ran in a straight line!" Countless data raced through her brain.

She was not the only one. The words "East side, west side . . ." were on the lips of any person within ear-shot as the band played "The Sidewalks of New York" for the 121st running of the Belmont Stakes. The odds on Easy Goer were nine-to-five, and Sunday Silence four-to-five. It was two minutes to post time. Trembling with excitement, Gerrie placed her bet. This time going with the new favorite, she bet $5,000 on Sunday Silence to win, and $5,000 on Easy Goer to place. Then she placed $10,000 on an Exacta: Sunday Silence to win and Easy Goer to place.

She went back to watch. It was time. All eyes were on the starting gate as they heard, "And . . . *they're off!"*

When the gates sprung open, ten eager horses burst out and as many jockeys were hungry for a win. Gerrie's heart pounded as Sunday Silence, running second to Le Voyageur, took over the lead. The crowd tensed. Sunday Silence was first in command. Then moving past Le Voyageur, Easy Goer started his drive, coming up to the front runner . . . momentarily. He looked out over the ground ahead . . . the sight was familiar . . . it was "home." Finally, racing on his favorite track, he began his move. . . . Reaching out for the stretch of ground before him, he gave the performance of a lifetime. He knew his territory and covered it, taking over the lead from Sunday Silence at the one-mile pole. Two lengths . . . three lengths . . . on and on he went until everything behind him merely faded in the distance. It was the second fastest Belmont Stakes in the history of the track. Gerrie had blown it!

Her face contorted by grief, she rushed out to her car, opened the door, and slid in. She sat with head against the cold steering wheel; darkness fell, then she went home. Over the weekend Gerrie sorted through receipts and documents to give to her attorney, verifying money she had spent on the farm. June 12, the Monday after the Belmont, Gerrie took the day off, giving herself a long weekend. During that time she made plans to see Cindy through the sale of all real and personal items, then help her find a smaller home. Gerrie decided to look for a luxury houseboat for herself. She was happiest on the river. She still thought she could quit before she got caught.

Unknown to Gerrie, in the office that same Monday, Pat Salzman searched through drawers, boxes, and cabinets that were "off-limits." Documents began to surface . . . one at a time . . . little by little . . . $80,000 in forged checks. The deception was over. Gerrie's fall was inevitable. The lava from the volcanic hell she had been storing for years had erupted!

At Windy Hills Farm, Gerrie was relaxing on the sun-deck; unknown to her, this was her last hurrah.

CHAPTER 11

"Gotcha"

Gerrie walked into the office at 9:00 A.M. Tuesday, June 13, 1989, with $20 in her pocket. Knowing her "resources" were at hand, she remained quietly confident that she could recover within a few days.

Pat turned away quickly as Gerrie entered the room. *That's different,* Gerrie mused, *especially after a race like the Belmont.* Pat should have asked about Gerrie's race results. Any other time, Pat's excited opening questions such as, "How did you do?" would have called for Gerrie to give a half-hour verbal rerun of the race.

Pat said in a monotone, "You're wanted upstairs in the conference room."

Something was definitely wrong. Gerrie stared at Pat. Pat's expression told the story. Gerrie stood motionless. Her heart pounded, she quickened her pace, almost running now.

She found herself entering the meeting room. Stepping through the doorway, she saw the president, vice president, treasurer, chairman of the supervisory committee of the credit union, and one of the vice presidents of the company

171

sitting at the conference table. A pregnant silence filled the room. She could almost smell the tension.

Feeling complete panic, she was more afraid of where she was than where she was going. She knew she was caught.

The men lowered their eyes. Obviously reluctant to face one whom they had trusted for thirty-seven years, they also felt betrayed. Acrid stillness permeated the air around them. No one moved. After a lengthy pause, the graying, classically featured vice president, Tobias Williams, began.

"Do you recognize these checks?" he asked, sliding them across the table to Gerrie.

A cold clamminess covered her flesh, cooling her face. She touched the checks. Her fingers tingled. She was about to faint. Struggling for composure, Gerrie softly replied, "Yes, I recognize them."

"Do you know who wrote them?" he asked.

"Yes . . . I did."

"Do you know how much is here?"

Praying for the whole scene to disappear, Gerrie hesitated a moment. She answered, "I really don't know exactly, maybe eighty thousand?"

"Have you taken any more than this?" There was a silence. Gerrie wanted to vanish from the room and find herself in St. Croix or Jamaica, never to return, but it was too late for that.

"Will you sign a statement that you did this, Gerrie?"

She took a deep breath. "No, I will not sign anything. I will call my lawyer."

Williams's voice deepened. "You know, Gerrie, you are now dismissed from your position, from the grounds of the Henry Vogt Machine Company, and from the credit union. Please turn in all your keys and anything you have belonging to the credit union. Take only your personal things with you. We will send anything else that belongs to you to your home. I will escort you to the office and to your car."

The long-feared moment she had so often visualized had finally arrived, yet she was unprepared. Within minutes she was escorted from the building she had known so well.

In a daze she got into her car. Driving from the parking lot, everything seemed unreal. She was unaware of red lights, stop signs, traffic, or direction, but out of sheer habit she headed home. She drove slower than usual; perhaps subconsciously she was stalling for time. She was grateful for one thing, however: she was grateful that her mother never knew. Her mother had been saved from the disgrace. Indeed Gerrie was confident that her mother's prayers had protected her for years. Without them, she felt she had been destined to be caught long before now.

As Gerrie headed toward the outskirts of town, reality surfaced. She wanted to change directions, head for a restaurant, bar, racetrack—anywhere but home. Her mind bounced from one subject to another as she murmured to herself, "I should have hidden the money. Then I could have run." But she didn't—couldn't—because Cindy had everything. The two of them would have to go through the miserable ordeal together. "If I can only explain it's over, calmly. I know Cindy will be hard to control, but I'll have to handle that part as it comes. It's too late to worry about consequences."

The highway narrowed to a little black-top road with a single white ribbon-like line. She drove slower, saying over and over, "Dear God, help me." Once she told her, how could she keep Cindy from running from the house, driving away, and killing herself? Cindy had never been able to handle a severe crisis, and this was the epitome of exigency. Switching from one idea to another, she said, "Maybe they won't find it all!" only to counter that idea with, "That's stupid! It's too much to hope for."

She felt tortured with the thought of prison. Her heart was beating harder, and her head felt as though it would burst into a million pieces.

A familiar sign reading "Clark Station Road" sent a sickening pang into the pit of her stomach. Reluctantly, she turned toward the farm, the place she had loved, and as she approached the Windy Hills Farm driveway, her main fear was confronting Cindy.

She stopped the car outside the garage and waited, hardly breathing, searching for the right words, the right attitude. Their lives depended upon it.

Getting out she mechanically placed one foot in front of the other. When she reached the doorway, she called out in a voice she didn't recognized as her own, "Would you come here, Cindy, we've got to talk." There was a long pause as she listened to puttering sounds coming from the yard. Finally she stepped into the kitchen and with her voice cracking from fear, she repeated.

"Please come here, we have to talk now."

Entering the room, Cindy, who had been on the deck enjoying the warm day, stopped cold when she saw the expression on Gerrie's face.

"What's the matter?" Cindy asked, walking closer.

"Shut the door; we can't be interrupted." Gerrie clenched her fists and prayed that she could handle Cindy's reactions, whatever they might be.

Cindy wiped the suntan lotion from her hands and looked quizzically at Gerrie.

Gerrie stood silently. An ominous stillness filled the room. She realized this moment was to be the last calm they would ever know together. Finally, Gerrie said simply, "I've been fired."

Cindy turned away, wiped her brow, and said innocently, "What on earth for, Gerrie?"

"For taking money from the credit union."

Cindy remained quiet and calm as seconds passed. Moments later she said, "Well . . . what are you going to do?"

"I don't know what to do first, but I'll protect you Cindy, don't worry. Just stick by me, please," Gerrie begged.

Gerrie looked at Cindy intently, thinking she would lose it, but she seemed quite composed, calculating, and under control. Gerrie went on, "The FBI will probably be out today. They may come for me right away, or tomorrow, so we will have to remove everything valuable from the house. Get all your clothes, your jewelry, your furs, and have Kim come pick them up. I will start destroying records that will incriminate you."

Cindy's eyes widened and her mouth opened in shock. The thought of the authorities entering the home and taking possessions was obviously frightening.

With tumultuous haste, the two went into action. Cindy proceeded to throw everything she could into boxes. She rushed from room to room, stopping only to catch her breath.

Hurriedly, Gerrie scanned through boxes of record books, bank statements, bills of sale, searching for and destroying anything that could prove Cindy's association with her. Cindy grabbed her valuables and put as much jewelry on as she could. Gold bracelets and diamond necklaces filled her arms, and serpentine chains dangled from her hands.

Tension grew as Kim arrived and loaded her car. Cindy finished gathering the last of her things to be sent with her daughter and put them in the car. Kim drove off.

Only then did Cindy turn to Gerrie and inquire, "What do we do now?"

"We get our stories straight," Gerrie said desperately.

Gerrie was aware that the amount of money she had taken was in the millions. She explained to Cindy, "The $125,000 Pick 6 that you claimed on your income tax would explain everything that was purchased after the win. In explaining the checks that were deposited to your account, I will tell them that you borrowed that money and it was repaid at a later date. Just stick by me, Cindy, and I'll deny that you knew where the money was coming from; you'll be protected. I *will* need lawyers' fees. It can come from the sale of the rest of the horses.

"It will be in the paper, so to protect yourself. Just tell everyone that I lost the money gambling and I will probably have to take the cure.

"The most they'll give me is two years. With a good attorney I won't have to go to prison. I'll only have to go to Gamblers Anonymous . . . but if they find out I've been laundering money and have supported the farm and business with the money from the Henry Vogt credit union, it will blow the whole thing wide open, send you up for twenty years and me for life without parole. So I'll tell them I lost the money because I was addicted to gambling."

Convinced she would be arrested at once, Gerrie hurried to gather legal papers on the farm and the business. She also tried to figure out Cindy's theoretical income to substantiate the expenses incurred for the farm, thereby creating a cover for Cindy. The horses and two cars which were also purchased with company money were the only remaining things that Gerrie legally owned.

She knew the farm was safe because the deed was in Cindy's name. Gerrie was caught, but by law the authorities could not take the farm unless they could prove there was a conspiracy, and she felt they would have a hard time proving that. A master plan, well-devised from the beginning, requiring only that Cindy memorize specific business expenses that the winning tickets claimed on her social Security number were said to have covered. Gerrie trusted Cindy and believed they would always share things equally. Cindy could sell the farm, split the money, and give it to Gerrie's brother Tom to keep for Gerrie until after she had served her two years, if she had to go. This was her plan.

As Gerrie explained she saw that Cindy was growing more nervous.

"Everyone will know the way we've been living."

"No," Gerrie assured her, "I will deny all intimacy with you. Don't worry, I will protect you."

Gerrie grimaced. Apparently, for Cindy a homosexual relationship between them was the most resented "labeling" that could come from the entire affair. In fact, the label seemed of more concern than being an accomplice in a huge embezzlement.

The two worked into the night, sorting out tax records for the farm and Cindy's personal tax data. Gerrie talked to Cindy for hours, telling her how to respond to questions regarding where the money came from to remodel the Chenoweth Run house, purchase the two farms, and build the barn at their present home. She told her how to make it sound feasible, thereby disassociating Cindy with the crime.

Most of their debts had been paid; Gerrie saw to that, but she had to get ownership of the horses out of her name and into Cindy's. The next morning, July 14, 1989, they found six bills of sale for horses and transferred the title of the horses to Cindy. However, Diane Siline, a farm hand, notarized the documents and post-dated them June 7, 1989, one week before Gerrie's dismissal from work. The June 7 date would protect their investment in the horses. Cindy felt confident after they had finished destroying receipts and changing ownerships. She was armed with answers and forti- fied with documents. The "plan" went into effect. At the First National Bank, Gerrie withdrew $1,200 from her checking account and gave it to Cindy. After this was completed, she proceeded to deplete and close out the rest of her accounts.

Remorsefully, Gerrie called her brother, confessing ev- erything. She wanted to tell her family before they read it in the paper. She was relieved. "More than anything," she said, "I have to protect what we have." Her brother offered to have her stay with him until she had time to figure out her next move.

Learning of Tom's offer for Gerrie to live with him, Cindy agreed that Gerrie's move to his apartment would be a wise choice. If Gerrie could stay with Tom until she was ar- rested, the farm address and the business might be safe. Ger- rie could also change her mailing address to her brother's, "That way everyone will believe you have been living with him. Then you could return home anytime after the address is changed."

But Gerrie wanted to stay where she was, to be alone. She withdrew, not wanting to talk to anyone, not even to her sisters. She was mortified. All her life she had been striving to attain two goals, wealth and respect. Now, she was horror- stricken to come to the agonizing truth that they were both gone.

With financial help from her family for an attorney, she hired a young, astute lawyer named William Rusnack. At Gerrie's first visit to his office, he said, "I will do whatever I can. Keep in touch and report your whereabouts in case they want to arrest you."

She did everything she could think of to get money to keep Cindy safe and secure. To safeguard herself against terms in an Order of Attachment, she had closed out her checking and savings accounts the day after she was fired. She tried to sell her Cadillac for $6,000. Finally, she accepted $4,500 on a quick sale and gave the money to Cindy. "Here, hide it in a safe place," Gerrie said, handing her the bills. She felt certain that Cindy had been hiding money in safe places for years. "It's the money from the sale of my car."

Gerrie's other car, a 1984 Buick Skylark, was transferred into Tom's name. In this way, she would have something to drive until she was arrested, and again, it could not be traced to Cindy.

As the days passed, she waited for something to happen —anything. But no one came looking for her, and there was nothing in the paper. It was as though nothing had happened. The only difference was that the intense pressure of agonizing over when she would be caught was gone at last, only to be replaced with regret and desolation.

Cindy made one phone call after another to friends, telling them of the embezzlement. She reiterated the story as she and Gerrie had rehearsed it, "Gerrie stole the money," she said, "but she lost everything gambling!" Acquaintances they had met in recent years believed the story, but close friends of theirs didn't.

Cindy called Karen, saying, "You know, in May I told you that Gerrie and I were going to split-up? Well, with this now, I'm going to stick by her. . . . Yes, Gerrie took the money. She was so addicted to gambling that she lost everything. . . . Oh, she won't have to go to jail, but she *will* have to go to Gambler's Anonymous. . . . Why? Because she couldn't stop!"

Karen listened to the fabricated accounts. She reminded

Cindy of the many wins that she recalled, including the "Pick 6."

Cindy answered, "Oh, *she* didn't win that."

"Yes she did. Gerrie told Jan and me about it, remember?"

"No, that $125,000 win was *mine*. I won that. I had most of the winning tickets." Cindy continued the conversation with the issue most important to her. "It will be spread all over Louisville that I've been living with a woman. My father, my family—everyone will know. I hate her for doing this to me."

"Well, certainly your family knows that Gerrie has supported you, Cindy?" Karen reminded her friend.

"What do you mean? I have supported *myself,*" she answered. Her 1040A Form for 1979 gave her income as $3,158.37, and in 1980 it was $3,721.21, yet she tried desperately to convince her friend.

"Oh, okay, I'm sorry, Cindy," Karen said, not wanting to further agitate her.

"And our friends will be in a state of shock when they hear that Gerrie has been fired for embezzling."

"Wait, Cindy. It's no big surprise to me, and I don't think it will shock your close friends. Some of us have suspected this for a long time, so if it didn't matter then, it won't matter now."

Cindy's sweetness turned to instant anger. Her voice rose, her mortification plain. "And all the time they knew . . ."

Cindy quickly hung up. With this sudden awakening, she had to plan were she would go from here. She had to disengage herself from relationships of the past and approach the future with a new purpose. After all, everything was in her name.

Meanwhile, Gerrie kept in constant motion, as though she were trying to run from herself.

Without income from the credit union, Cindy searched for actual means of supporting herself by placing an ad in the paper for boarding horses. This would give her printed proof that much of her income could have resulted from boarding fees, and it would also look as though she were trying to keep the business going "as usual."

Knowing the authorities would be checking all avenues to find the money, the couple agreed that Cindy should hire her own lawyer. If Cindy's worth was questioned, they would go after the business. She needed legal protection for the investments they had. Even though the business was in her name, if the FBI could prove her involvement, they would confiscate as much as possible.

With a virtuous expression and tone, Cindy asked, "Where on earth do you think the FBI wouldn't look if they'd come, Gerrie?"

"I don't know, Cindy, but if you have any cash, hide it under the loose bricks in the atrium, or bury it in the barn."

Later that evening, the silhouette of a woman could be seen hurrying into the barn. She grabbed a spade and started digging under the sawdust in the corner of a horse's stall. Only the thoroughbreds raised their heads to see and listen.

Lifting the clumps of dirt, she buried the plastic-covered packages. Everything was coming to a head.

As she ran across the field of bluegrass toward the house, her platinum hair glistened in the last bit of evening light. Small twigs snapped underfoot, disrupting the stillness, and a colt whinnied.

The next day Cindy's complex emotional responses changed continually from fear . . . to anger . . . to hate. The party was over. She had to survive.

Cindy said to Gerrie, "You have to move and change your address at the post office. You can't be caught living here." Internally, Cindy must have been in a state of panic: *I have to keep the business going. I may have boarding horses coming in, and if this comes out in the paper while she is living here, it will kill the business.*

Outwardly, Cindy was very cool. Calm resignation prevailed. There were no hysterics—not yet, anyway.

After several hours she couldn't take any more. Suddenly she yelled, "You have to leave, you cannot be caught here! Now, Gerrie! Leave!"

"But this is my home. Everything I have is here. I can't stay with Tom; he offered, but you know he's not well. It would kill him. Where can I go without cash? When we sell some of the horses and other things I'll have enough money, but at the moment I have nothing."

Cindy had no time for Gerrie's complaints. "*I said leave, dammit!*"

Shocked, broken, and speechless, Gerrie turned to walk away. Cindy continued to yell and Tootie began whining in the corner. With one swoop, Cindy scooted the puppy out of the room commanding, "And here, take your goddamn little dog with you."

Gerrie bent to pick Tootie up. Holding her dog close, Gerrie realized that all parties concerned would be better off if she were not there. She had never wanted to burden anyone, certainly not Cindy, but especially not her brother who had been in poor health. She only intended to give to loved ones; never had she intended it to be the other way around. She decided to leave and return only to gather her belongings for a possible sale.

Gerrie loaded a few clothes and personal items into her car and set out with $30 in her pocket. Immediately Cindy began phoning friends, telling them that Gerrie no longer lived with her.

"I found out later that as soon as I left the house, Cindy called Russell," Gerrie said. "She saw him as her only means of survival. He could support her and he could also erase the homosexual label."

Cindy was also desperate for a solution. Her partner was about to be arrested, and the credit union might try to take her farm and horses. She needed help. She knew Russell would be busy, and the last thing she wanted to do was interfere, but she needed advice.

Meanwhile a saddened Gerrie drove around with her clothes in the trunk of her car and her little pet beside her. She had to calm herself before going to her brother's apartment. It would hurt her to see the pain on her brother's face. The last thing she wanted to do was cause his health to deteriorate more. She could not handle another loss.

The day was warm and sunny as she drove to the riverbank. The houseboats reminded her of a time to which she wanted to return. She watched a young boy patiently bait his hook, throw in his line, and wait. Time after time he baited his hook and waited. After an hour or so he left. She wished that her disappointments would once again be so small.

It was then that Gerrie took a hand-held tape recorder from her glove compartment and began recording the traumatic events of her life. She spoke of the happy, the sad—and the theft. She recorded her life with Cindy until, distressed by her own words, she left the river's edge and drove around Louisville. She parked for a while, then drove from street to street, feeling she had nowhere to go.

Her attention was drawn to a little old lady with white hair stepping from a bus with three plastic garbage bags. The lady lifted them one at a time, then dragged them across the sidewalk to the bus shelter. Gerrie glanced at her watch. It was 1:30 in the afternoon.

Four hours later, Gerrie drove by the bus stop again. The lady was still sitting in the bus shelter, asleep. Gerrie continued driving several blocks, telling herself to mind her own business. But then making a fast turn toward the bus stop, Gerrie parked the car and slowly walked to where the lady was sleeping.

"Hello, you've been here a long time." As Gerrie spoke, she noticed the lady's worn, faded clothes and how her ankles had swollen over her shoes. Believing the shopping bags might be holding objects for sale, Gerrie asked, "Are you selling something I might like to buy?"

"No, dese is all my belongings, ever'ting I own," the old lady said. Her accent was heavy. A sweet smile framed her tanned face as she told Gerrie that she had been living with a relative who had passed away. "Now, I'm on my own."

"But you can't stay here all night!" Gerrie objected.

She shook her head. "No, I sleep at the shelter downtown," she explained. "Every few months when my medicine runs out I have to make a trip to the drug store on a bus. The fare is sixty cents, but if I wait until six, it only cost twenty."

Gerrie, feeling as though she was at the end of her rope, had met someone who had less. She pulled some money from her pocket, counted out $15 and handed it to the lady.

"Here, I'll split this with you. It's all I have," she told the old woman.

"Oh, God! Tank you! Tank you!" the woman muttered in broken English. She crumpled the bills tightly into her fist and held it to her breast.

Feeling uplifted, Gerrie walked away as she saw the bus

approaching. She had almost reached her car when she stopped and looked back to see the old woman wave.

Three blocks down the road Gerrie stopped at a Convenient Food Mart for $4 worth of gas and a $1 lottery ticket. To win Kentucky's "Instant Win Lottery," you have to match three of a kind: a match of, say, three $5 symbols would give the holder $5. Gerrie rubbed the silver paint covering the numbers on her ticket; they revealed three $50 matches.

As she walked out of the store she became terrified when she saw a police cruiser passing by, knowing the authorities could be after her at any moment. But they didn't come.

Getting back in her car, she drove to the edge of the river and decided to spend the night there.

The next morning Gerrie was awakened by the foghorn of a riverboat. It was eerie, yet serene, because at the moment she was safe. In another part of town, at Henry Vogt, the atmosphere was anything but serene as three certified public accountants worked to unravel the accounts.

That day she moved into a motel. More days inched by. On July 11, a month later, the story of the embezzlement hit the Courier Journal.

> John Ruffin, regional director in Atlanta for N.C.U.S.I.F., has an examiner at Henry Vogt Credit Union working with State auditors and said he has no basis for believing losses will exceed $80,000.

Gerrie stared at the paper. She couldn't believe what she was reading. "They haven't found the shortage." It was too much to wish for. "Maybe, just maybe," she said to herself. But in reality, she knew further disclosures were inevitable.

The local private accounting firm of Cotton & Allen PSC

was hired to investigate. Her attorney kept her informed on the results of the lengthy audit. After the news article had appeared in the *Courier Journal*, fifteen auditors began a relentless investigation of the credit union's finances.

Every day Gerrie called home for messages. With each call, Cindy sounded more distant. She refused all of Gerrie's invitations to meet for a drink, saying she had no time. Out of desperation, Gerrie asked if she could come back home to help with the problems. "I can cut the grass or help clean the house, and handle some of the workload."

She was met with the same rejection. "You can't come back now. If you were caught here, it would ruin my business. Go somewhere else." Many times, as Cindy was speaking, Gerrie wondered if Kim was in the room by the phone. Cindy had changed so much that a verbal war erupted every time they spoke. It didn't seem to matter to Cindy how desperate Gerrie felt. "I was drained of everything she could wring out of me," Gerrie later said, "and now that I was down, she was trying to bury me."

Each day Gerrie kept in contact with her lawyer to assure him and the authorities that she was not running. One day she stopped at her friend Jan's house. "I don't know where to go, Jan. Cindy refuses to give me money, I can't go home, and I can't go to my brother—he's far too sick to go through this."

Jan felt terribly sorry for Gerrie. "Stay here, Gerrie, you don't have to sleep in your car or worry your family." Gerrie was comforted by her friend. She wanted to talk, and Jan listened.

"You know," Gerrie said, "I can't believe the events in my life, but I'm putting it all on tape so that someday I can listen to it and perhaps understand." Relaxing with a scotch and water, she recalled, "In 1987 Cindy's income through my winning tickets was close to $100,000. In 1988 it was $40,000 because of my wins at the track. This was in addition to the money not reported. And this is the income of a woman who only worked one week in sixteen years."

Jan invited Gerrie to stay with her. She stayed two weeks, sometimes writing letters to Cindy, but much of the time was spent alone at the poolhouse, talking into her recorder, hoping to understand her past.

Meanwhile, the auditors at the credit union were discovering more shortages. Handwriting experts searched for forged signatures, and they found them—at least some of them. The totals were constantly being revised and climbing upward.

On July 14, Gerrie received a letter stating the findings of the investigation in a complaint filed in Jefferson Circuit Court by the counsel for the plaintiff, Henry Vogt Employees Credit Union, under case number 89 CI 05283. It stated in part:

> During the course of Powell's employment by the credit union, the fraudulent acts . . . have resulted in a loss to the credit union in an amount known to be not less than $125,000.00, during the period of August, 1988, through June 14, 1989. . . .
>
> WHEREFORE the Credit Union demands as follows:
>
> 1. Judgment against the defendant Geraldine Powell in a sum equal, but not less than $125,000.00;
>
> 2. That a general order of attachment issue against all real and personal property of Powell or against the interest of Powell in any corporation, partnership, or other joint or sole venture by her;
>
> 3. That the title to all real and personal property owned by Powell be held in trust for the use and benefit

of Henry Vogt Employees Credit Union and she be directed to turn over said property to the Credit Union.

Gerrie had nothing left for them to take. She had already turned everything except her jewelry over to Cindy on June 14, the day after her dismissal from Henry Vogt.

Exhausted and with little money left, she finally decided she had no choice but to drive to her brother's apartment, where she told him she would like to take him up on his offer. Tom welcomed her. "You need support now like never before," he said, consoling his sister. "This is no time to be by yourself; besides, I want you here."

They were awake most of the night talking, and there were hundreds of questions, many suggestions, and much sorrow. Tom's voice—deep, rich, and kind—was comforting to her. His understanding was just what Gerrie needed at that point in her life.

Suddenly Cindy started calling every day. She visited often, wanting advice from Gerrie in handling the farm and liquidating the assets, and with each visit the household was disrupted. Gerrie could see the debilitating effect this was having on her brother, whose health was poor and who couldn't stand excitement. She knew she could not continue to stay with him much longer.

On July 28, while Gerrie was away from Tom's house, an attempt was made to deliver a summons. Then on August 14, a copy of a statement made by Harold Norris, president of the credit union, was delivered at Tom's. It listed the charges to date.

a. *Writing* CU checks *to herself* and *her creditors.*
   Forging signatures of authorized CU officers, authorized CU personnel, and CU members.

Cashing the checks without debiting her own CU deposit or share account.

Cashing the checks and retaining all monies *without debiting* the account of the payee CU member.

According to the auditors' calculations, the loss to the credit union during the period from September 1985 through June 14, 1989, was $204,890.71. And the figure kept climbing.

Gerrie's lawyer, William Rusnack, responded to the motion and affidavit. He stated that in his questioning of Gerrie, she had denied that she was aware of owing any sum in the amount of $204,890.71.

Not long afterward, a new course for the investigation was set at the credit union office. Harold Norris was required by the credit union's bonding company to go through thousands of checks written on members' accounts. In cross-checking he found company checks forged by Geraldine Powell and deposited into an account, indicating that others were involved.

One month later, Cindy was served with a subpoena to give a deposition. She was frantic when she called Tom to ask for guidance in giving the sworn testimony. To keep her association with Gerrie distant, Tom agreed to meet with Cindy to arrange a mutual contract between the two women. At the private meeting Cindy agreed to stand by the original plan, giving Gerrie half the proceeds from the sale of the farm, if Gerrie, in return, would say that Cindy was totally innocent of any conspiracy to tax evasion and knowledge of embezzlement of funds at Henry Vogt and that there was no intimate relationship. Cindy quickly added, "On the advice of my attorney, I refuse to sign anything." However, on September 16, 1989, Cindy signed a statement in front of a witness, agreeing to release certain items belonging to Gerrie: furniture, three sofas and chairs, an iron table and chairs, end tables and lamps, a marble-top chest, a credenza, a compressor, a record cabinet, a refrigerator, plus several collections of old money.

At a meeting between Gerrie and her attorney, William Rusnack, he apprised her of the growing shortages that were being discovered daily and added, "I must tell you, Gerrie, it looks bad."

"What about my addiction," Gerrie asked, "isn't that a defense?"

Rusnack looked at her appraisingly. "I strongly advise you to plead guilty by reason of insanity," he said decisively.

Gerrie became indignant, insulted, and she refused. She lifted her chin defiantly.

"How could I convince a jury that I was insane, when I was able to fool the examiners for twenty-five years?" The growing frustration was only the beginning of further disagreements between attorney and client. Due to the conflict, William Rusnack moved the court to allow that his name be withdrawn as attorney for the defense.

CHAPTER 12

Some Questions, Some Answers

Hiring a new lawyer, Peter Newman, Gerrie tried to prepare to give her deposition. She arrived at the office on October 2, 1989, at 1:00 P.M. Present for the testimony, besides Gerrie and her attorney, was Alan V. Sears, the tall, dark-haired attorney for the credit union, who had a reputation for tenacity, and Thomas R. Pitek, of the Cuna Mutual Insurance Group.

After being first duly sworn, Mr. Sears asked that Gerrie state her full name.

Gerrie's voice showed little emotion. "Geraldine Wray Powell."

"And your current address, Ms. Powell?"

Immediately Peter Newman stood up and signaled an objection.

"I don't know that that is necessary at this point. And for the purposes that we have discussed earlier, she had appeared in court or in response to all documents and phone calls and in fact is here today pursuant to a phone call and not any official notice. And with reference to her residency I'm going to direct her not to answer the question at this point unless you can show me some relevancy. She does not own any real estate."

Sears looked at him for a moment.

"So you're directing her not to answer then? And she does not have any lease in her name; is that correct?"

"Yes," Newman nodded. His eyes held the other lawyers.

Looking away, Sears turned back to Gerrie.

"Do you reside alone, ma'am?"

Again Newman stood.

"Again, I'm going to direct her not to answer that because of not wanting to get anyone else involved because of other possible implications. And it's strictly for the protection of other people, not for the protection of her, the people that have befriended her."

Sears sighed and went on.

"Are you currently employed?"

Gerrie waited a moment, looked toward Newman as if waiting for his objection, and then replied.

"No."

Sears said, "At this point do you have any source of income?"

Gerrie's voice quivered. "No."

Watching her intently, Sears picked up the pace.

"What was your last employment?"

"Henry Vogt Credit Union."

"At the time you were with Henry Vogt were you employed at any other locations? Did you have any other sources of income other than your salary at Henry Vogt."

"Yes."

Now his questions and her answers came in staccato bursts.

"And what were those?"

"It was a business."

"And what type of business?"

"It was thoroughbred horses."

"Did the business go under a name?"

"Well, yes. Windy Hills Farms."

"And what was your interest in Windy Hills Farms?"

"I had no interest in the farm itself."

"Then how did you derive income from it?"

"Well, because the horses ran under that name or ran under the individual names."

"All right. Was Windy Hills Farms a partnership or proprietorship?"

"It was a partnership."

"Who were the partners?"

"Cindy Whitehall. There was no money derived from it though."

"Was Cindy the only partner?"

"Yes."

"So it was a *proprietorship?*"

"Yes."

Sears was on a roll. He continued, "You had indicated that was a source of income to you."

"Well, it really was not."

"You've indicated you had no interest in it. I gather you mean you had no ownership interest in it?"

"In the farm itself?"

"In Windy Hills Farms."

"Right."

"Did you have any ownership interest in any of the thoroughbreds?"

"Yes."

He pushed her relentlessly.

"And what thoroughbreds did you own or have an ownership interest in?"

Gerrie, a bit nonplussed, tried to slow his questions so she could gather her thoughts.

"Well," she paused, "that would depend on the date. After June the 7th, I had no interest in them."

He wasn't about to be put off. He cut in.

" 'In them.' Did you own more than one June the 7th?"

"There were two."

"And what were the two that you owned on June 7th?"

"Brother Merv and Air Finesse Won."

"And you said you had no ownership interest in them. What happened on June 7?"

"Well, May 23 we separated—well, I quit the business, or the farm." Gerrie hesitated, took a breath and then said in an even softer voice, "We had a problem."

"When?"

Sears was not about to let her lack of definitiveness go by.

"May 23. And I turned all these over to Cindy on June 7, or right at the 7th."

He looked her straight in the eye. "Explain 'turned over'."

Gerrie was obviously rattled. "Well, there was a lot of bills coming due and we had a dispute over the trainer, and there just wasn't anything in it. And I turned . . . " She hesitated and then said, "There was trainers' bills due on the horses and I turned them over to her."

Sears kept on relentlessly.

"When you turned the horses over to her, what specifically did you do? Did you sign any papers, was there a bill of sale involved?"

Gerrie couldn't let down her guard for a moment.

"Signed a contract releasing me of all further expenses and signed bills of sale over to her."

"Who all signed the bills of sale?"

"Well, I signed it, she signed it, and a notary signed it."

Sears was finally at the point he had waited for. He tried to show Cindy's involvement.

"Were you and she the only two owners in these horses?"

"Mm-hm."

"And you did both of these on June 7."

"Right at June 7, the first part of June. I'm saying the 7th, I'm not really for sure, but it was the first part of June."

"Did you receive any money for this?"

"No."

"How much—if you recall, and if you don't recall specifically, just give me a general idea—how much in bills were owed that prompted you then to transfer these horses to Cindy?"

"About $7,000."

"Total?"

"I don't know. That's all I knew about it. We still hadn't gotten other bills."

"But what I meant was, that was for both horses?"

"Yes."

"$7,000 for both horses."

Gerrie nodded yes.

"Do you know what the market value of the horses were?" Sears asked, never taking his eyes off her.

"Well, at the time one was running in a $5,000 maiden race, hadn't even broken its maiden yet. And the other one was running in a $6,500 claiming race, and nobody claimed it, so it wasn't worth that much. So I would assume they'd be worth right at $7,000."

"Were there other horses that you owned then prior to June 7, other than these two?"

Newman, who had not found an opening, now stood up.

"In what period of time?"

Sears knew he was trying to limit the damage and wasn't about to assist.

"Well, just in your relationship with Cindy?"

"Over the period of time there were a lot of horses, because you would run them, they'd be claimed, and you'd use that money and you'd get more horses. So there were a lot of horses over the period of the partnership."

"Were any of these owned solely by you?"

"At one time they were owned solely by me, yes. Cindy and I had partnerships, severed partnerships. I had owned them at times by myself and she owned at times by herself, and then we worked back into a partnership several times."

"Other than the thoroughbreds then, did you have any other source of income? Whether you gained the income from it or not, did you have any other source of income?

"Does gambling count?"

"If you had income from it."

Again Newman sought to limit the focus. "Net income or gross?"

Again Sears countered his attempt.

"Is that the only other source of income that you had, other than the horses and your job and gambling were your only sources of income?"

"Yes."

"The Windy Hills relationship that you had—you indicated you had no interest in the farm itself, but only in some of the horses. Is that a correct statement?"

"Yes."

"That's a correct statement. Did you have a written agreement or written partnership agreement with Cindy Whitehall?"

"Not this last time, I don't think we had one."

Sears was too thorough to let the reply pass.

"Let's define 'last time'."

"Like I say, we've been in and out of business several times, and—"

"The last time that you were in business together prior to June 1989, when you say you transferred these last two horses that you owned over to her, was there a written agreement during that period?"

Gerrie stared at the clock on the wall. Almost two hours had passed. When would this end? She took a deep breath.

"I don't think so."

"And what period did that cover?"

"I'm not for sure, '85 or '86 . . . about '85 or '86, I'm not certain."

"From '85 or '86 until '89, there was a relationship."

" '86."

"From '86 until '89 there was a relationship with respect to these Windy Hills Farm horses that was subject to written agreements?"

"Right."

"Now, were there written agreements before that?"

"Well, we had a written agreement when we first started. And then . . . I don't know, we had another one at one time. We had two written agreements."

"Two written agreements?"

"Mm-hm."

Sears took a step back. "And over what period of time, from what years to what years?"

"Well, one was I think twice in one year, in '86, I think,

197

or '85, I'm not for sure. But one covered six months maybe, I'm not sure. It was short periods of time."

"The agreements that you had, do you have copies of them?"

"No."

"Were they—let me characterize a formal agreement as one that is prepared either with the assistance of counsel of someone with a particular expertise in the preparation of such documents. Were any of your documents formal documents?"

Newman flashed her a look.

"No," Gerrie replied.

"Then who would draft what agreements were drafted?"

"Well, I usually would draft them, as you said, with what we would agree on, and we'd both sign it."

"Do you recall the specifics of your agreement with Cindy from 1986 to '89, the most recent time? What was the agreement?"

"Well we agreed fifty-fifty, I mean, you know, fifty percent purchase from each one of us. Now sometimes I'd pay for them and she'd pay me back, and if she'd pay for them then I'd pay her back. It would be . . . we never had any specific way of doing it. Just. . ."

"The last two horses, Brother Merv and Air Finesse Won —were those fifty-fifty purchases?"

"Yes."

"So you put up half of the money and she put up the other half?"

"Yes."

"Do you recall what the purchase price was for Brother Merv?"

"I think it was $5,000. It was bought at an auction. I wasn't there at the time."

"So you would have put up how much?"

"$2,500."

"And Air Finesse Won?"

"She was claimed . . . I think she was claimed at $5,000, I'm not sure on that, but I think it was $5,000 that she was claimed at."

"And your contribution would have been what?"

"$2,500."

"Do you recall specifically that Cindy did in fact put up $2,500 for the purchase for each of these horses?"

"Yes, she did."

"What was it that caused this last partnership relationship to cease in June?"

"Dispute over the trainer."

"Could you elaborate?"

"The trainer was not doing the horses any good and I wanted to change trainers and Cindy didn't because the trainer was her son. And we had a number of disputes over the period of time over that."

"Was that trainer Courtney Morrison?"

"No, that trainer was Jimmy Kelly."

"Was the relationship—the partnership agreement that you had with Cindy during this time, the fifty-fifty—did that go also to expenses?"

"Yes."

"And what would the expenses have been generally? What type of expenses are incurred?"

The two lawyers glared at each other.

"You have your trainer's bill, you have your feed bills, you have your storage bills, you have your vet bills. Now there were times when Cindy—when the horses were disabled, when they came back to the farm, she took care of them. She took care of all the horses; she was the one that cleaned the stalls, did all the work, took care of getting the vets there, and exercising them and wrapping them. She did all the laboring part on the horses. So I mean some of that would go in, because she put her time in it and I might cover more expenses of that bill, or something."

"So the two of you agreed to value her time as her contribution rather than dollars-and-cents contribution?

Gerrie ran a hand across her forehead. It ached.

"Sometimes. I mean, it would depend on how many horses were there at the time."

"Did you have any other partnership or business arrangement with anyone other than Cindy Whitehall?"

"In what period? When?"

"Well let's start with 1986 forward."

"Courtney Morrison, on a horse."

"Was that a partnership agreement?"

"No."

"What was that?"

"It was not a partnership agreement, it was . . ." Gerrie hesitated, still wanting to protect Cindy. "Cindy had nothing to do with this, but it ran under Windy Hills Farm name. Courtney did not have any money to claim the horse. So I claimed the horse and she, Courtney, trained it, until . . . no training bill was paid on it until the time that it had equalized itself."

"Explain 'equalized itself'."

"Well, the charges that would normally be incurred by a trainer—all right, she was not charging, I had to pay no training bill. So when it equalized the purchase price of the horse then that became . . . she got half of the purchase, which there wasn't that much time elapsed between that before she got the horse, on an unfair basis."

"What horse was it?"

"Duexlingot."

"Spell that."

"D-U-E-X-L-I-N-G-O-T."

"And when was that?"

"Maybe 1987."

"So basically that horse then—which you claimed for how much?"

"I think it was $2,500."

". . . Ultimately came to be the property of Courtney Morrison as a result of the training agreement, her contributions towards the training agreement?"

"No. It came to be hers because of her not quite ethical way of entering it into races."

"And did you realize any return on that horse at all?"

"No, money was lost on it."

"Any other joint ventures or partnership agreements with other persons during that period?"

"No."

"Is the arrangement—the horse racing, or the thoroughbred arrangement you and Cindy had—is that the only business venture that the two of you have ever been involved in together?"

Sears's eyes burned into hers.

"Yes," she replied quietly, glancing away.

But he was not to be avoided. Sears was slow, methodically developing each question setting a foundation which for Gerrie, who had to walk on it, was made of quicksand.

"You've never owned any sort of business together?"

"She has had businesses. She'd had her dog kennels, her antique businesses."

"And you've never had any part in any of those?"

"No."

"Have you ever made any contributions of cash money or other types of contributions to any of those businesses?"

"No."

"Ms. Powell, do you currently own any motor vehicles?"

"No."

"Automobiles, trucks?"

"No."

"Are you currently driving a motor vehicle?"

"Yes, I am."

"And it is not yours?"

"No."

"To whom does it belong?"

"To my brother."

"Did you ever own the vehicle?"

"Yes."

"When was that?"

"I owned one three months ago."

"What kind of vehicle was it?"

"A 1984 Cadillac."

"And what did you do with it?"

She looked at Newman, who was expressionless, then she answered, "I sold it."

"And to whom did you sell it?"

"It was sold to a dealership in Indiana, through Cannondale Cadillac. I don't know, because I don't have any paper on it."

"Did you realize any money from that sale?

"No, it was a loss. Well I don't know whether it was a loss or not."

"Were you indebted on the car?"

"Yes, I was."

"And your car did not sell for enough to pay the loan off?"

"No."

"Who held the paper?"

"There was no lien on the automobile, but at the time this happened I had bills."

"Did you use the money to pay the bills?"

"Yes, I did."

"And to whom did you pay it?"

"I'd have to name about ten different people that it went to."

Exasperated because of the long and difficult examination of his client, Newman rose, his teeth clenched. "Let me inject this. If you have sold assets to the detriment of the credit union they can trace those assets back. But with reference to a $4,000—let me ask a couple of questions, if I can, maybe to move this on."

Looking neither right nor left, he continued.

"How long had you owned that vehicle, that '84 Cadillac?"

"Year and a half."

"What did you purchase it for, approximately?"

"Well, about $6,500."

"And you realized $4,500 from Cannondale?"

"Mm-hm."

"Tell us at this point, without going further, if I could do this for you to get some of these answers for you, what kind of bills, not to whom, but the nature of what kind of bills did you pay?"

"Well to Visa, doctor bills, people I borrowed money from, a vet bill on my dog."

"Let's do it one by one. How much did you owe Visa? And this is after you sold the vehicle."

"At that time I could tell you, how much was anything, I was too distraught, I couldn't tell you what it was, I'd have to think about it. I owed my brother, which I paid him. I paid him about $2,000."

"$2,000 of the $4,500?"

Hour three and Gerrie was visibly tired.

"Mm-hm. I paid another friend $700. I don't know what I owed on Visa."

"Medical bills, ballpark figure."

"It's right at $300."

"Veterinary bill, ballpark?"

"$50."

"And that was on the dog?"

"Mm-hm. And the rest I used to live on."

Newman nodded to Sears, who began his relentless questioning again.

"Did you transfer a car to your brother in June of 1989?"

"Yes, I did."

"And what kind of car was that?"

"An '84 Skylark."

"Did you get money for that?"

"No. That was on money that I owed."

"And how long had you owned that Skylark?"

"Three years, maybe. Two years."

"Did you pay cash for it?"

"I traded another car in for it."

"And paid the difference in cash?"

"Mm-hm."

"And what was the total price?"

"I don't know whether it was cash or whether it was a check."

"And what was the total purchase price?"

Gerrie was adamant. "It was right at $4,000, $4,200."

"And you transferred it to you brother?"

She nodded, "Mm-hm."

"What was its fair market value at that time?"

Newman was testy. "Well, you can get that out of the book."

Gerrie answered, "About $2,700, I would say."

"And this was in addition to the $2,000 you paid from the other car?"

"Yes."

"Did you transfer any other cars or motor vehicles to any other persons within the last six to eight months?"

"No."

"So am I correct in saying that both of those cars have been sold?"

"Yes."

"And all of the monies that were gained from those were used to pay debts?"

"To pay those and then to live on. I had no income."

"Do you own any equipment, heavy equipment or farm equipment, do you have any ownership interest or have you ever purchased any such equipment?"

"No."

"Do you currently have any interest in any livestock?"

"No."

"Other than the horses that we previously mentioned—I believe there were three, and you said there were a series of others that you owned at one time, or not—are there any other interest in livestock that you ever had in the last five years?

"Other than horses, no. Livestock, what are you referring to?"

"Horses, it could be farm animals. Any type of farm animal, any livestock."

"No, horses is all."

"No cattle or . . ."

"No cattle."

"Have you ever contributed to the purchase of horses other than those that you've indicated that you owned in the thoroughbred horse racing? Other than the things that you've had an ownership interest in, have you ever contributed to the purchase of items that you've had no ownership interest in?"

"No."

"For instance, have you ever contributed money to buy something that has then been put in someone else's name?"

"I might have done that, but I've been repaid for it. I mean, if I have loaned people money, which I have done, and then been repaid on it. But, I mean, not . . ."

"Does Cindy Whitehall currently have an ownership interest in any livestock, horse, or any type of thing that you've contributed money toward the purchase of but have no ownership interest in?"

Newman held up his hand, considered for a moment, exploring every avenue of escape. Then he added to Sears's question, "Other than that which you've already testified to today?"

Despite her weariness, Gerrie tried not to implicate Cindy in any way. "Cindy has some, but they're hers."

Sears continued, "And you made no contribution to the purchase of any of them?"

She forced herself to sound definite. "No."

"Have you ever contributed to the maintenance of such

animals that weren't yours—for instance, any horses that Cindy Whitehall may own, or other persons may own, that you have no ownership interest in but you've contributed your dollars toward the maintenance of those animals?"

Newman leaned toward her. "Other than that which you've testified to here?"

"Not that I know of," she said quietly.

Sears went on. "Other than the two horses that you've indicated, and you previously testified to, have you sold any horses or other livestock in the last six months?"

"Not sold, but there were some horses that . . . there was one that broke down, and it was either destroyed or given for medical purposes. One was given to the Equine Services of Shelbyville. And a mare was given there also."

"Are those contributions or did you receive money for them?"

"They were contributions."

"Any others?"

Newman signaled his objection.

"In the last six months?"

"I don't know what . . . I don't think so."

Newman smiled slightly, trying to put the face of good nature on what he knew was a disaster.

"How about land. You currently own no real estate?" asked Sears.

"No."

On and on went the monotone questions and Gerrie's colorless answers.

"Have you ever owned real estate?"

"About twelve years ago."

"Where was it?"

"New Cut Road."

"Do you remember the address of the property?"

"5341, I think. I'm not for sure of the address."

"The 5000 block?"

"Yeah."

"And did you own that in conjunction with anyone else, or was it solely yours?"

"I owned it with my brother."

"No other owners?"

"No."

"When the property was transferred out of your name, to whom was it transferred?"

"It was sold."

"It was sold to third parties? Unrelated to you?"

"Yes."

"Have you contributed to the purchase of any real estate other than that which you've already owned?"

She knew what point he wanted to make. She wasn't about to be shaken.

"No."

"You have not. Have you added improvements or paid for the construction of buildings on any real estate that you did not own?"

"I have put in carpet in things at the farm there."

"Where, Windy Hills?"

"Yes."

"And what was the value of that?"

Looking at Sears, Newman asked, "Value or cost?"

Sears gave a tight smile. "Well, let's start with cost and go to value, I guess. Cost is really all you're going to know. What was the cost of the carpet?"

"About $1,200, I think."

"In your room alone?"

"Yes."

"And you were living there?"

"Yes."

"And what was the business relationship of your living there?"

"I paid board. Rent. To Cindy."

"And what was the amount?"

"$400 a month. Well it was really $300, but that . . . I mean, it was $300 a month, and the other $100 was for food or whatever went in on the purchase of food or anything that had to do with what I used."

"And that was $400 per month that you paid each month?"

"No, $300 exactly. The other varied."

"So you had $300 plus certain expenses?"

"Yes."

"How long did that go on, from what period to what period? From what date to what date, approximately?"

"From the purchase of the farm until I left there, which was maybe the last . . . the middle of May."

"What was the beginning date? Do you know when that was?"

Wearily, Gerrie scratched her head. "I think it was the latter part of '87."

"Was this your sole residence, or was this a business?"

"No, that was my residence. I was going to buy into the farm and have the basement fixed up there, but it did not work out."

"Were you ever able . . ." Sears thought better of the question he had intended and took another tack. "Was your relationship with this rental such that you were ever able to claim a deduction, since this was a residence and not any sort of office . . ."

"No."

Sears looked at her appraisingly and finished his question. ". . . That would entitle you to a deduction?"

"No."

"Did you take any sort of tax credit or tax deduction for any of the improvements to that property?"

"No."

He didn't miss a detail.

"Was the carpet that you added the only improvement that you made to the Windy Hills real estate?"

"I put in a security system."

"Over the entire farm, or just in the house?"

"No, this was just a camera back in the barn that came through a little monitor."

Sears paused. Then his voice rose, "Was that part of your partnership arrangement with Cindy?"

Leaning back in her chair, Gerrie shook her head. "No, I wanted it in there for myself because of the . . . I just wanted to see what was going on back there at times when there was no one there."

"You never paid for the building of the barn or any sort of out-buildings on that Windy Hills Farm?"

"No. Cindy has got a mortgage on it for that."

"Did you have anything to do with the mortgage? Did you co-sign on the mortgage?"

"Yes, I did."

"And what was the total liability that you co-signed for?"

"Whatever the amount was, $35,000."

"Did you co-sign for any more than that?"

"I co-signed only on the first . . ." Gerrie stopped and glanced over at her lawyer. He said nothing so she turned to Sears who was already phrasing his next question.

"On the first lien on the property?"

"Mm-hm."

"And that was for how much?"

"$60,000, I guess."

"So a total of approximately between $90,000 and $100,000?"

"Yes."

"Did you co-sign for anything else on that property?"

"No."

"Did you make payments on that note?"

"No. I would give . . . Cindy made the payments on the notes. Unless . . . I mean, if I wouldn't pay a month, or two months or whatever, then she would take the money and pay it on that. I mean, but I would not pay it."

"If you wouldn't pay a month or two months of what, rent?

"Rent."

"If you didn't pay a month or two months . . ."

Hesitating, Gerrie finally shook her head. "Well, I don't know how she termed it. No, I did not make payments on that."

"Was the loan in even such a condition of default that the bank made a demand on you to make any kind of a payment?"

"No."

"So other than your $300 plus expenses, you never made any other contributions to that farm purchase, other than co-signing."

She coughed and sipped some water from the glass pitcher on the table. "Not for the purchase. Cindy did not have—Cindy needed a co-maker because she did not have a full-time job, she's always been in business for herself."

"Are there persons today who owe you money?" He gave her a broad grin.

She gave him a soulful look. "No," she replied.

"You hold no notes against any persons or entitles?"

"No," she said, a blank stare on her face. She was damned if she'd let him rattle her.

"You hold no mortgages or open accounts?"

"No."

"Do you have any contingent liabilities against other persons?"

"No."

"Do you currently have a suit pending against Cindy, a personal injury suit?"

"No."

"Are there any other persons you feel might be liable to you such that you contemplate a legal action or you contemplate a collection action?"

"No." She kept her eyes front and looked for a spot on the wall to focus on to keep her sanity.

"Do you have any bank accounts, either jointly or—"

"No."

"No partnership accounts, interest in any partnership accounts?"

"No."

"Are you an officer or stockholder in any corporation?"

"No."

"Do you own stocks or bonds?"

"No."

"Now, when I ask about these accounts, I'm talking about not just in Kentucky but anywhere in the United States or overseas, or anywhere in the world." Sears was not about to give her any way out of facing punishment for the fraud she had committed.

"No."

"Other than your obligation as a co-signer on the mortgage notes on Windy Hills Farm, are you obligated under any other notes?"

Forcing concentration, Gerrie, whose thoughts were ricocheting back and forth, gripped the side of her chair until her knuckles were white.

"No."

"When the Windy Hills property was purchased there's some evidence in the credit union records that you took out loans to the credit union for the purpose of purchasing that property."

"Right."

"And the monies were then made payable by cashier's check to Cindy Whitehall."

"Right."

"Could you explain that for me?"

Gerrie gulped air. She had long ago made up her mind that creating a new lie was the only way to save anything. "Well, at the time that she was going to purchase the property she owned two pieces of property, and she needed . . . until the places were sold to pay for the Windy Hills Farm. The sellers wanted their money for the down payment. All right, so it takes a lengthy time to get a second mortgage on the first mortgage. I could get it through the credit union, which I did. Cindy signed the note, she put up her pieces of property.

"And then when the properties were sold the credit union was paid off. And one note was $5,000—I had a loan balance of my own, which was on a second mortgage; they paid that off, too, the lawyer paid both loans off. It was a short period of time."

"Have you ever contributed to Cindy Whitehall's support monetarily?"

She flushed again.

"No," she lied.

"Other than the $300 and $400 rent."

"No."

"Have you ever purchased nonperishable assets for her? For instance, I'm talking about things like washing machines, jewelry."

Though he was tenacious, her determination was steely.

"I have borrowed money or loaned her money to purchase things, and she has repaid me."

"Are there any loans for purchases that you've made that have not been repaid?"

"No."

"Have you ever purchased an automobile for her or anyone else?"

"No. I have borrowed money and it's been repaid, or I have loaned her money to purchase automobiles. I think it was a van."

"But that's always been repaid?"

"Yes."

"Have you . . . would the same thing apply to any other persons other than Cindy Whitehall? In other words, have you made purchases of these types of items for other persons—jewelry, automobiles, furniture, equipment?"

Gerrie bit her lip. This was not the time to let her real feelings out. "I loaned her daughter some money, but then she repaid me, when she purchased her home. And I've loaned her son some money to purchase a truck, and he repaid me."

"Let me just phrase it this way. Are there any of these types of purchases or loans that were made that have not been repaid?"

"No."

"Have you ever purchased CDs—certificates of deposit—or made other types of deposits in other persons names?"

"Well I have made a CD deposit, yes, but my name was first on it, it was in joint."

"Joint with whom?"

"One was with my mother and one was with Cindy when she had sold one of her pieces of property—or one, when she won some money at one time. And then she wanted a short-term investment, so I invested some for her at that time."

"Do these still exist, these certificates, or have they been cashed in?"

"They have been cashed in."

"Are there any certificates of deposits that you know of that still exist that you contributed to though they're not in your name?"

"I didn't contribute to any of them." With an iron will she kept her voice steady. She was caught between a rock and a hard place. "It was not my money."

"Have you ever paid bills for anyone other than what you've already testified to—you know, someone has a bill and it's not your obligation but you paid it for them—that you've not been repaid for?"

"No."

"With respect to the Windy Hills Farm, again, do you know how much income that farm generated on a monthly basis?"

Gerrie fidgeted in her chair.

"No."

"Any idea?"

"No."

"Did it produce any income at all?"

"Yes, it produced income."

Sears's baritone voice rose ominously.

"Would the income in your mind be significant income or insignificant income?"

Gerrie stared at him. "Well, it was so spasmodic. It would depend when she would have a lot of boarders in, when she wouldn't, what her bills were. You know, so that was hers, it was her income as such, it wasn't mine, so . . ."

"Did you ever have access to her books?"

"Yes."

"Did you keep her books for her?"

"Yes."

"Were you compensated for keeping her books for her?"

"No."

"Do you know what the expenses were for the farm on a monthly basis?"

"It varied."

"Did the farm generate enough income to pay its expenses?"

"No."

Finally, Mr. Sears agreed to terminate the deposition. Gerrie gave a huge sigh of relief. It had been a long, difficult, and potentially disastrous inquisition. She knew it, and was only glad the torture was over . . . for the moment.

CHAPTER 13

Cindy Testifies

Minutes later Cindy entered the room. Her head held high, Cindy walked gracefully and confidently, and to Gerrie she still looked beautiful. She was wearing an expensive silk dress in subdued shades of purple, with matching shoes. She was duly sworn, examined, and testified as Gerrie listened.

After stating her name and address, a few minutes of silence set the stage, then the questioning began.

"Is that address in Jefferson County or Bullitt County? The sheriff doesn't know."

Her voice was low and sultry. A voice Gerrie knew too well.

"Shelby and Jefferson."

"Okay. So it's Shelby and Jefferson, you cross the line?"

"Mm-hm."

"And how long have you lived there?"

"Since August of '87."

"And where did you live before that?"

"5703 Chenoweth Run Road."

"When you are at your current address, do you live there alone?"

"Now?"

"Right."

She smiled the radiant smile Gerrie had once so loved.

"No, I have a boarder."

"And how long has the boarder been there?"

Cindy looked at Sears and batted her lashes, exposing blue eyes. "Since the first of July."

Gerrie noticed he seemed oblivious to the charm for which Gerrie had so willing sacrificed everything. Gerrie sighed.

"Prior to that did you live there alone?"

"Yes. From May until the first of July alone."

"And then prior to that, I gather, you were not?"

"Right."

"And who lived there then?"

"Gerrie."

Her voice now had all the acid of vinegar.

"How long did Gerrie live there?"

"From August of '87."

"Is that the date the property was purchased?"

"That's the day I moved in."

"Was Gerrie living with you at the Chenoweth Run address as well?"

"Yes."

As if suddenly shy, Cindy lowered her head.

"How long had she lived there?"

"Okay. That property was bought in November of '77 and I think she moved in about '79 or '80."

"And had she lived there continuously during that period of time?"

"Yes."

Sears paused for a moment, looked down at some papers, then went on, "How did you and Ms. Powell meet?"

"I was in the dog business. I showed dogs and I groomed dogs and I had a dog kennel, and I met her through some friends that I showed dogs for and groomed her . . ." Cindy hesitated, then said, "She had a poodle."

"And how long after you met did she move in?"

"Let's see, I met her approximately twenty years ago for the very first time. I probably didn't start grooming her dog until, you know, a few years later. And she moved in, '79 or '80 in Chenoweth Run."

Then like lightening from a dark cloud he struck. "So what was the nature of your relationship from the time you first met twenty years ago until she moved in—a casual acquaintance?"

Cindy avoided eye contact. Her voice was barely audible. "Friends."

Sears gave a tight-lipped smile. "Would you consider yourself to be close friends?"

"Yes," she replied so quickly that the word faded before it was uttered.

"When you first met Ms. Powell, where was she working?"

"The only place I knew she ever worked was the Henry Vogt credit union."

"Do you believe she was working there when you first met her?"

"That's what she said."

"During that time, you knew her to have sources of income other than her employment with the Henry Vogt credit union?"

"Just gambling."

"No other sources of income?"

"Not to my knowledge."

Sears was not about to let go.

"Could you elaborate on the income she received from gambling? You said, 'Just gambling'."

Cindy flashed him a dirty look.

"Well, all she told me was gambling. That's what I assume."

His face was stern now.

"She spoke to you concerning it?"

"Well," Cindy said softly, "what is it you want to know?"

He mimicked her, "Well, I just want to know what she said about gambling." His voice hardened. "If you felt it was a source of income for her, what did she say and why did you come to believe that?"

Cindy shook her head. "Well, because when she would go to the races and win some money I would see this happen, and when she had money or spent money she said, you know, she had a good day at the races or . . . and she went to casinos, too, I do know that."

"Where?" he prodded.

"She went to Atlantic City and Las Vegas."

"Did she go frequently?"

"Sometimes she did and sometimes she didn't. Sometimes, you know, maybe it was once a month, and maybe it would be several months before she would go again."

"How long did this go on? Was this from the first time you met her, or was this something that developed after you had known her for a while?"

Cindy shrugged, "I don't know what she did before I met her."

"From the time you met her was this something that she was engaged in, was she a gambler at that point?"

"Yes."

"And did she continue to gamble, to your knowledge, throughout the time that you knew her?"

"Yes."

"Did she ever discuss with you the extent of her winnings and her losses?"

"No, not always."

"Not always?"

"No, she would maybe say, 'I had a good day at the races,' or . . ."

"Were you aware of the extent of her winnings?"

"No, not entirely."

Sears was tired of playing cat and mouse. He snapped, "When you say 'not entirely,' tell me the extent to which you were aware?"

His manner unnerved her. She began to stumble, "Well, 'entirely,' . . . I didn't always know. Gerrie had her own privacy and I did, too; I didn't pry in her . . . you know, we . . . ," she sputtered.

Sears broke in, "Do you know where Gerrie got her money to do the gambling?"

By sheer force of will Cindy regained her composure.

"No. She told me she gambled. That's how she made her money."

"Were you aware at times that she lost?"

"I beg your pardon?" Cindy said drawing out her words.

"Were you aware that sometimes she would lose money?"

She nodded. "Sure."

"Where? Here with the horse racing only?"

"No, I went to Atlantic City on a couple trips and also to Las Vegas."

Gerrie was a bundle of resentment, remembering Cindy's attitude.

"How many times did you accompany her to either Las Vegas or Atlantic City?"

"Not too many. I did not go very much."

"During the times that you did accompany her, did she lose large sums of money?"

"I have no idea what she did, what her outcome was at the casinos. I did not ask." A little evasion, Gerrie thought.

Sears made a face as though this was pure fantasy, then he asked, "Did Gerrie ever tell you where she got the money to gamble?"

"No."

"Were you aware of approximately how much money she made as an employee of the Henry Vogt credit union?"

There was a short pause.

"No," Cindy said softly.

"Was it your impression that the amount of money she made would have supported her going on trips to Las Vegas and Atlantic City?"

There was a long sigh. "I don't know that I even thought about it."

Changing the pace, Sears began to fire his questions.

"Did Gerrie ever confide in you that she was taking money from the credit union unlawfully?"

"Absolutely not."

"Did you own the property at Chenoweth Run Road?"

"Yes."

"When did you buy that, do you have any idea?"

"Yes, November of '77. Well, that's when I moved in, November '77."

"Gerrie wasn't living with you at that time?"

"No."

"Did you live there alone until she moved in in '79?"

"Mm-hm."

"Are you married, ma'am?"

"No."

"Were you ever married during the time you knew Gerrie?"

"Yes."

"Were you married when you bought the property on Chenoweth Run Road?"

"No."

He barely gave her time to catch her breath.

"When Gerrie lived with you on Chenoweth Run Road, was there any arrangement or agreement between the two of you as to how the household expenses would be paid?"

"Let's see, she paid rent."

"Do you remember how much?"

"$300 a month."

"Were there any other monies that she paid you?"

"Sometimes if, you know, the utility bills were expensive she would pay on those."

"Was there an agreed amount or just as a need would arise she would contribute?"

"No."

"Would you ask, or would she volunteer?"

"I don't remember."

"Other than yourself, were you the sole owner of the property at Chenoweth Run?"

"Yes."

"When you sold the property at Chenoweth Run Road you then bought the property in Shelby and Jefferson County, correct?"

"Yes."

"Is that a farm that operates under the name of Windy Hills Farm?"

"Yes."

"Is Windy Hills Farm a partnership, corporation, proprietorship—what is the status?"

"It's just the name of a farm . . . I just wanted to name
a farm something. Most farms have a name so I named it
Windy Hills Farm."

"Do you do business under that name?"

"Yes, I do now."

"When did you start?"

"Well, I just have a few boarders. Actually it's part of my
address."

"Do you have bank accounts in that name?"

"It's in my name."

"But not in the name of Windy Hills Farm?"

Cindy was definitely rattled.

"I can't remember if that comes first or my name, I don't
remember. I don't have a check with me."

He saw it and continued.

"Do you have a track account in that name, for instance,
at Churchill or . . ."

"No, not in the name of Windy Hills Farm."

"Whose name are the track accounts in?"

"They were in joint names."

"You and . . ."

"Gerrie."

"Anyone else, just the two of you?"

"No."

"Are any of those track accounts still open?"

"No."

"Could you describe for me essentially the business op-
erations of Windy Hills Farm?"

As she listened, Gerrie wore the face of composure, but
inside her stomach churned.

"Well, I have a boarding business and the horses raced

under our names. Sometimes they would race under Windy Hills Farm; we used that occasionally. But mainly it was just horse racing."

"Who owned the horses?"

"Gerrie and I did."

"Jointly?"

"Yes."

"Was there an agreement between you and she concerning these horses?" His eyes bore into her.

Trembling, she looked away. "Yeah, she took care of the financial part of them. She bought the horses. I took care of running the stable and seeing and caring for the horses, that they had feed."

"And then—that's the expenses, that's the purchase and maintenance—what about the profits?"

"Well, there were no profits."

"None of your horses ever won any money?"

"Yes, they did on occasion."

"Then how was it split?"

"It was put into the account. It paid for training bills, when there was enough to pay for the training bills, and if there was enough to pay for feed bills it would buy the feed."

Gerrie took a deep breath. Though Cindy was obviously nervous, she was holding up. All in all things were going okay, better than she had a right to expect. She refocused on Sears's intense questioning.

"There was never enough to take any money out?" he was asking.

"No."

"Did you ever purchase any horses?"

"Did I? No."

"Did you ever make a contribution—a cash contribution, a monitory contribution—other than your services or your labors, toward the purchase of any of the horses that you and Gerrie ran at these various tracks?"

"Yes, I did. I had an antique business, and I sold that and that went into the horses."

Now it was Sears's turn to be surprised. He recovered quickly. "The antique business—was Ms. Powell ever in the antique business?"

"No, it was mine."

"Did Ms. Powell every make any monetary contribution to that business?"

"No."

Sears's questioning went on and on.

"When did you sell the antique business?"

Silence. He waited for an answer.

"Let's see . . . I am not sure. I think it was '84. I would have to look that up to make sure."

"Before you moved into Windy Hills Farm, were you involved in the purchase, training, and running of horses?"

"Yes. There was another farm in Simpsonville."

"What was the name of it?"

"It was the same thing."

"Did you own it?"

"Yes."

"Was it in your sole name?"

"Yes."

"Did Ms. Powell make any contribution toward the purchase of that property?"

"No. I was lucky at the racetrack one night. I won $120,000 on a Pick 6, and that's what bought that farm."

Gerrie looked at Cindy, who was rubbing her temples. Gerrie could see Cindy was growing tired. It made her nervous.

"Do you still own that farm?"

226

"No."

"When did you sell it?"

"When Clark Station was purchased."

"Other than the Windy Hills Farm, ma'am, do you have any other sources of income?"

"Yes, I work two jobs."

"How long have you been employed on these two jobs?"

Sears was not about to slack off.

"Since . . . August."

"Of this year?"

"Yes."

"Prior to that, what was your employment status?"

"Horse boarding."

"Is that it? How long were you in the horse boarding business?"

"Since '86."

"And from 1986 until August of 1989, the boarding business was your sole source of income?"

"Yes, other than when I would go to the race track and bet on the horses. Our horses that would win, I would get some money from that."

"So the horses did win. And how were the profits from the horses that won divided up?"

"It was my money that I bet on the horses."

Disbelief was reflected on Sears's face. "You're talking about your winnings from the races and not your winnings from the horses?"

"Right."

"They were not your horses then that were winning?"

There was no response from Cindy.

"When you talk about your winnings you're talking

about winnings betting on other people's horses or winnings from your horses running and winning races."

"Both."

"So you said the horses you entered did occasionally win?"

"Yes."

Another tight-lipped smile from Sears.

"Now then, the purses—the winnings from those horses that you and Gerrie owned—how were they divided up?"

"It was not divided. It paid for training bills and feed and expenses."

"So there was never any distribution of money between you and Ms. Powell on any of those horses?"

"No."

"How many horses do you own now?"

"I have one horse, a yearling."

"Does it have a name?"

"It's my horse. Yeah, Jazz L."

"Did you formerly own a horse by the name of Brother Merv?"

Gerrie's face sagged. He knew the smallest detail. She wondered what would surface next. She looked at her watch. It was now mid-afternoon. *How much longer?* she wondered.

"Yes," Cindy was answering.

"Where is that horse now?"

"Sold."

"When?"

"I do not know exactly when."

"Was it within the last six months?"

"Probably July."

"And how did you come to own Brother Merv?"

"He was bought at an auction."

"By whom?"

"We purchased him."

"You and Ms. Powell?"

"Yes."

"When was that, do you have any idea?"

"It would have been . . . yes, it was a year ago September."

"When you sold the horses, did Ms. Powell have any interest in it?"

"No."

"What happened to her interest?"

"She signed all the horses over to me the first of June of this year."

"Why?"

"Well, the horses were not winning and our expenses were becoming greater and she was thoroughly disgusted with the business and she said she wanted out and she signed them all over to me."

"Was there another horse that she signed over to you?"

"Yes." Weary, Cindy was squirming in her chair. This was where mistakes could be made. Gerrie sat forward, listening intently once again.

"Was that Air Finesse Won?"

"Yes."

"Was that done on the same date?"

"Right."

"And has Air Finesse Won been sold as well?"

"Yes."

"When was it sold?"

"Since June, I don't know the exact date. I would have to look it up to give you the exact date."

"Concerning Brother Merv, do you know how much the horse brought when it was sold?"

"$5,000."

"To whom was it sold, do you know?"

"No, I don't."

"How about Air Finesse Won?"

"$5,000."

Gerrie breathed a little easier. Cindy was still holding up.

"Do you know to whom Air Finesse Won was sold?"

"There were several people. I do remember the last name of one owner, it was Thomason, and that's all I can remember."

"Do you know the purchase price of these two horses when you and Gerrie bought them?"

"Five on Brother Merv. I don't remember on Air Finesse."

"Who paid the money to buy the horses, these two horses?"

"Gerrie bought Air Finesse Won. I know I didn't have anything to do with that. And I'm not sure about Brother Merv. It seems like I remember writing a check for him the day he was purchased, but I'm not sure about that either."

"What did Ms. Powell get out of the transaction where she signed these two horses over to you? What was the benefit to her?"

"What kind of a benefit?"

"Any kind of benefit. Did she receive money?"

"No."

"What was the benefit to her of signing those over to you?"

"Because she wasn't going to support them anymore."

"Did Ms. Powell ever contribute any money toward your personal support, payment of your bills?"

"No."

"Did you receive money regularly from Ms. Powell?"

"No."

"You did receive rent from her, though, did you not?"

"Yes."

"Do you recall how much and for what?"

"Rent, $300 a month."

"And what did she rent from you?"

Cindy's face was impassive. "She used a master bedroom and it had a private bath."

"And other than the $300, did she make any other contributions to the farm or to you?"

There was a long pause, the kind that signaled a lawyer that the witness may be lying.

"Yes, she did. She did some improvements on the farm, things that she wanted done, painting and carpeting."

"Specifically what improvements were made?"

Cindy squirmed again.

"I can't remember right off. There was some landscaping."

Sears nodded to himself and picked up the pace again.

"Was this at the house or some other place on the farm?"

"The house. A security system was put in the house."

"In the house or in the out-buildings?"

It was clear Cindy wasn't comfortable. Gerrie grimaced.

"In the house."

"Anything else?"

"Oh, let's see. . . . She had bought an air conditioning unit for her bedroom."

"Did Ms. Powell ever pay for any of the out-buildings on the facility?"

"No."

"Were any out-buildings built while she lived there at the farm?"

"Yes, a barn."

"When and how was it financed?"

"I acquired a loan from the bank that I deal with."

"Are you alone obligated on that note?"

"Yes."

"No one else?"

"No."

"Ms. Powell isn't obligated on that note?"

Cindy made a face. "I guess she was a co-signer on the original note."

Sears prodded, "And the original note. Let's define the original note. Tell us which note you're talking about?"

"When the house was purchased."

"Do you know the face amount of that note?"

"$70,000."

"Is she obligated on any other notes?"

Gerrie shot Cindy a warning look, but Cindy didn't see it.

"No."

"So she's not obligated on the note to improve the property?"

"No."

"Has Ms. Powell ever made any payments on that note that she's obligated on as co-maker?"

"Not to my knowledge. A couple of times I was a little short and she did help me out to make a payment, because they're made quarterly."

An interesting assessment, Gerrie thought bitterly.

Sears was already fashioning his next question. "They're made quarterly?"

"Yes."

"And when you say 'a couple,' I interpret that to mean at least two. Is that correct?"

"Probably."

"Have there been more?"

"I really don't remember."

"And what was the extent of her contribution?"

"I don't even remember at the time."

"Did you ever pay Ms. Powell back when those payments were made?"

"I don't remember whether I did or didn't."

"Do you own a car?"

"Yes."

"Did Ms. Powell pay any money for the purchase of that car?"

Sitting at her counsel's table, Gerrie had never felt more lonely. A haunting emptiness filled her stomach. The stress of these opening depositions had suddenly taken their toll. She clutched herself as if she might slip away or evaporate and tried to stay fixed within the present, torturous though it was.

"It was financed."

"Through whom, a bank?"

"No, Gerrie financed it for me."

"She financed it for you? Does she have a lien on it?"

"No, there's no lien on it."

"What kind of car is it?"

"It's an '82 Cadillac."

"Do you still own it?"

"Yes."

"What was the purchase price?"

"I don't remember. It's not in very good condition."

"Has that loan been paid back to Gerrie?"

"Yes."

"Was there a note or any sort of document that would indicate the financing?"

"No."

"When was it paid back?"

"Oh, I don't even remember."

"Within the last six months?"

"No, it was paid back before . . . probably last year some time."

"Do you have a receipt showing payment, do you have any document indicating that the financing arrangement has been terminated?"

"No."

"Is there any other equipment on that farm to which Ms. Powell contributed any monies, whether purchased or otherwise?"

"She bought a riding lawnmower."

"Do you still have that?"

"Yes."

"Any other items to which she contributed to the purchase?"

"Let's see. There were two additional stalls built in an old farm that was damaged. She built those two stalls."

"Do you have any idea what the cost of that construction was?"

"$1,600."

"Anything else?"

"I could probably, you know, come up with some things, but right off the top of my head I just can't." Cindy smiled. It was almost 5:00. Knowing the deposition would soon end, Cindy was pepping up, acting confident again.

"Now these items that I'm questioning—are those items which Ms. Powell has contributed but which have not been paid back by you? In other words, you have not repurchased the $1,600 in stall construction?"

"No."

"You have not repurchased the riding lawnmower? And you have no evidence of payment on the Cadillac, though you indicate that it has been paid off?"

"No."

"Are there any others?"

"Any other what?"

"Any other items of equipment or any other items of value to which Ms. Powell contributed or purchased?"

"I mentioned the air conditioner."

"You still have that?"

"Yes."

"But other than those you're not aware of anything else?"

"I mentioned a security system, didn't I?"

"Yes, okay. How about livestock? Is there any livestock on the farm today, including horses, or any other livestock Ms. Powell contributed toward the purchase on?"

"No."

"When you made the purchase of the property on Clark Station Road, did you borrow money from Ms. Powell at that time to make the purchase?"

"No, it was not borrowed from her. It was borrowed from the Henry Vogt credit union, and when the two pieces of property sold it was paid back."

"You were not a member of the credit union, were you?"

"No, but she told me the interest rate was lower."

"So the transaction would have been that she would have borrowed the money from the credit union, used it in the purchase of the property, and then it would have been repaid?"

"Right."

"The house on Chenoweth Run Road—were any improvements made to that property with Ms. Powell's monies?"

"Let's see, there was some carpeting done there, and I think . . . I believe an asphalt driveway was put in."

"Has Ms. Powell ever purchased for you or on your behalf jewelry items?"

"I think one Christmas gift she gave me a little necklace."

"Any stocks or bonds purchased by her on your behalf?"

"No."

"Have you ever received from Ms. Powell cash or monies by way of having such monies deposited in an account in your name?"

"When the horse account was low and could not make payments, yes, she did give me money to put into the bank. It was either money or a check, I'm not sure which."

"Have you ever received gifts of money from Ms. Powell, large gifts—and by 'large,' I'm talking more than $1,000."

"No."

"Has Ms. Powell ever paid bills for you? In other words, bills that were your obligation, for instance, obligations coming due, that you were not able to meet, for whatever reason. Has she ever paid those on your behalf?"

Distractedly, she smiled at him and looked lingeringly at her watch.

"I don't remember."

Sears was annoyed by her cavalier attitude. "Was your relationship one that that sort of thing happened?" he asked with a smirk. "You'd pay each other's bills?"

"No."

"So, as I understand, what you're saying is that it would be unusual for Ms. Powell to pay bills for you, obligations that you had—you have bills coming due you can't pay them, she pays them for you—that would be an unusual situation?"

"Mm-hm."

"And you cannot recall that ever happening?"

"No."

"To your knowledge, did Ms. Powell report winnings from her gambling under your Social Security account number?"

"No."

"When was the last time you spoke with Ms. Powell?"

"About two weeks ago."

"How would you describe your relationship with Ms. Powell today?"

"Well, I guess it isn't wonderful."

"I mean, do you still consider yourself friends?"

"Yes, I still consider her a friend."

"You are aware of the allegations currently pending concerning theft of funds from the Henry Vogt credit union?"

"I don't know much about it."

"Are you aware of those allegations?"

"Just what I've been told."

"Prior to being told those things—when were you told these, within the last six months?"

"It's been within the . . . you know, maybe a month ago."

"Were you aware of any such misappropriation by Ms. Powell prior to that?"

"Absolutely not."

"Prior to the last six months?"

"Absolutely not."

"Have you ever told anyone any different?"

"Any different than what?"

"Any different than you were aware that Ms. Powell had been taking money from the credit union?"

"No, I knew nothing about it."

"I gather from Ms. Powell's prior testimony, which you were not aware of, she indicated that she moved out of Windy Hills Farm somewhere in May, last part of May 1989?"

"That's true."

"How would you describe your relationship prior to that?"

"We were friends."

"It was not an intimate relationship?"

"We were friends."

"Were you ever aware of any bookmaking activity taking place at Windy Hills Farm?"

"Oh, at parties."

"Is that it?"

"Mm-hm."

"Was Ms. Powell involved in that?"

"I really don't know, I didn't get into any of that."

"Did Ms. Powell keep your books on the farm?"

"Yes."

"Did you compensate her for doing that, or was that her contribution on some kind of arrangement you had?"

"Right."

"What was the arrangement that you had?"

"That she would just do it. I'm not a bookkeeper."

"Do you know what on average the expenses were for operating that farm, for a monthly average?"

"No."

"Do you know on average what the income for the farm would have been?"

"No, I just turned it all over to a CPA and he filed the taxes."

"Not to Gerrie Powell but to a CPA."

"I had a CPA to file the taxes, yes."

"Did Ms. Powell contribute to the monthly operating expenses of that farm?"

"If it was needed. If funds were short, yes."

"And to what extent did she contribute in dollars and cents?"

"I have no idea. Just when a training bill had to be paid or feed had to be bought."

"Was this done without regard to any sort of measured agreement, like half from her, half from you, this was just, like, as needed?"

"Well, my part—I worked . . . I worked that farm from seven in the morning all day, that was my contribution, working and seeing that the horses were cared for and trained properly and fed properly, and equipment taken care of."

"So you made no monetary contribution, dollars and cents, money to pay the bills, that was not your contribution, that was Ms. Powell's?"

"For the racing expenses."

"What about the rest of the farm? Was that the only activity the farm was engaged in?"

"I had boarders there."

Shaking his head disgustedly, Sears said, "That's all I have."

Through all of the questioning, Gerrie could see that Cindy was straining for composure, but she had answered as planned. When it was over, Cindy was in the clear. Gerrie grimaced. It was Gerrie's opinion that she had perjured herself to protect Cindy, and that Cindy had perjured herself to protect Cindy also.

A week after the deposition, Cindy called Tom. He was to give his sister a message: "I will give Gerrie half of the money, but tell Gerrie that I never want to see or hear from her again."

Hearing this, Gerrie felt terribly depressed and angry; then on Friday, October 13, 1989, Gerrie received a form letter from the Henry Vogt Machine Company. It stated:

> As a terminated participant in the Henry Vogt Machine Co. Office Pension Plan, you have certain vested rights. Upon your attaining age 65, the date of your normal retirement, you may begin to receive a monthly pension in the amount of $770.86 if you are not married at that time. This pension benefit will be payable for your lifetime only.

Her spirits were lifted, but only momentarily.

On October 14, Cindy held a sale of household furnishings and told Gerrie she had sold all of her possessions. Cindy gave her $2,000 from the entire sale.

The next day, trying to handicap a few races, Gerrie went to the track. She saw Russell with Cindy at his side. He appeared cool, going on about his duties as an owner, while Cindy bubbled around him taking his arm at every opportunity. Gerrie felt the knife twisting in her stomach as she watched them.

Besides the $2,000, Gerrie had nothing left except her

clothing and her little dog, Tootie. And the money had to last until she was taken to jail. She went to a nearby park and let the puppy run among the green cedars. The thought of her past mistakes filtering down to her pet saddened her. She did not know what would become of the dog if she had to serve time. Gerrie felt that she had failed her, too. She had asked everyone she could think of to take Tootie, but for one reason or another, they couldn't. There was one person, however: her friend Jan, whom she hadn't asked because Jan already had five big dogs as house pets. But Gerrie had to do something; so she decided to meet with Jan and ask her anyway.

She knew that Jan was an animal lover. Ten years earlier, she found an injured Irish Setter on the road. A few weeks later ten puppies were born and homes were found for all except four. Although the dogs were kept in the house most of the time, at six months of age they had successfully turned every blade of grass in the yard into mud. Friends smiled with amazement when they learned that, instead of finding homes for the dogs, Jan spent thousands of dollars for landscaping to cover the mud with aggregate terraces for them.

With trepidation Gerrie went over to Jan's house. She was her last hope. Not wanting to let on how desperate she was, Gerrie began the conversation with a joke. "Do you know what our friends say about you, Jan?" Gerrie smiled. "They say, if there is such a thing as reincarnation, when they die they want to come back as your dog. No one could have a better home." She became serious. "Jan, I want to ask something that means a lot to me. I want to ask if you would please adopt my puppy. I can accept my punishment a lot easier if I know she hasn't had to pay for my mistakes."

Without reservation, Jan replied, "You got it, Gerrie."

"You don't know what that means to me, Jan. I have no one left to ask," Gerrie said, remembering how her friends had once crowded around. Tears glistened in her eyes as she left.

CHAPTER 14

Up and Up,
Down and Down

Every few weeks the auditors found a new figure for the total amount of the embezzlement. Workers from Henry Vogt were hearing rumors: "It's up to $1.2 million," then in another week they reported, "They've found $2.6 million missing; it's the biggest case in Kentucky history!" A week later, Gerrie sat in a bar having a gin and tonic with Jan. Swirling her glass to mix her drink, her face cracked and she started to grin, a bit of her old confidence returning. "Have you heard? It's up to $4.1 million . . . and counting." Despite the threat of disgrace and jail, Gerrie was proud . . . like an athlete who had set a record. Jan looked at her, astounded.

A few days later, Gerrie called the farm. It was Monday, October 30, and she left a message on the recorder, "I'm tired, Cindy, tired of living this way. I'm coming home." After four months of living with friends and family, she wanted to have a feeling of belonging somewhere. Cindy had accepted all the money she had given her for sixteen years. Gerrie felt it was her home at least as much as it was Cindy's.

Her dusty car loaded with belongings, Gerrie motored back to the farm. She wanted to take a shower in her own bathroom, to sleep in her own bed, and spend the rest of her free time there.

It was a blue-gray twilight when she arrived. Shadows from the cedar trees fell across the long driveway edged on both sides with weathered horse fencing. Nearing the back of the house, she sensed an ominous stillness that was never there before. As she got out of the car, Cindy's two dogs came to wag and greet her. They looked starved. Their water and food dishes were empty. Gerrie filled the pans and the two animals ate with ravenous gulps. She looked around searchingly. Cindy was gone.

Gerrie walked through the double gates toward the barn, noticing immediately that the horse van was missing. The barn that had housed thoroughbreds a few months before stood empty. There were no horses in the paddocks or fields. Everything was abandoned. A generator used in the event of power failure was gone, as was the tractor. She felt angered at the thought of receiving only $2,000 from what Cindy had said was the total sale. Her bedroom suite alone had cost $6,000.

Gerrie was curious to see the bedroom suite Cindy had purchased to replace hers. Walking closer to the outside of her bedroom window, she was shocked to see her own furniture still sitting in the same place. Obviously Cindy had kept the suite for herself.

Gerrie made her way through the garage and to the back door by the kitchen. Peering through a window, she saw the space where her washer and dryer once sat. The appliances had evidently been sold. She felt a bitter bile rising in her mouth. Cindy had taken everything, and Gerrie hadn't even enough to pay something on her attorney's fees.

Her first feelings were anger, then she felt saddened at the thought of Cindy doing this; she wanted to go inside.

Perhaps she would find other surprises. When her key failed to enter the cylinder, she realized that Cindy had changed the locks. Gerrie was infuriated. She became more incensed as she tried to insert the key. Turning the knob, she realized the door wasn't locked. Gerrie's first though was, *She wants me back.*

Inside she found many of her things still there, things that Cindy said had been sold. Confused at the mixed messages, Gerrie fixed a scotch and water and made herself comfortable on the couch. "It felt so good just to be home again." She had just begun to relax when she heard a car pull in the drive; she walked over to the window and saw it pass her car and continue to the barn. It was Martin, Kim's husband. He served as their caretaker. She sat back down and sipped her drink. She heard a clicking sound coming from the phone in the kitchen, indicating that a phone in the barn was being used.

Minutes later, the house phone rang. Answering, Gerrie heard Cindy's voice. Her demands screamed through the lines, "Get out of my house and off my property, or I will have you put off." The razor-sharp words slashed into Gerrie's head. Hearing Cindy rant on, Gerrie could hardly believe that this was the woman who had come to her as she sat on the same couch months ago and said, "Just hold me, Gerrie. We need to get away, we need to be by ourselves." Over the screaming voice at the other end, Gerrie's bizarre thoughts drew her to the months before the purchase of Windy Hills Farm. "Since then," Gerrie murmured, "she hasn't cooked; we ate out. She didn't clean; we had a maid. She wasn't my secretary; she was never home. When we traveled together, it was only to keep me from Donna. She slept in her own bed except when she wanted something."

Gerrie found it incredible that she had been so stupid, as

she listened to the voice on the other end of the phone screaming at her. "Goddamn it, get out of my house or I will call the police."

Completely disillusioned, Gerrie replied, "If you want to call the police, go right ahead. I'd rather see Henry Vogt take it back." Gerrie slammed the phone, gulped her drink, and made herself another.

Twenty minutes later, the sound of tires crackling the tiny stones on the long driveway brought a blue police cruiser into view. Cindy, in Russell Newlander's Caddy, was bringing up the rear. Another police car pulled in behind Cindy.

A heavyset, ruddy-faced officer approached the house. Directing his question toward its only occupant, he asked, "Are you Gerrie Powell?"

"Yes, I am," she answered firmly.

"There has been a report that you no longer live here. Can you show me some I.D. with this address on it?"

"Yes, my driver's license." As Gerrie retrieved her license from her glove compartment, she saw Cindy on the opposite side of Russell's car.

Examining Gerrie's license, the officer called Cindy to answer his next question. "She has I.D. showing she lives here. Do you have proof who owns this property?"

"Yes, I do." Well-armed, Cindy produced a document for the officer to examine.

Gerrie told the officer, "Yes, she has a deed, but I have provided all the money for the purchase. She has made no payments."

"Then show proof," the officer said, "that you are a part owner or a lessee." They had her. She had destroyed everything and could produce nothing.

Turning to Gerrie, the officer warned, "You are to leave

this property now or I will arrest you for trespassing." The officer told Gerrie not to harass, call, or contact Cindy or come on her property again.

As the officer talked to Gerrie, Cindy stood with folded arms, head back, and a sardonic grin, at the doorway watching the scene. She had won this round and she knew it.

Gerrie turned to leave. Slowly walking past the woman who at one time had professed to love her deeply, she said, "Cindy, is this the thanks I get for protecting you . . . by destroying all the documents that would have protected me?" Gerrie waited for a response. Cindy turned away.

Gerrie left the farm. Cold realization ran down Gerrie's back like icy streaks. Her problems were compounding. Even if she was facing a short sentence, she had nowhere to live while she was still free. It was the lowest ebb of her life. She had nothing. By law everything was Cindy's. Cindy could keep it and go free unless it could be proven that she knew of the theft; it was her word against Gerrie's.

Gerrie was running out of funds and was unsuccessful in finding a job. Hearing her complain about having no money, friends began asking why she didn't rely on her usual way of making it—gambling.

After hearing this, she was motivated by pride and self-preservation as she set out with the determination of a thoroughbred and headed for the track. It was Wednesday, November 15, 1989, and Louisville was under tornado watch until 6:30 P.M. The Justice Department, the FBI, and the IRS had been conducting their probe for five months, but at the moment none of this mattered to Gerrie.

Arriving at Churchill Downs too late for the first race, she walked toward the closed-circuit TV monitor. Then she saw Cindy with Russell Newlander on the screen in the winners circle. His horse had obviously won the first race. Judging by the look on Cindy's face as she held Russell's arm, Cindy was working on Russell Newlander as she had worked on Gerrie. Cindy was a master at deception and a champion of manipulation.

"Cindy has had this planned very nicely," Gerrie figured. "Russell is next in line to give her a good life after she has drained mine. She's working on him now. He has a farm, horses, money. He can provide Cindy with straight company, so if it comes out in court that she's gay, she can deny the relationship."

Saddened and disgusted at the sight, Gerrie was about to turn away when she saw a tote board flash, "Inquiry! Inquiry! Inquiry!" The winner was taken down to second place, and Gerrie uttered a faint, "Yahoo!" Opening her paper she grinned and said to herself, "This is my night."

Gerrie wasn't interested in anything in the second race, but having done her homework the previous night, she was ready for everything after the second. The wind was blowing hard. Tornados were ripping through Alabama and heading for Kentucky. The rain fell in torrents as Gerrie placed her bets on the Pick 6. She bet $4 on her selection of winners of the third through the eight races.

As the horses passed the finish line in the third race, all she could see was the deep gray sheet of rain that rolled down the windows of the clubhouse. Despite the downpour, the track conditions were still considered "fast"; it had not been raining long enough for the earth to become sloppy.

Gerrie waited for the winner to show on the monitor . . . Johnny Come Lately, her horse won the third race. She watched the closed-circuit TV for the results. The fourth race was on; again she won. Her studying was paying off. "I'm hot," she kept repeating. She won the fifth race, the sixth, and the seventh. "All I need is the winning ticket on the eight race in order to win the Pick 6." She studied the form just for something to do. Her ticket had been purchased since the end of the second race, and she could only wait. She ordered a bourbon and branch water and waited.

Meanwhile, the waiting was nearing an end for federal prosecutors conducting the investigation. They were already calling the case the largest crime against a financial institution in Kentucky history, and they still didn't know the full extent of Gerrie's theft. A special report from the Henry Vogt Employees Credit Union was issued to all members, bringing them up to date on the misuse of funds and assuring them of the safety of their deposits and investments.

Gerrie sipped her bourbon and saw that the horses were at the post for the eight race. She was distracted for a moment when Russell and Cindy walked into the room. Oblivious to the announcer's call or the noise around her, she watched fascinated as Cindy turned her magnetic smile at Russell into a look of helplessness. Gerrie shook her head; the look had been used on Gerrie many times. She knew it well —too well.

The eighth race was over. The bettors checked the monitor. Gerrie had it. "Wow," she murmured. "What a quick fix for depression." She won the combined six races. The ticket paid $6,690. She called her old flame Donna, and the two had a weekend of celebrating.

But the moment of victory quickly ended. In the months that followed, anxiety was her constant companion. Renting a small, one-bedroom unfurnished basement apartment, she slept in a sleeping bag and tried to live on the money she had won. Such threadbare living after her old luxury was only a small part of her growing torture.

Gerrie finally found a job with Village Marketing and Research. She worked twelve hours a day and was paid a commission on what she sold. For the first time in twenty-five years she was on the same level as her co-workers. She never had a night when her sleep wasn't restless and plagued by bad dreams. She wanted to be apprehended; for Gerrie, this was hell. But the audit continued.

Tom delivered a message to her: "Cindy has had an offer on the farm and will split the money with you as soon as the farm is sold." Hearing this news, Gerrie was happy. She diligently studied the racing form.

On November 22, Gerrie learned the farm had been sold. She was growing more tense with every passing day. The strain was taking its toll. Lines in her face were deepening and the heaviness of reality weighed her down. But the thought of getting half the money from the sale of the farm made her feel somewhat better. Momentarily her spirits lifted, and thanks to Donna, who was at her side constantly, she began to think of the future. Perhaps with the money she was to receive from Cindy she could build a new life when she was released.

It was a beautiful fifty-degree day, the kind of a fall day that makes one wish winter would never come. Tom had an appointment with Cindy to discuss the proceeds that were forthcoming from the sale of the farm. Her forwarded mail began arriving. Ceasar's Palace in Las Vegas invited her to its black-tie celebration called the "Sport of Kings." Sitting on the floor in her bare room, she opened an invitation from the posh Flamingo Hilton; she was invited to an awards dinner-dance, with an opportunity to enter their slot-players dream tournament. And another one came from Caesar's, Atlantic City; she received a Caesar's Emperors Club Card given to those who deserve recognition as Caesar's most valued players. She looked despairingly at the elaborate cards spread out before her, some embossed, glitter-flecked and tinsel-trimmed. Additional invitations for a gala in the Emperor's Ballroom were there. And for New Year's Eve, a request for her to enjoy "world-class entertainment and grandeur as only Caesar's Palace can offer." Still another came from El San Juan Hotel and Casino in Puerto Rico. There Gerrie could return to the blackjack tables beneath the crystal chandeliers by night and enjoy the days in La Veranda setting of white wicker and overhead fans, complete with ocean view. The life she loved passed before her eyes—hotels with free-form pools, cascading waterfalls, swim-up bars, and beautiful people. Gerrie laughed bitterly as she looked around her squalid, empty room; it hurt too much to cry.

On November 27, arriving at the farm to keep the appointment with Cindy, Tom was surprised to find her in a happy frame of mind. During the course of the conversation Cindy promised to filter cash to Gerrie a little at a time through Tom. She added, "After my lawyer's fee is taken off the top and after I pay the closing cost and realtor fees."

On December 1, 1989, Gerrie drove to Turfway Park in Florance, Kentucky, and relaxed with a gin fizz. She placed bets on a few races and won $965.50. It was one of her few good days.

The closing for the sale of the farm was scheduled for the first week in December. Gerrie was relieved. If they could clear $92,000 from the sale, she would be satisfied with $40,000. That would leave $52,000 for Cindy, plus money from the sale of the horses, equipment, and furniture. The sale from the extra items would give Cindy at least $50,000 more. Gerrie figured that with the money she received she could pay her lawyer, post a bond, and still have enough to hold her over.

She had hopes of fighting the case and taking the "cure" she knew she didn't need. Assuming she could convince the court she had a gambling addiction if she were sentenced, after two years she would be free and still have money when she came out of prison. "That would be great." She told Jan, "Looking back, I can say I had fun, I was on top. I did things I would never have been able to do before. And I went places. I'm not sorry. It's been over five months since I could breathe this easy." This too was her façade.

On December 18, the closing date for the sale of the farm, Cindy called Tom, informing him that she would need a few days to begin splitting the profits; she would get back to him.

Two days after Christmas, Tom kept an appointment with Cindy. After several hours he returned to his home with $4,000 in cash for Gerrie. "Cindy assured me that there would be other meetings." However, as appointments were made, they were broken. And the following month was a turmoil of broken meetings between Cindy and Tom, as each time she failed to show. Gerrie was disgusted. "Cindy's plan worked. Not only does she have the money, the property, and the jewelry, but she has my sworn statement that it was hers." Cindy was in the driver's seat. She had nothing to fear, no repercussions—at least not that she knew of.

The constant agitation of broken appointments with Cindy began to cause Tom sleepless nights and a loss of appetite. With every disappointment he became more depressed, and the constant pressure was affecting his already precarious health. During the last week of January, Tom suffered a stroke. It was obviously caused by the strain of trying to intercede for Gerrie. Realizing that Cindy's games had almost cost Tom his life, Gerrie was incensed.

She composed a letter informing Russell Newlander of the complete account of her and Cindy's life together. The letter stated in part: "She has mink coats, thousands of dollars in diamonds, a car, a van, the horses, and she is worth over $1,500,000 because of me. So beware, she is now trying to get you."

Like Gerrie, however, he appeared so taken with Cindy that he was oblivious to her glaring flaws. On February 24, approximately one week after Gerrie sent the letter to Russell, he and Cindy were married.

The news of their marriage caused a new level of depression for Gerrie. "I was blind, but I won't lie for her anymore; she knew what I was doing all the time. Cindy went with me after hours to get money, lots of it, for her business. I'll confess everything and take her down with me. If she can't give me money for an attorney, then she'll get nothing either. Actually, it belongs to the credit union, and it'll either go to them or to the Internal Revenue, but not to her. None of it is hers any more than it's mine." The more she thought of how Cindy now had everything, the angrier she became.

Calling the authorities, Gerrie agreed to submit to a lie-detector test and tell everything. Three days later, on February 27, she kept an appointment with the FBI and the IRS. She signed a fifteen-page confession, but due to the timing of her confession, the authorities were skeptical of her story. For months Gerrie had been protecting Cindy; now they felt Gerrie's reason for changing her story was revenge.

Stopping at a phone booth after leaving the office of the FBI, she called Jan. "I did it, Jan," she said.

"Were you really able to be honest with them?" Jan asked sympathetically.

"Yes, I told them everything and I feel good about it."

Jan was relieved. "Great, I'll meet you and we'll have a drink, now that this is off your chest."

The meeting took place at the Carriage House. Gerrie was glad to see her friend. They settled at a comfortable booth, ordered their white wine, and Gerrie leaned towards Jan. "It helps to talk, Jan, do you mind?"

"Not a bit," Jan replied.

Gerrie stared off into space and began to speak sadly almost to herself. "Good. . . . You know, I remember one Saturday in October 1987, Cindy and Jimmy wanted to buy a couple of horses at Keenland and I didn't have the money. That day Cindy went to the office with me and watched as I wrote $15,000 in money orders to myself. She cashed my paychecks for years. She saw my salary. Yes, she knew what I was doing. She'd burn up the highway in a fit of anger at three in the morning, drunk. She knew I'd get more money for her. I had to keep giving to keep her from killing herself."

Jan's eyes widened; she was fascinated. "So you're saying she knew about the fact that the money belonged to the credit union, right?"

Gerrie nodded. "Correct. If she hadn't known, she would have asked questions. I came home with thousands daily. And she knew. She'd say, 'Don't tell me anything.' In that way, she could always say, 'We never talked about it,' but she knew."

Jan grimaced, "And she did accept millions in the way of cash, farm payments, horses, and what-have-you?"

"Right," Gerrie said with a wave of her hand.

"And she didn't claim it as income?"

"No."

Jan sighed. "Well, what difference did it make, Gerrie, where the money was coming from? She knew it wasn't hers."

"I guess it doesn't make any difference, because she sure knew it wasn't all mine." Gerrie laughed, "What else can I tell you?"

Looking puzzled, Jan commented, "I just can't, for the

life of me, figure out not only how you did it, but how you got away with it so long. It's the wildest thing I've ever heard."

Gerrie kept sipping her wine reflectively and talking. She could not seem to stop. "It was easy, I controlled everything. The auditors only saw the books I gave them—no more, no less. I always had to have $3,000 or $4,000 on hand in the office to be used for petty cash for employees who wanted to cash checks. But we could have $10,000 or more on hand, depending on cash we had received from members adding to their accounts. There was a perpetual cash flow. The petty cash money would not be entered as a book entry. The amount on the books remained the same at all times. It was never posted to a petty cash account because it was needed to blend with the regular cash deposits. I used several different methods. It was so easy.

"By pulling out the forged cancelled checks each month, the only way I could have been caught would be if they had taken each individual check and traced it to each account. The company never had an audit of that kind. The statements sent out were correct. The total share accounts were greater than what they reflected in the books. I figured it this way," Gerrie continued, "if you take out $10,000, in a fifteen-year period it's going to show $15,000 short, because of the interest that should have been accumulating on the $10,000. This is the money the 'holding company' will be paying back, so it's going to be replaced anyway. I kept raising the insurance coverage as I took more money . . . until the coverage reached $5 million." She ordered another round.

Jan nodded. "Go on."

"Well, credit unions are required to have a fidelity bond. This covers treasurers, managers, and workers in case of fraud. The fee for our coverage was $7,500 a year. When I first started as manager, the fee was $150 a year. In addition to that, we were required to have a bond for IRAs and a $200,000 bond for the board of directors. The total annual fee was close to $10,000; it's an outside protector for investors. If the fraud surpasses $5 million, the U.S. government steps in to assure the people of their money. The government picks up where the bonding company leaves off.

"I never stole from the members. Nobody got hurt. Just think of all the thousands of dollars we paid to the insurance companies . . . and we never collected a penny from them, so nobody really lost. The balance of the money I took when I first started will never be found unless they do a complete audit every day of every deposit and trace it to the bank. This kind of audit would take them three or four years. They will never find it all . . . never! Put me in any banking institution or credit union and I will show you a hundred ways."

They ordered more wine and Jan said in amazement, "Did you tell them this?"

"Yeah, I've told 'em ever'thing. Ya know, I may beat this yet." Her speech was slurring from the effect of the alcohol. She started reminiscing about the way it was at the beginning of her and Cindy's affair. "I'd been trying to find a beautiful woman I could be proud to be seen with. It had to be someone I could trust. It had to be a woman who appreciated nice things, who wouldn't be too stiff if I asked to use her Social Security number. That was Cindy. She said she hated men and she wanted me. So Cindy was perfect. But what was I? Ya wanna know? I was a sexually satisfying money machine, that's what."

Jan couldn't help laughing. "Funny, Gerrie. Very funny."

Gerrie grinned in response. "They still think I was addicted to gambling. And I may beat this yet. . . ."

"Really?" Jan said, feeling shocked at the remark. "Well . . . why don't you call Donna, and . . . ah, she can—"

"Oh, no," Gerrie interrupted. "When Donna found out I didn't have money hidden away somewhere, she said she didn't want to see me anymore."

"You mean?"

Gerrie made a face. "Yeah, I mean. Money's gone. Cindy's gone. Donna's gone." This, however, was not a shock to Jan, and she looked upon her friend with sadness for not having seen it before.

"You are a lousy judge of character, girl," Jan told her. "You should have seen that long ago. I wish I could stay with you longer, Gerrie. I know you need someone, but I have to go now," Jan said, rising.

"I ought to go home anyway," Gerrie replied. "Thanks so much for coming."

The two left the Carriage House. Gerrie went to her apartment to once again make a desperate attempt to appeal to Cindy in a letter.

CHAPTER 15

Final Accountings

At the end of September, U.S. Attorney Joseph Whittle announced, "The theft could exceed $6 million, but federal investigators stopped counting the losses because of the complex records-checking necessary in the fifteen months investigation. The indictment placed the alleged loss at $4.3 million based on investigators' estimates."

After fifteen months of anguish, Gerrie learned she had been charged with 115 counts of embezzlement, bank fraud, money laundering, and tax evasion from January 1, 1974, through June 14, 1989. Assistant U.S. Attorney James A. Earhart was quoted as saying, "If convicted, Gerrie Powell could be sentenced to several thousand years in prison and fined millions."

Harold Norris, former chairman of the credit union said, "According to the records on paper, we were worth about $3 million. After the investigation we found we should have been worth around $9 million." The missing money amounted to two-thirds of the credit union's assets. The case was the largest credit union scandal in U.S. history. The question on everyone's lips was how this unassuming looking woman had carried it out for so many years.

At 9:30 A.M. on October 16, a crisp and cool fall day, Gerrie entered U.S. District Judge Thomas Ballantine's courtroom on the second floor of the Federal Court House in Louisville.

It was the kind of room Gerrie had once admired and sought to emulate. Thick, dark-blue carpeting gave cool contrasts to off-white walls where gold-framed oil paintings of past judges were displayed. Huge arched windows were heavily draped in blue-gray velvet. The color was repeated in roping on brass stands which separated the public from the lawyers and the subject being charged.

Judge Ballantine looked very much like a thin version of Charles Laughton with white hair and horn rimmed glasses, or perhaps it was only the feeling of power that radiated as he entered the room and seated himself behind the large mahogany desk. Surrounded by stillness, the only hint of sound was air flowing through heat ducts.

To escape the possibility of being recognized on the evening news by her employer at her new job, Gerrie decided to go incognito. Wearing a dark wig, sunglasses, make-up, a black dress, and heels, she stood with her lawyer, Peter Newman, for the swearing in. Newman's silver-rimmed glasses framed a thoughtful stare at the judge as he read the seven charges.

The charges were combined: one count of embezzlement, one count of bank fraud, and five counts of tax evasion.

Judge Ballantine began to read the indictment.

HIGH ROLLER

Count 1

The Grand Jury . . . charges: On or about and between the 12th day of October, 1984, through and including the 14th day of June, 1989, in the Western District of Kentucky, Jefferson County, Kentucky and elsewhere, within and outside the Western District of Kentucky, the defendant, Geraldine Wray Powell, an employee, that is, Manager and Head Teller of Henry Vogt Employees Credit Union, Louisville, Kentucky, did knowingly execute and attempt to execute a scheme and artifice to defraud such insured financial institution, that is, Henry Vogt Employees Credit Union, the deposits of which are insured by the National Credit Union Administration, and to obtain monies, funds, credits, assets, securities and other property owned by and under the custody and control of the Henry Vogt Employees Credit Union, by means of false and fraudulent pretense, representations and promises, to wit:

1. Geraldine Wray Powell was hired by the Henry Vogt Employee Credit Union in 1951 as a clerk, and promoted to a position she occupied until her discharge on June 14, 1989, during which time her highest annual salary from the Credit Union was approximately $26,000.00;

2. Around 1974, Geraldine Wray Powell began wagering on sporting events, horse races, and at casinos located around the country, resulting in ever increasing gambling losses and expenditures; by 1989 such losses and expenditures totaled approximately $1.5 million;

3. Around 1983, Geraldine Wray Powell entered the horse racing and breeding business, in connection with which she provided approximately $400,000.00

261

toward operating expenses of that business, including expenditures for the cost of construction, purchases of vehicles, expenses of training, veterinary bills, food and boarding of horses;

4. On or about July 22, 1987, Geraldine Wray Powell purchased a farm located at 2419 Clark Station Road, Fisherville, Kentucky, for approximately $187,000.00 for use in the horse business (consisting of two tracts of real estate, commonly known as "Windy Hills Farm");

5. In order to cover gambling losses, and to fund her lifestyle and business endeavors, from on or about and between the 12th day of October, 1984, through and including the 14th day of June, 1989, Geraldine Wray Powell took monies, funds, credits, assets, securities and other property owned by, and under the care, custody and control, of the Henry Vogt Employees Credit Union totaling approximately $2.9 million through the execution of various schemes:

a. Between October 1984 through June 1989, Geraldine Wray Powell forged and cashed drafts drawn upon the Credit Union and made payable to various individuals, members and entities, placing the names of shareholder as payee onto the forged drafts and then placing a fictitious amount onto the forged draft; forging the name on the back of the draft as an endorsement; and presenting such instruments for payment at the First National Bank of Louisville;

b. Between October 1984 and June 1989, Geraldine Wray Powell would take and convert to her own use, genuine drafts and checks coming into the possession, custody and control of the Credit Union from various individuals, members and entities, taking and cashing such checks and drafts at the First National Bank of

Louisville, rather than depositing and posting said checks and drafts to the account of the Credit Union;

c. Between October 1984 and June 1989, Geraldine Wray Powell would withhold cash from bank deposits made on behalf of the Credit Union at the First National Bank of Louisville, and take and convert to her own use, cash deposited by members of the Credit Union, by providing a receipt to the Credit Union members as evidence of the deposit, taking the cash deposited by members of the Credit Union and converting it to her own use without properly using the members' deposit slip; posting the account of the Credit Union member, but failing to place the deposit upon the official Credit Union books, causing such deposits to be shown as income to the member on their personal account, while the account and account records of the Credit Union would not reflect any such deposit;

d. Between October 1984 and June 1989, Geraldine Wray Powell would cause to be issued to herself and others money orders drawn upon the account of the Credit Union without paying or receiving payment therefor;

e. Between October 1984 and June 1989, Geraldine Wray Powell manipulated her personal accounts at the Credit Union by posting false and fictitious loan payments on loan accounts owed the Credit Union by Geraldine Wray Powell; and failing to post withdrawals from deposit accounts at the Credit Union in her name; and

f. Between October 1984 and June 1989, Geraldine Wray Powell maintained fictitious and fraudulent account books and records for the Credit Union, which books and records would be provided to the supervisory staff of the Credit Union and state officials during peri-

Jan Welles

odic audits, and which account books and records did not disclose the diversion of funds by Geraldine Wray Powell through her execution of the above schemes and artifices to defraud the Credit Union;

6. Between October 1984 and June 1989, Geraldine Wray Powell's execution of the above schemes and artifices to defraud obtained by false pretenses, representations and promises approximately $2,807,964.00 in moneys and funds owned by and under the custody and control of the Credit Union.

All in violation of Title 18, United States Code, Section 1344.

COUNT 2

The Grand Jury further charges: On or about the 15th day of April, 1985, in the Western District of Kentucky, Jefferson County, Kentucky, the defendant, Geraldine Wray Powell, a resident of Jefferson County, Kentucky, did willfully attempt to evade and defeat a large part of the income tax due and owing by her to the United States of America for the calendar year 1984, by preparing, signing, mailing, and filing with the Internal Revenue Service, a false and fraudulent United States Individual Income Tax Return Form 1040 on behalf of herself, wherein she reported as taxable income for said calendar year of 1984, the sum of $22,169.67, and that the amount of tax due and owing thereon was the sum of $3,771.00, whereas, she then and there well knew and believed her taxable income for said calendar year 1984 was the sum of $176,637.67, upon which, said taxable income there was owing to the United States of America an income tax of $76,253.34.

264

In violation of Title 26, United States Code, Section 7201.

COUNT 3

The Grand Jury further charges: On or about the 15th day of April, 1986, in the Western District of Kentucky, Jefferson County, Kentucky, the defendant, Geraldine Wray Powell, a resident of Jefferson County, Kentucky, did willfully attempt to evade and defeat a large part of the income tax due and owing by her to the United States of America for the calendar year 1985, by preparing, signing, mailing, and filing with the Internal Revenue Service, a false and fraudulent United States Individual Income Tax Return Form 1040 on behalf of herself, wherein she reported as taxable income for said calendar year 1985, the sum of $21,925.00, and that the amount of tax due and owing thereon was the sum of $3,625.00, whereas, she then and there well knew and believed her taxable income for said calendar year 1985 was the sum of $447,394.00, upon which, said taxable income there was owing to the United States of America an income tax of $211,141.10.

In violation of Title 26, United States Code, Section 7201.

COUNT 4

The Grand Jury further charges: On or about the 15th day of April, 1989, in the Western District of Kentucky, Jefferson County, Kentucky, the defendant, Geraldine Wray Powell, a resident of Jefferson County, Kentucky, did willfully attempt to evade and defeat a large part of the income tax due and owing by her to the United States of America for the calendar year 1986, by preparing, signing, mailing, and filing with the Internal Revenue Service, a false and fraudulent United States Individual Income Tax Return Form 1040 on behalf of herself, wherein she reported as taxable income for said calendar year of 1986, the sum of $12,270.00, and that the amount of tax due and owing thereon was the sum of $1,410.00, whereas, she then and there well knew and believed her taxable income for said calendar year 1986 was the sum of $380,946.98, upon which, said taxable income there was owing to the United States of America an income tax of $177,454.49.

In violation of Title 26, United States Code, Section 7201.

Count 5

The Grand Jury further charges: On or about the 15th day of April, 1988, in the Western District of Kentucky, Jefferson County, Kentucky, the defendant, Geraldine Wray powell, a resident of Jefferson County, Kentucky, did willfully attempt to evade and defeat a large part of the income tax due and owing by her to the United States of America for the calendar year 1987, by preparing, signing, mailing, and filing with the Internal Revenue Service, a false and fraudulent United States Individual Income Tax Return Form 1040 on behalf of herself, wherein she reported as taxable income for said calendar year of 1987, the sum of $13,719.00, and that the amount of tax due and owing thereon was the sum of $1,987.00, whereas, she then and there well knew and believed her taxable income for said calendar year 1987 was the sum of $351,270.47, upon which, said taxable income there was owing to the United States of America an income tax of $127,216.13.

In violation of Title 26, United States Code, Section 7201.

Count 6

The Grand Jury further charges: During the calendar year 1988, in the Western District of Kentucky, Jefferson County, Kentucky and elsewhere, within and outside the Western District of Kentucky, the defendant, Geraldine Wray Powell, had and received gross taxable income in the amount of $246,829.68, more or less, that by reason of receipt of such gross taxable income there was owing the United States of America an income tax of $59,867.24; that well knowing all of the foregoing facts, and in August, 1989, she willfully attempted to evade and defeat the said income tax due and owing by her to the United States of America for 1988 by failing to file and pay an Individual Tax Return Form 1040 for 1989, and by engaging in act of the following:

a. Geraldine Wray Powell, engaged in a scheme whereby she took Henry Vogt Employees Credit Union members, then selected the name of one of the Credit Union drafts, then selected the name of one of the Credit Union officers, and then cashed the drafts at the First National Bank of Louisville;

b. Geraldine Wray Powell, engaged in the above scheme mindful not to draw drafts in excess of $10,000.00, which would have triggered the financial institution's Currency Transaction Report requirements when she cashed the drafts at the First National Bank of Louisville; and

c. Geraldine Wray Powell would take money from cash deposits made by members at the Credit Union, converting portions of that cash to her own use, the balance of which she deposited to the Credit Union account at the First National Bank, Louisville, Kentucky, and she would adjust the books of the Credit Union and account records of customers affected to conceal the diversion of funds.

All in violation of Title 26, United Sates Code, Section 7201.

COUNTS 7–98

On or about the following dates, in the Western District of Kentucky, Jefferson County, Kentucky and elsewhere, within and outside of the Western District of Kentucky the defendant, Geraldine Wray Powell, knowing that the property involved in the following financial transactions represented proceeds of some form of specified unlawful activity, that is, bank fraud and embezzlement, in violation of Title 18, United States Code, Section 657 and 1344, did knowingly and willfully conduct and attempt to conduct and cause others to conduct the following financial transactions, which transactions involved interstate commerce and involved the use of one or more domestic financial institution engaged in and whose activities affect interstate commerce, to wit, the First National Bank, Louisville, Kentucky, which transactions in fact as defendant then and there well knew involved the proceeds of a specified unlawful activity, and with intent to promote the carrying on the specified unlawful activity and knowing that each such transaction was designed in whole or in part to conceal and disguise the nature, location, source ownership and control of the proceeds of the specified unlawful activity, defendant did engage in the financial transaction described as follows:

COUNT	DATE	DRAFT #	PAYEE	DOLLAR AMOUNT
7	10/31/86	21300	CU member	$8,752.50
8	11/04/86	21301	CU member	$6,852.00
9	11/07/86	21303	CU member	$6,545.00
10	11/13/86	21304	CU member	$7,345.00
11	11/20/86	21306	CU member	$8,245.00
12	11/27/86	21307	CU member	$6,512.00
13	12/03/86	21309	CU member	$8,865.00
14	12/04/86	21310	CU member	$5,000.00
15	12/10/86	21311	CU member	$8,875.00
16	12/17/86	21312	CU member	$8,950.00
17	12/19/86	21313	CU member	$5,500.00
18	12/22/86	21314	CU member	$7,466.00
19	12/26/86	21315	Geraldine Powell	$6,500.00
20	12/30/86	21316	CU member	$9,205.00
21	01/16/87	21317	CU member	$6,700.00
22	02/11/87	21318	CU member	$5,600.00
23	03/25/87	21321	CU member	$7,000.00
24	03/25/87	21322	CU member	$7,250.00
25	03/26/87	21323	Gerrie Powell	$6,700.00
26	04/13/87	21325	CU member	$6,700.00
27	04/16/87	21326	CASH	$6,000.00
28	04/20/87	21324	Gerrie Powell	$4,500.00

29	04/22/87	21327	Gerrie Powell	$10,000.00
30	04/22/87	21328	Gerrie Powell	$10,000.00
31	04/24/87	21339	CASH	$6,000.00
32	04/27/87	21333	CU member	$4,750.00
33	04/27/87	21330	Gerrie Powell	$5,500.00
34	05/05/87	21334	CU member	$5,900.00
35	05/11/87	21335	CU member	$4,800.00
36	05/14/87	21337	Gerrie Powell	$7,789.00
37	05/15/87	21340	CASH	$7,600.00
38	05/21/87	21341	CU member	$6,300.00
39	05/28/87	21342	CU member	$5,450.00
40	05/29/87	21343	CU member	$5,500.00
41	06/01/87	21344	CU member	$3,200.00
42	06/03/87	21345	CU member	$8,357.00
43	06/04/87	21346	CU member	$3,500.00
44	07/02/87	21347	CU member	$6,057.01
45	07/10/87	21348	CU member	$5,872.45
46	08/12/87	21353	CU member	$3,143.08
47	08/25/87	21354	CU member	$5,300.00
48	08/31/87	21355	G. Powell	$9,000.00
49	09/01/87	21358	CU member	$6,500.00
50	10/28/87	21359	CU member	$8,927.00
51	10/29/87	21360	CU member	$5,795.00
52	11/12/87	21361	CU member	$4,000.00
53	11/17/87	21364	CU member	$8,900.00
54	11/19/87	21365	CU member	$6,550.00
55	12/16/87	21367	CU member	$7,200.00
56	12/23/87	21368	CU member	$8,700.00
57	12/30/87	21369	CU member	$8,513.51
58	02/08/88	21372	CU member	$6,700.00
59	02/09/88	21373	Gerrie Powell	$2,000.00
60	03/08/88	21379	CU member	$6,057.92
61	03/23/88	21381	CU member	$6,396.75

62	03/23/88	21385	Gerrie Powell	$3,500.00
63	04/05/88	21386	CU member	$7,725.00
64	04/12/88	21387	CU member	$5,565.23
65	04/19/88	21388	CU member	$7,827.03
66	04/21/88	21389	CU member	$8,250.00
67	05/02/88	21390	CU member	$4,899.50
68	05/03/88	21395	CU member	$4,500.00
69	05/11/88	21396	CU member	$8,752.00
70	05/26/88	21397	CU member	$8,252.50
71	06/03/88	21384	CU member	$870.29
72	06/03/88	21398	CU member	$6,293.73
73	06/07/88	21399	CU member	$4,766.00
74	06/21/88	21402	CU member	$8,971.50
75	06/24/88	21403	CU member	$7,288.00
76	06/28/88	21404	CU member	$7,421.75
77	07/25/88	21406	CU member	$7,752.00
78	07/28/88	21407	CU member	$8,522.00
79	08/26/88	21408	CU member	$7,255.75
80	09/09/88	21418	CU member	$6,000.00
81	09/28/88	21419	CU member	$6,975.00
82	09/29/88	21420	CU member	$5,963.46
83	10/21/88	21421	CU member	$6,864.80
84	10/28/88	21423	CU member	$7,452.02
85	11/02/88	21424	CU member	$8,989.22
86	11/04/88	21425	CU member	$8,885.76
87	11/11/88	21426	CU member	$4,565.75
88	11/23/88	21433	CU member	$8,585.05
89	02/07/89	21436	Gerrie Powell	$9,877.25
90	03/14/89	21439	Gerrie Powell	$8,787.50
91	03/24/89	21440	Gerrie Powell	$4,757.88
92	03/31/89	21441	CU member	$5,875.00
93	04/05/89	21442	CU member	$6,800.00
94	04/13/89	21443	CU member	$6,955.00

95	04/19/89	21444	CU member	$8,750.00
96	02/10/89	21463	Gerrie Powell	$6,500.00
97	02/24/89	21464	Gerrie Powell	$5,000.00
98	03/03/89	21465	CU member	$8,127.35

COUNTS 99–114

On or about the following dates, the defendant, Geraldine Wray Powell, knowing that the property involved in the following financial transactions represented the proceeds of some form of specified unlawful activity, that is, embezzlement and bank fraud, in violation of Title 18, United States Code, Section 657 and 1344, and knowing of the financial institution's obligation under federal law, to wit, Title 31, Section 5313, to report currency transactions in excess of $10,000.00, and knowing that the transactions were designed in whole or in part to avoid the transaction reporting requirement under federal law, defendant did knowingly and willfully structure and assist in structuring the following currency transactions, which transactions involved interstate commerce and involved the use of one or more domestic financial institutions engaged in and whose activities affect interstate commerce, to wit, the First National Bank, Louisville, Kentucky, when as defendant then and there well know that the property involved in the financial transactions represented the proceeds of some form of specified unlawful activity, and with intent to promote the carrying on of the specified unlawful activity and knowing that each such transaction was designed in whole or in part to conceal and disguise the nature, location, source, ownership and control of the proceeds of the specified unlawful activity, defendant did engage in the structured transactions:

COUNT	DATE	DRAFT #	PAYEE	DOLLAR AMOUNT
99	04/16/87	21326	CASH	$6,000.00
100	04/22/87	21324	Gerrie Powell	$4,500.00
101	04/20/87	21327	Gerrie Powell	$10,000.00
102	04/22/87	21328	Gerrie Powell	$10,000.00
103	04/24/87	21329	CASH	$6,000.00
104	04/27/87	21330	Gerrie Powell	$5,500.00
105	05/14/87	21337	Gerrie Powell	$7,789.00
106	05/15/87	21340	CASH	$7,600.00
107	08/31/87	21355	G. Powell	$9,000.00
108	02/07/89	21436	Gerrie Powell	$9,877.25
109	02/09/88	21373	Gerrie Powell	$2,000.00
110	02/10/89	21463	Gerrie Powell	$5,500.00
111	02/24/89	21464	Gerrie Powell	$5,000.00
112	03/14/89	21439	Gerrie powell	$8,787.50
113	03/23/88	21385	Gerrie Powell	$3,500.00
114	03/24/89	21440	Gerrie Powell	$4,757.88

COUNT 115

On or about and between the 1st day of January, 1974, through and including the 14th day of June, 1989, in the Western District of Kentucky, Jefferson County, Kentucky and elsewhere within and outside the Western District of Kentucky, the defendant, Geraldine Wray Powell, an employee, that is, Manager and Head Teller of the Henry Vogt Employees Credit Union, Louisville,

Kentucky, the deposits of which was then and there insured by the National Credit Union Administration, did
willfully and knowingly, and with intent to defraud the
Credit Union, did embezzle and misapply the sum of
$4,289,492.00, more or less, in moneys, funds, credits,
securities and other things of value belonging to the
Credit Union, and pledged and otherwise entrusted to
the care and custody of Geraldine Wray Powell as such
employee, and the sum of $6,064,495.00 was depleted
and lost by the Credit Union as a result on the embezzlement and misappropriation of funds by Geraldine Wray
Powell.

After the reading of the charges there was a pause, then
Judge Ballantine asked, "Ms. Powell, how do you plead?"
A faint voice replied, "Guilty, sir."
"Ms. Powell, no one else can make a deal for you. And
there are no deals here. Do you understand that by pleading
guilty you will forfeit your privilege of having a trial by jury?
You will not be allowed to bring in witnesses to speak in your
behalf regarding your character. Do you understand?"
"Yes, sir." Gerrie answered softly, still hoping to receive
lenience, with an order from the court to serve time in a
facility for addicted gamblers.
"Ms. Powell, how do you plead?"
Without hesitation she replied, "Guilty, Your Honor."
Assistant U.S. Attorney James A. Earhart asked the
judge to impose the maximum sentence, calling Gerrie's
crime one of "personal greed."
The Judge announced, "Due to the enormity of the
crime, sentencing will not take place until December 17."
The court was adjourned until that date.

On Monday, December 17, 1990, at 9:30 A.M., Gerrie stood before Judge Ballantine again as he asked, "Miss Powell, do you have any statement you want to make before the court imposes sentence?"

"No, sir."

Judge Ballantine directed his attention to the Assistant U.S. Attorney and asked, "Mr. Earhart?"

James Earhart's distinguished mannerism seemed to command an added hush in the courtroom as he began to speak in a deep sonorous voice, "Yes, Your Honor, I do have a brief statement I would like to make.

"Before the court imposes sentence, I believe there are three factors or three items that the court should take note of which are important in this sentencing decision. Number one, in this particular case as a result of Ms. Powell's activity, the Henry Vogt Credit Union failed. That institution was closed and eventually had to be taken over by the National Credit Union Administration, who had to cover the losses, as well as the insurance company, which had to cover the losses caused by Ms. Powell. The credit union has been repurchased and reopened by another institution. That's an important factor in this case, is the failure of the Henry Vogt Credit Union.

"Second is Miss Powell's motivation for the commission of this crime. And it can be stated, I guess, no better than personal greed and personal comfort. There is no real motive for this crime other than Ms. Powell's enjoyment of the use of this money. That's not much of an excuse to offer for the theft of approximately $4.5 million over the course of two decades.

"Third, the absence of assets at this point to be able to recoup was suffered by the Henry Vogt Credit Union. The court should note from 1983 to 1989 Ms. Powell embezzled approximately $2.5 million just during that last six years of the scheme. Despite that, there is nothing to show for it or at least there have been no assets identified for it. It is known that Ms. Powell and others have purchased assets. All of those assets have been placed or put in other people's names or third parties' names to date.

"It should also be noted by the court that not only were those assets placed in other people's names recently, but they were placed in other people's names during the course of the scheme. In other words, Ms. Powell was doing precriminal planning is what it amounts to. All of the major assets purchased by Ms. Powell during the course of this embezzlement were placed in other people's names. Ms. Powell was aware of the consequences of getting caught and took steps to protect against that. Ms. Powell was aware of methods to get caught and took steps to assure that she would not. She avoided the CTR reporting requirements. She was able to manipulate and manage the books of the credit union for approximately twenty years to conceal or transfer all of the possible assets which could be recouped to be placed for restitution.

"Ms. Powell has received a two level decrease for acceptance of responsibility. The United States does not oppose that in light of Ms. Powell's cooperation since she has been caught. Nevertheless, the United States would respectfully request that this court impose a sentence of 97 months, which is the maximum under the guideline range as calculated under level 28, and that the defendant should be given no further consideration for her cooperation beyond that."

After hearing Mr. Earhart's statement, Gerrie listened intensely as Judge Ballantine spoke.

"All right. I believe, given the extent and nature of these

offenses, a sentence at the high end of the guidelines in almost mandatory. It's the judgment of the court that the defendant is committed to . . ."

As Judge Ballantine's voice rose, Gerrie felt the rhythm of her heart hammering at her chest, and into her throat and up the sides of her neck. Her elastic thoughts waivered from the enormous importance of the sentence to the reasoning only she could understand. She looked around the courtroom, shocked, thinking to herself, *Where's Cindy? . . . She's the one that needed . . . she* demanded. . . . *Where is she now?*

Gerrie stiffened her legs and back to keep her legs from buckling . . . and recalled a time when her attorney had asked, "How much would you say Cindy has not reported to the IRS?"

"Oh, a million and a half, easy. Maybe more."

"She's in deep shit," she recalled him saying. "Just let the courts take care of her."

Standing with her lawyer, Gerrie could not stop thinking of Cindy getting away. She was ruthless and clever. *How can she live with herself after cheating me out of my share? She has no conscience.* Suddenly her thoughts thudded back to the present. Judge Ballantine was watching her intently.

". . . for a total term imprisonment of 97 months." Eight years and one month.

The prison term was the maximum recommended under new federal guidelines that set fixed prison sentence for crimes committed after November 1987.

"It is further ordered that the defendant shall make restitution in the amount of $5,707,779.34 to the Attorney General through the United States Attorney's Office for disbursement to the identified victim in this case, National Credit Union Administration.

"Ms. Powell, you have the right to appeal this sentence

to the United States Court of Appeals. For the appeal, you may apply for leave to appeal as a pauper. At your request the clerk of the court will prepare and file forthwith on your behalf a notice of appeal."

Gerrie's face was stoic, the message was clear: Gerrie's time had come, and crying wouldn't change it. Inside, though, she felt a bitterness she had never known before. With all the scheming she had done, her plan had protected Cindy so thoroughly that it backfired.

A month later, on Thursday, January 17, 1991, the night before Gerrie was to start her sentence, as the rest of the world watched the first television news of the war in the Persian Gulf, Gerrie sat on her sleeping bag in her small apartment shifting through old papers that had been stored at her mother's and at Tom's. She kept diligently hunting for cancelled checks . . . discarding some, saving others.

Trapped with the results of her life and the darkness of her room, she stared desolately at the scraps of paper. A knock on the door disturbed her thoughts. It was Jan bringing the little dog, Tootie, for a last visit before Gerrie left for prison.

"How's it going, Gerrie?"

Gerrie smiled grimly. "Oh, I don't know." She clasped the dog in her arms. The puppy wiggled happily in her master's arms and Gerrie asked, "Would you like a drink?" As she spoke, she reached for a plastic bag that sat on the floor beside her. Handing it to Jan, she said, "Here . . . take this. It's all I have left. It's a lot of invitations, checks, and papers I didn't know I had. And here, take the rest of the tapes of my life." Shaking the plastic bag, Gerrie said, "I want you to keep these papers that are in here and send them to me if I need them, okay? Do this for me?"

"I will," Jan said softly, confirming her words with a handshake, not realizing what the contents of the bag were.

Gerrie left her apartment the next day, January 29, 1991, and began serving her sentence at the Federal Correctional Institution in Lexington, Kentucky.

Epilogue

On February 1, 1991, three days after Gerrie was incarcerated, Cindy Whitehall Newlander left her husband. The couple had been married eleven months and eight days. At the time of the separation, Russell was left with no forwarding address for his wife, only her place of employment, the Pee-wee Valley Veterinary Clinic.

Gerrie had not yet learned the news, although she wrote to friends and relatives and received letters often. Some of her letters to friends were censored, as was a note from her to Jan on March 19. In the note, Gerrie had requested that Jan send the legal papers from the plastic bag in her possession. Before the papers could be packaged for mailing, Jan was served with a subpoena on March 22, to appear before the grand jury "with any and all items belonging to Geraldine Powell and/or Cindy Whitehall Newlander."

On Monday, March 25, with the war in the Gulf over, Cindy's acquaintances and business associates were receiving similar subpoenas to produce any and all real and personal property and answer questions regarding any transactions with the two women.

Jan Welles

On April 18, Jan, Karen, Tom Powell, and three of Cindy and Gerrie's closest friends appeared singularly before the grand jury with items belonging and pertaining to the couple.

Sitting alone in her prison cell, Gerrie recalled the contents of one letter she had written a year earlier on March 8, 1990:

Cindy,

. . . I will no longer say, "She thought the money came from gambling." You did know. You did have intent. You thought I had it set up so good that you could cry, "I didn't know." It was set up very good . . . and we could have gotten away with it, but you double-crossed me.

Remember last February when I was in the wheelchair crying to you that we were bankrupt, and I said, "I am not going to take any more money, and we will have to sell the horses," and you said that I was "only trying to hurt you." You didn't care where the money came from or what happened to me.

There are twenty persons who are willing to testify that you told them, "Yes, Gerrie is going to get her half. That was our agreement." Even your lawyer knew we had this agreement. "My protection of you [Cindy] for my share of our money."

The sad part is that it would have worked, everyone believed us. The F.B.I. couldn't get "intent on your part" out of me. You could have been free of all of this to take your chances at keeping your half for yourself. This confession will not help or hurt me. It will help them [the N.C.U.A.] get back their money that you have. When it is proven that all you have is credit union money, your lawyer cannot accept his fee from that

282

money. They will not bargain with you for just my part, they will want it all.

Gerrie recalled a few lines of another letter she had written three days later:

Cindy,
I am writing to you begging you to have a change of heart and give Tom some of the money that is mine. I am, as the F.B.I. said, "destitute."

On October 11, 1991, eight months after Cindy had left the Newlander home, Russell paid two mortgages in full, totaling $175,000. He had obtained the mortgages in March 1987, before his marriage to Cindy Whitehall.

One month later, Russell filed for a divorce in the Oldham Circuit Court. The petition for dissolution of marriage states:

During this marriage the parties have acquired property and Mr. Newlander asks the Court to make a determination as to the division of said property, and, that he be restored all his non-marital property.

That prior to this marriage the parties entered into an Antenuptial Agreement, and, Mr. Newlander asks the Court to enforce the terms and provisions of that agreement. He asks that a fair and equitable determination be made as to the responsibility for the payment of debts and obligations incurred by these parties during this marriage and that a fair division of all property acquired by these parties during this marriage be made, and that he be restored all his non-marital property free and clear of any claim of the Respondent, Cindy Whitehall (New-lander).

Since the testimony before the grand jury, the Justice Department and Internal Revenue Service have been taking an extensive look into the case. The inquiries into Cindy's life are on-going.